SINAPI § BOOKS

RIGHT WING POLITICS
& RELIGION :
THE UNHOLY ALLIANCE
EXPOSED

HENRY BECHTHOLD ~

RIGHT WING POLITICS
& Religion:

THE UNHOLY ALLIANCE
Exposed

SINAPI § BOOKS

an imprint of
HOWLING DOG PRESS

ACKNOWLEDGEMENTS

Thank you to my family for allowing me the time to write this book, especially my wife, Donna. And, I thank Jesus Christ for giving me the strength and courage to confront the Christian Church and the "political right" in America regarding the issues that I have raised in *Right Wing Politics & Religion: The Unholy Alliance Exposed.* I pray that this will result in genuine repentance and reformation within the conservative, Christian Church and right-wing political movement.

—*Henry Bechthold*

SINAPI BOOKS

TABLE OF CONTENTS

THE EVIDENCE

RIGHT WING POLITICS
& RELIGION :
THE UNHOLY ALLIANCE
EXPOSED

RIGHT WING POLITICS & RELIGION : AN INTRODUCTION TO CONFLICTED BEHAVIORS

I T HAS BEEN NEARLY a millennium since the conclusion of the Christian Crusades, which wreaked havoc for two centuries, but there are still "Christian Crusaders" today. Their methods may *appear* to have changed, although many in the Middle East who have experienced the "shock and awe" and *smart bombs* of the American military would probably disagree; nonetheless, the desire for power and control remains the same for today's *Christian Crusaders*. The Crusaders of the Middle Ages identified their enemies based upon their Islamic religion and geographical sphere of influence, then attacked and attempted to coerce them to submit to the Crusaders' form of governance. Likewise, contemporary Crusaders have also identified their international enemies based upon their geographical sphere of influence and their supposed "terror connections" to those within the Islamic religion. They have labeled them as being an *axis of evil*. However, this book will clearly reveal another *unholy alliance* of politics and religion existing within the Christian right-wing's own conservative domain. It is indeed ironic that a modern "unholy alliance" of contemporary *Christian Crusaders* is intent on dismantling a declared "axis of evil" that is once again primarily comprised of Islamic people; moreover, with today's Crusaders again trying to coerce them into their own style of governance. —*Déjà vu?* While their techniques *appear* to be more civilized, they still fully intend to win their battle for our culture. And, to most unbiased observers, they do appear to be winning.

George Bush is President of the United States because of the successful efforts of these civilized, contemporary "Christian Crusaders." Both houses of congress have been *conservatized* through their efforts. And, they desire to invade, pervade and dominate every aspect of our culture, especially the political realm.

Who are these modern, civilized "Christian Crusaders?" They are right-wing, Christian leaders in powerful and influential positions, whose broadcast audiences number in the millions. Although there are many, three of the most prominent would probably be Pat Robertson, James Dobson and James Kennedy. They have been successful convincing their multitudes of listeners that our nation has been *hijacked* by dishonest and immoral politicians, which essentially means 'Democrats'. Therefore, they have also convinced their followers that it is their duty to take their nation back by voting for right-wing candidates who will support their political agenda.

I have written this book as a warning to our secular culture and to the millions of conservative Christians that these men influence so greatly. Beware! Most of today's right-wing, Christian leaders are not what they appear to be. This book will expose their duplicities. You will see that the primary duty and challenge for Christians is not to take back their nation from dishonest and immoral politicians, but rather to take back their Church from deceptive, arrogant and hypocritical Christian leaders.

Who am I, and what has motivated me to write this book? I am a conservative, Christian Pastor. I have been preaching the gospel for twenty-five years. In this book, I am undertaking a painful and difficult task. I am embarking on a journey that is certain to lead me into perilous waters, with impending storms of retribution waiting to be unleashed from my comrades in the conservative, Christian Church. I know that this is imminent because I have crossed their "line in the sand," by exposing their hypocrisy and dishonesty. Their arrows of Christian vengeance have already targeted me, but this book is certain to bring out the *heavy artillery* from the "war chest" of right-wing Christianity. I cannot allow this fate to phase me, for my first responsibility is to God. He has given me this mission. Right-wing Christian leaders have misrepresented and slandered Him, by their teachings and behavior. They have engaged in blatant hypocrisy, intentional dishonesty and gross financial abuse. Someone must confront them, because they are expanding their sphere of influence into every arena. Someone must expose their unethical and immoral conduct, before they are allowed to further multiply their deceptions within our society. Someone must undertake this painful and difficult task, and I don't see anyone else coming forward.

Many centuries ago, the Old Testament Church was in a similar state of disobedience. Someone was needed to confront God's wayward people. The Bible states that God asked the prophet Isaiah whom He could send. It is recorded that Isaiah responded, "here am I, send me." Although I am surely not worthy of being compared to the prophet Isaiah, my response must be the same. Someone must take up this sad and undesirable task, regardless of how hard it is.

What is so hard about what I'm doing? I have spent one-quarter century preaching the gospel, and extolling all virtues of the Christian Church. Now I must declare its compromises and sins.

Moreover, there is a *brotherhood* among Christians that runs deeper than bloodline family relationships. Jesus Himself stated, in the very presence of His earthly bloodline family members, that His true brothers and sisters were those who do God's will. The leaders that I am exposing in this book are my spiritual brothers and sisters. They are my family just as much as my earthly mother and father. I am indicting my family with these revelations. However, I have no choice, because my responsibility to Jesus is greater. Jesus declared that anyone who loves His family more than Him is not worthy of Him. My supreme love for Jesus compels me to accept this disheartening assignment.

To be forced to choose between your Christian brothers and sisters who you can physically see and touch, and your God who you perceive through faith alone, is a very difficult experience. Although it is a painful decision, there is only one clear, inevitable choice. You cannot continue to be a preacher of the gospel if you regard your human relationships as being of greater importance than your fidelity to God. The Bible states that "we ought to obey God, rather than men." If I am to be faithful to my God, I must accept this distasteful mission, and also accept its consequences.

As previously stated, I have already been the target of Christian vengeance from my fundamentalist, Christian family. A couple of personal experiences should help to illustrate the retributive nature of right-wing Christianity.

Our church had been a regular advertiser in the Minnesota Christian Chronicle, which is the premier conservative Christian newspaper in the Twin Cities. However, when we decided to confront the Church on sundry issues because of its blatant, intentional dishonesty and gross financial abuse, we soon discovered that there are *sacred cows* in the Church which, if questioned, will bring swift ostracism and retribution from the "powers that be" within the Church. It is a rude awakening and a disheartening experience to discover that many of your comrades in the Church do not necessarily want to "be" honest and faithful in their doctrine and behavior, but rather to maintain an "appearance" of honesty and fidelity. I now understand that there are *secrets* within the conservative Christian Church that are of much greater importance than the members of the Church. I had dared to question the Church's financial abuses, and I soon realized that this is one of several unpardonable sins. I had also exposed an "age-old" lie and cover-up that has been willingly accepted and promoted by church hierarchy, and I was about to experience the vengeance of the Church. My brothers and sisters were about to disown me, and to practice some friendly Christian cannibalism. I received messages on my voice mail informing me that I was going to hell, and was taking others to hell with me. I was accused of blasphemy for pointing out the Church's errors. I was threatened that pressure would be put on the newspaper to force them to print a retraction of our ads. It is amazing and hurtful to see how people that you've called *brother* and *sister* can transform their Christian kindness and love into anger and hate in an instant. Furthermore, that wonderful Christian newspaper that I had supported and advertised in, was setting aside the "tar and feathers." I was about to be the sacrificial offering to the Twin Cities Christian community. The editor would print an apology to all Christians for having published our damaging ads, and for the pain and harm caused by them. I was, in effect, labeled as a harmful and damaging agent in the Christian community. Why? Because I had *blown the whistle* on dishonesty and financial abuse within my Church. Of course, any beneficial results that could have been accomplished by our ads were effectually squashed by my public discipline and ostracism by these respected church leaders. However, they did not offer to refund the money for these ads that they had publicly demeaned and humiliated. They simply branded me as a troublemaker and kept our money. This was a painful lesson in "Christian Recompense 101."

It is also noteworthy that an "inside source" later acknowledged that two of the biggest churches in the Twin Cities had put pressure on the newspaper management to print a retraction or lose their support. It is hard to describe the disappointment in realizing how easily church leaders could be bought and sold. It is discomforting to know that the politics of men has more influence and power upon Christian media than does honesty, integrity and God's Word.

On several occasions, I had also been asked to substitute as a Christian talk-show host, on the only conservative Christian talk radio station in Minneapolis: KKMS. Everything was great until I ventured to discuss another one of these *sacred cows*. I soon learned that my experience with the Christian newspaper was not a fluke or rare "exception to the rule" of Christian retribution. It was déjà vu. On the following day, the regular host, who I thought was my friend, spent three hours marginalizing and humiliating me before his Christian audience. He also offered up another opportunity for his Christian listeners to call in and participate in another delightful feast of Christian cannibalism. It is certainly not a coincidence that I have never again been asked to substitute for anyone at this radio station. These difficult and wounding experiences have served as an educational experience for me in the Christian school of hard knocks. It grieves me to have come to this conclusion, but it is the unfortunate truth. If you tote the party line in the conservative Christian Church, and do not question their doctrines and practices, you will prosper and be loved. However, if you decide to question or expose any corruption or dishonesty within their organization, you will be marginalized, humiliated and ostracized. I am sad to say that this is the truthful and deplorable condition within my Church. Conservative Christianity has become corrupt, hypocritical and arrogant, and it will not tolerate any protests to its unholy behavior.

The line had been drawn in the sand. I had to choose which side I would be on. My decision has been made. I must be on the side of honesty and faithfulness, which is God's side. Unfortunately most of right-wing Christianity is on the other side of that line. I have tried to work within the system, and to convince my Christian comrades to change their deceptive and hypocritical practices. Unfortunately, it has become painfully obvious, that the conservative Christian Church will not willingly reform itself. They are enjoying their ill-gotten power and wealth, and they have no intention to relinquish it. I now have no choice but to confront and expose them in the secular arena, because they have slandered my awesome God through their unethical and immoral behavior. I am sorry, but the only hope for reformation among my conservative, Christian cohorts, is by "Exposing Right-Wing Christianity." Their compromises, dishonesty and hypocrisy must be unmasked. It is a cancer that has metastasized and saturated the Church, and it is spreading into the secular arena, as these same unfaithful church leaders desire to extend their influence over our government.

If they have been unfaithful in leading the Church, would they be faithful in leading our government? If they have been unfaithful to the Bible, which is the most important and authoritative document ever written for a Christian, would they be faithful to our Constitution? If they have justified ignoring and disobeying the commandments of God recorded in the Bible, will they not also justify ignoring and trampling upon the noble principles set forth in our Constitution? If they can justify misrepresenting and slandering the character of their own God, whom they claim to worship and love, will they not also justify slandering the character and reputations of their secular political opponents?

Most people assume that the majority of Christian leaders must be honest and faithful because of their respected positions in the Church. Unfortunately, this is an inaccurate and dangerous assumption. There are numerous wolves in *sheep's clothing*, and they have successfully pulled the wool over our eyes.

In order for you to understand their true character, you must be given special access to view their behavior within the Church. This book will provide you with that access. I have intentionally gone into great detail in the eight "Evidence Chapters," in order to clearly demonstrate beyond the shadow of a doubt, that most fundamentalist Christian leaders are anything but honest and faithful. They have betrayed the Bible and their God! They have willingly and routinely participated in distortion, deception, blatant hypocrisy and gross financial abuse. They have concocted sophisticated cover-ups in an attempt to hide their lies and schemes. That is why I have strived to dot every "i" and to cross every "t" in my presentation of the biblical evidence in chapters eighteen through twenty-four. Their dishonest and unfaithful conduct within the Church must be clearly revealed, so that they will not be able to maintain their false appearance of righteousness and holiness. They must be unmasked before they succeed in extending their dictatorial sphere of influence beyond the Church. Their intentional distortion and manipulation of the Bible must not be allowed to happen to our Constitution. Their unfaithful leadership within the Church must not be allowed to invade and pervade our government.

As you continue to read, it is important to remember that I am addressing Christian conservatives in this book. For the sake of brevity, I will often simply refer to them as the "Church," but what I am dealing with is *right-wing* Christianity. Please also remember that this book is addressing the Church in America. There are great numbers of faithful Christians throughout the world, and some of them are literally laying down their lives for their faith in Jesus. Also, there are individual churches in America that have not strayed into the materialism so evident in much of the American Church. These are churches that are still doing true ministry. In most cases they are found in the inner cities, running soup kitchens, clothing ministries, homeless shelters, or drug and alcohol rehabilitation programs. And, a large percentage of these churches that are doing true ministry, have congregations that are primarily African American or other racial minorities. It is also true, that even among the churches who are guilty of the hypocrisy and double standards revealed in this book, certainly there are sincere members who have simply been misled by church leaders regarding these issues.

It is important to note that the charges presented against the Church in America within this book, _do not_ also represent charges against the Bible or Jesus Christ. As, I, myself am a Christian, moreover the pastor of a conservative Christian Church, I trust and cherish the Bible. You could say that I am an *insider* within contemporary, conservative Christianity. The Church's troubling and contradictory behavior has led me to expose the American Christian Church and its leaders. In the pages that follow, you will find hypocrisy, materialism, financial abuse, deception, manipulation, distortion and censorship. You will find a Church that has a *sin problem* that is just as serious as our secular culture's. You will find a Church that disdains and decries certain practices of the *political left*, while employing similar methods and strategies within the Church. You will discover the "unholy alliance" created by the conflicting values and behavior of the Church's religion and its politics. Be prepared to have your eyes opened to levels of hypocrisy and double standards that will alarm you. It is time to *blow the whistle* on right-wing Christianity in America.

§ 1 §

RECENT DEVELOPMENTS:
A HURRICANE, A "HIT,"
& HYPOCRISY

S THIS BOOK goes to press, recent developments in our nation have required me to add this chapter. At this moment, we are attempting to recover from the worst natural disaster in America's history, hurricane Katrina. Hundreds have certainly perished, but we may never know exactly how many lives were lost. And, the total financial impact will probably be hundreds of billions of dollars.

As the hot winds and tidal waves of Katrina proved to be deadly, the hot air proceeding from right-wing leaders has also been causing *political waves* in our nation. In fact, one of these "wind sources" also intended to produce *deadly results*. Pat Robertson, who had been a supporter of the right-wing's "contract with America" more than a decade ago, has recently advocated creating another type of *contract* with the nation of Venezuela. During one of his recent "700 Club" national broadcasts, Robertson publicly endorsed a *contract* to assassinate the President of Venezuela, Hugo Chavez. And, unfortunately, Robertson has not been the only conservative, *hot air* source. Other right-wing

leaders, such as James Kennedy and James Dobson, have also been creating political waves in America regarding the two concurrent Supreme
Court vacancies.

I would be remiss if I did not address these recent developments,
because they are directly related to the central message of this book.
They provide additional evidence of the misguided priorities and values of right-wing, Christian leaders. They reveal a critical lack of
sound moral judgment within a group of men who are supposed to
represent moral leadership.

The rare occurrence of having two simultaneous judicial vacancies
on the Supreme Court has the right-wing salivating. This is their *golden
opportunity* to dramatically impact the future of Supreme Court rulings
for many years to come. All three of the aforementioned Christian leaders, Pat Robertson, James Kennedy and James Dobson, have been mobilizing their millions of broadcast listeners to persuade the White
House and their U.S. Senators to demand the appointment and approval
of conservative judges to fill these vacancies. Robertson, Kennedy and
Dobson have been reminding their audiences that America's judiciary
has become an arrogant and elite oligarchy, which is in the process of
rewriting our constitution. They have made it a top priority to correct
this problem. This judiciary issue is dealt with in greater detail in a
later chapter.

Kennedy and Robertson are both ordained ministers of the gospel,
and Dobson is a psychologist specializing in family matters with his
international "Focus on the Family" organization. I must give all three
of these men credit for their ability to marshal their forces to accomplish their political desires. However, I must also question their judgment, priorities and values.

As I previously stated, Kennedy and Robertson are gospel ministers.
Jesus said that His *kingdom* was not of this world (John 18:36). He also
taught that the essence of true Christianity is found in ministry to the
poor and needy (Matthew 25:31-46). As ministers of the gospel of Jesus Christ, it would seem to be far more appropriate for Kennedy and
Robertson to be mobilizing their audiences to contact church leaders
regarding the materialism, financial abuse and other compromises
within the Church that are exposed in the following chapters of this

book, encouraging these leaders to use the Church's immense wealth to feed starving children and to house the homeless? Why are they instead repeatedly mobilizing their followers to impact politics? Jesus made it clear that His kingdom was not of this world, and that His priority was ministering to those in need. However, it appears that Kennedy and Robertson are doing the exact opposite of what Jesus did. Their focus is on impacting the *political kingdom* of this world, rather than inspiring their followers to provide for those trapped in poverty throughout America and around the world.

James Dobson's daily radio broadcasts seem to reveal similar questionable priorities. As previously mentioned, his organization is called "Focus on the Family." However, a more appropriate and accurate name would probably be "Focus on the Government" or "Focus on the Judiciary." With the troubled state of Christian marriages and families revealed in this book being quite similar to that of our secular society, "Focus on the Family" should probably be spending a lot more time *focusing on the family*, and spending a lot less time focusing on politics. Instead of repeatedly mobilizing his audience to call government leaders in order to influence politics, perhaps Dobson should be motivating his followers to contact church leaders regarding Christian family issues. Maybe, if he had done so, the Church's divorce rate and other family problems would not rival the rates of those in our secular culture. Although division within our nation's government may be an important issue, to an organization named "Focus on the Family," division and divorce within Christian homes should be far more important. Although vacancies on the Supreme Court are also an important issue, to an organization named "Focus on the Family," the vacancies within Christian homes caused by absent and unavailable fathers should once again be far more important.

Robertson, Kennedy and Dobson sit in judgment of judges who are allegedly not being faithful to their job descriptions. However, it could be argued that all three of these men are also not being faithful to their primary job descriptions. If so, their judgmental practices constitute pure hypocrisy.

At this point, we are certainly justified in asking a few pertinent questions. Why are these respected and powerful Christian leaders so active in politics? Why are they constantly judging and criticizing government officials who don't share their political views? Why are their Christian ministry organizations so *entangled* with secular and political issues? Why are they fighting so tenaciously to control the political direction of our nation?

Are these men not aware of Jesus' statement that His kingdom is *not* of this world; moreover, that He said that His servants, therefore, don't fight for control of this world's kingdom (John 18:36)? Are they not aware that the Bible states that Christians are to be submissive to government authorities and ordinances (1st Peter 2:13-15; Romans 13:1-7)? Are they not aware that the Bible advises Christians not to become *entangled* with other affairs in this world, so that they can be good "gospel soldiers" for Jesus (2nd Timothy 2:3-4)? Of course, these leaders are well aware of the existence of these biblical texts, but have obviously chosen to ignore them.

Why are right-wing, Christian leaders choosing to disobey the Bible's counsels and commands regarding this issue and numerous other issues that shall be revealed in this book? What comes first with these men, their Christianity or their politics? What's more important to them, being obedient to the Bible that they claim to honor and love, or enforcing their personal and political agenda at any cost? This book will clearly reveal that their politics and religious pride consistently overrule their fidelity to the Bible and Jesus. Their actions speak much louder than their words.

It is both interesting and significant that the apostle Paul, who wrote nearly half of the New Testament, was a Roman citizen. As a "legal Roman," he could have attempted to become involved in the Roman government and political proceedings in some manner. However, there is no record of the apostle Paul ever becoming even remotely involved with politics or government. He did not attempt to run for political office, nor did he try to influence Roman public policy; furthermore, there is no hint of him ever supporting or opposing government leaders. Paul invested his time, energy and talents preaching the gospel and ministering to people. Perhaps it would be wise for today's Christian leaders to follow Paul's example. After all, Jesus' "great commission" to His followers directed them to go into all of the world *preaching the gospel*, not campaigning for public office and contacting their senators.

Pat Robertson, however, must have misunderstood Jesus' great commission, as well as the apostle Paul's example concerning politics. Although being an ordained minister, Robertson decided to jump into this world's political kingdom with both feet, as he ran for the Presidency in 1988. He also tried to implicate God in his scheme, by stating that God had told him to run. What's more, he boldly and confidently declared that he would be the next President of the United States, while on the campaign trail in New Hampshire.

It is noteworthy that Pat Robertson is the same guy who also claims to be getting messages from God on a regular basis that people are being healed of diseases across America, as he is praying during his *700 Club* broadcasts. It goes something like this. He declares that he sees a lady in a blue dress in Ohio, or a man in a red shirt in Florida being healed of cancer, diabetes or some other serious illness. Of course, he conveniently never mentions their names so that his professed miraculous healings can be verified. Evidently God is only capable of showing Robertson the color of their clothes and where they live, but not their identity.

When Pat thought that he heard God tell him to *run* for the Presidency, and that he would *win*, could it be that God actually had told him to *shun* the Presidency, and that he would *sin* by running? What could explain Pat's mistakes concerning his interpretation of his supposed messages from God? Perhaps Pat Robertson simply has a "hearing problem," which prevents him from receiving the full, exact and correct messages from God.

Unfortunately, Pat Robertson also has a memory problem. During his failed bid for the Presidency, Robertson claimed to be a combat veteran of the Korean War. When his combat claims were challenged by congressmen Pete McCloskey and Andy Jacobs, Robertson sued them for $35 million. Robertson eventually dropped the lawsuit, but as is revealed in Robert Boston's book, *The Most Dangerous Man in America*, legal depositions brought forth revelations of Robertson's past military service that not only contradicted his combat claims, but also asserted him to have allegedly consorted with prostitutes and to have acquired the name of "liquor officer," due to his regular trips to purchase liquor for the rest of the officers serving in the "rear" *with him*. As a gospel minister, Robertson should have remembered the Bible verse that says, "be sure your sin will find you out" (Numbers 32:23).

Although Robertson's poor decisions and unwise choice of friends as a young man in the military could be attributed to youthful immaturity, there can be no excuse for his continued evil associations throughout his adult life as a gospel minister. Robertson has advocated for, associated with, befriended and even entered into business relationships with brutal dictators such as Rios Montt of Guatemala, Mobuto Sese Seko of the former Zaire, and Charles Taylor of Liberia, who was indicted as a war criminal! Robertson must never have heard that old cliché that, "birds of a feather flock together." Is someone with this poor of judgment a person who should be listened to, respected and emulated within the conservative Christian community?

Robertson not only makes poor decisions in choosing his friends, but also in choosing his words. In the August 18, 1986 edition of the *New York Magazine*, Pat Robertson stated that almost all great builders of our nation have been Christians. He added that "termites" (non-Christians) have now taken over these institutions that Christians built. Robertson then declared that the time has arrived for a *"godly fumigation."* Fumigation is done to kill termites. If the non-Christians are the termites, what is Robertson suggesting? It is true that Robertson has a history of making exaggerated, inaccurate and ridiculous statements, but this time he even out-did himself. Was he really advocating the killing of all non-Christians? I'm sure that is not the case, but his rhetoric is still careless, foolish, damaging and abhorrent. Why do other right-wing leaders sit passively by while Robertson makes such outlandish statements?

It is actually hard to believe that I need to devote space in this book to address a statement made by a gospel preacher, in which the assassination of a government leader was publicly advocated. There is absolutely nothing that can be said to defend or excuse Pat Robertson's recent foolish and criminal suggestion that our nation should put out a "hit" on Venezuelan President, Hugo Chavez. Robertson is a gospel minister. He is supposed to be advocating the *saving of* life, not *snuffing out* life! Jesus said to love our enemies and to do good for them, not to murder them. If other Christian leaders have been forced to step down from their leadership positions because of adultery or embezzlement, shouldn't a leader who publicly advocates the murder of someone, also be forced to step down? Where's the outcry demanding Robertson's resignation from the *supposedly* moral and righteous leaders of the Christian right-wing? Their marked silence regarding such an immensely immoral suggestion should be an embarrassment to all sincere Christians. Are there not any conservative, Christian leaders with enough courage and moral fortitude to publicly demand his resignation from all leadership positions and responsibilities within the conservative, Christian movement?

In the final paragraphs of this chapter, we'll focus on issues directly related to hurricane Katrina. It is interesting that Pat Robertson also finds himself in the middle of this situation. Robertson established and controls a relief organization called "Operation Blessing." This organization has come to the forefront in the aftermath of Katrina's devastation. Why? Because Robertson's "Operation Blessing" was listed by the federal government's FEMA organization as one of the leading charities to receive donations for hurricane relief. What a coincidence! Pat Robertson, whose *700 Club* avidly supported George Bush's presidential campaigns in 2000 and 2004, coincidentally had his "Operation Blessing" charity promoted by an agency of the federal government as a prime recipient for hurricane relief donations. Could there possibly be a political connection?

This probable political favoritism is only half of the problem with FEMA's recommendation of Robertson's "Operation Blessing" charitable organization. What's the other half of the problem? The past history of *Operation Blessing's* financial practices and accountability are questionable, to say the least.

Juan Gonzalez, a reporter for the *New York Daily News* and co-anchor for *Democracy Now!*, has recently exposed some troubling information concerning the financial practices of Robertson's charity. Gonzalez revealed that the single largest recipient of money from "Operation Blessing," which is supposed to be a ministering relief organization, was Robertson's own Christian Broadcasting Network.

Furthermore, Gonzalez reminded us of the unethical and dishonest financial conduct of Robertson and "Operation Blessing" during the Rwandan genocide a number of years ago. Gonzalez recounted how money was raised on Robertson's *700 Club* broadcast for the alleged purpose of purchasing planes to fly relief supplies to the Rwandan refugees. However, an investigation conducted by the Virginia Attorney General's office, revealed that the planes were used to bring in mining equipment for a diamond mining operation, the African Development Corporation, whose major shareholder was Pat Robertson. According to Gonzalez, Robertson eventually had to reimburse his own "Operation Blessing" charity $400,000, because these planes were being used in an attempt to enrich himself. Evidently, "Operation Blessing" has indeed been a *personal blessing* to Pat Robertson and his Christian Broadcasting Network.

This brings us back to hurricane Katrina. In view of Robertson's past political support of President Bush, and of the past questionable financial practices of his "Operation Blessing" charity, is it appropriate for FEMA to recommend this organization as a prime recipient of hurricane relief donations? In the following chapters of this book I will be documenting the financial abuses that permeate the American Christian Church in general. Should our federal government be recommending that more funds be donated to this Church, so that church leaders can have the opportunity to mismanage more money? The American Christian Church does not have a money shortage. It has an ethics and accountability shortage. To the materialistic and selfish American Church, a greater influx of money is like more cocaine for a drug addict.

I shall present a simple and affordable plan for the Christian Church in America to provide, in advance, for any future catastrophic events, such as the devastation brought about by hurricane Katrina. However, before I reveal that plan, it is only fair to acknowledge that many Christian churches have certainly opened their doors to minister to Katrina's victims. Thousands of Christians have stepped forward to show the love of Jesus by their actions. I do commend all of those who have ministered to the refugees of Katrina. However, although it is nice for churches to open their basements and fellowship halls for homeless families; notwithstanding these acts of kindness, how many of us would want to live in a church basement with many other families for an extended period of time? The exceedingly wealthy Christian Church in America can and should do more.

There are well over 300,000 individual Christian church properties in America. There are also thousands of Christian ministry buildings and thousands of Christian denominational, executive and office buildings, as well as thousands of Christian school campuses. Because churches and ministries do not have to file tax returns, it is impossible to know the exact value of these assets. However, with today's inflated real estate values, the total combined value of these properties is unquestionably at least several hundred billion dollars, and possibly exceeding a trillion. I propose that every Christian ministry, congregation, conference and denomination make a one-time donation, equivalent to *only one percent* of their total assets, into an "emergency residential fund." If every Christian church and ministry in America participated in this one percent donation, the revenue generated would total at least several billion dollars. For less than three billion dollars the Church could do all of the following:

  • Purchase five plots of land of three thousand acres each
  in rural areas strategically located across America, to be
  used as *emergency residential sites* for future disasters.
  • Construct large "single-story" apartment buildings at
  each of these sites, providing 12,500 furnished apart-
  ments capable of housing 50,000 people at each site, and
  with each apartment having its own private entrance and
  bathroom for the safety and dignity of its occupants.
  • Construct large "common-area" buildings totaling one-
  million square feet at each site, which could be used as
  dining, recreation and storage facilities.

This proposal would provide safe, private, dignified housing for at least a quarter of a million people at these five sites, with at least two or three billion dollars remaining to provide emergency food, water and clothing, as well as immediate bussing to these sites. Can there be any legitimate reason for the Christian Church in America not to do this? Is it too much to ask for the Church to sacrifice *one percent* of its assets to provide suitable, safe and dignified accommodations for survivors of future catastrophic events?

The New Testament book of Acts records that the first-century Christian Church was willing to give _all_ of its assets to provide for those in need (Acts 2:44–45; Acts 4:34–35). Can't the twenty-first century Church spare _just one percent?_ I am confident that the Church could continue to operate adequately with the remaining ninety-nine percent of its wealth.

We must never repeat the ordeal we witnessed at New Orleans. And, the Christian Church has the opportunity and ability to take the necessary preemptive action to make suitable preparations in advance, to assure that survivors of any such future events can receive more timely, safe and dignified care. Will the Church in America _step up to the plate?_ Will Christian leaders such as Robertson, Kennedy and Dobson be willing to marshal their audiences to pressure church leaders into adopting a plan such as the one that I've proposed? Would such a project to alleviate future human suffering merit their time, energy and financial resources, as do a variety of political issues? I will eagerly wait to see the response of Christian church leaders in America.

Many right-wing Christian leaders supported _preemptive military action_ in Iraq. Will they also support _preemptive humanitarian action_ here in America? These emergency residential sites could be used numerous times every year for victims of floods, earthquakes, hurricanes and tornados. And, they would certainly be utilized and appreciated in the event of a major terrorist attack. If Christian churches and ministries in America are not willing to sacrifice _only one percent_ of their assets, after witnessing the suffering of their fellow Americans in Louisiana and Mississippi, they should no longer claim to be followers of Jesus! And, if Robertson, Kennedy and Dobson are not interested in motivating their listeners to pressure leaders within the wealthy, Christian Church in America to make such a small sacrifice as this, they will have clearly revealed that political power is of far more importance to them than ministering to suffering humanity.

2

BUSH'S RELIGION & GOVERNMENT POLICY: IS IT A DEADLY COMBINATION?

OUR PRESIDENT, George W. Bush, is a self-professed Christian. While campaigning for the Republican nomination during the 2000 primaries, Bush publicly stated that Jesus Christ was his hero. His declarations of his Christian faith certainly helped him to garner the Republican nomination and the Presidency, as conservative Christians voted for Bush over Gore by a significantly lopsided margin. Without the Christian vote, Bush would have been soundly defeated. Once again in 2004, conservative Christians came to his rescue in his victory over John Kerry. Bush's profession of Christianity has certainly been his political salvation in both elections. This combination of Bush's professed Christian faith and his politics, has been a source of contention and frustration throughout his tenure in the oval office, as each passing month brings new revelations of obfuscation and clandestine operations within his administration, which contradict his professed Christianity and pollute his politics. Many on both sides of the political spectrum feel that they have been betrayed by George W. Bush as he has attempted to dance the *political/religious* "two-step" during his Presidency.

Let's begin this chapter by examining the impact of Bush's religion upon his government policy. It certainly has had an unquestionable influence upon his executive decisions. Many of these decisions have caused great consternation among those who have opposed Bush from the beginning. We will conclude the chapter by examining the "flip-side" to this *political/religious* scenario, where it becomes obvious that Bush's religion and his politics have been an incompatible, unsuccessful, and agitating combination to his opponents and supporters alike.

It's common knowledge that the Bush Administration is comprised of numerous Christian conservatives. As with President Bush himself, their deeply held spiritual convictions are certain to affect their individual decisions, thereby also influencing public policy. Probably the most controversial policy decision of the Bush Presidency was his preemptive military strike against Iraq. Is it possible that any of the peculiar Christian beliefs held by those within Bush's "inner circle," could have been the catalyst for the invasion of Iraq?

As a Christian pastor, I can attest to the existence of a very popular Christian doctrine that certainly produces the kind of outlook and attitude necessary to prompt such decisions. The theological doctrine of "Calvinistic Predestination" is widely accepted and taught by many famous and respected Christian leaders. This doctrine essentially teaches that God has predestined and preprogrammed the decisions, actions and vocations of every human being before they were born. It maintains that God has arbitrarily predestined some people to go to heaven and some to go to hell. This teaching is adhered to by millions of Christians throughout many denominations.

What is the possible Iraq connection to this Christian doctrine? Proponents of Calvinism generally share some common characteristics. They usually exude an overt sense of spiritual arrogance and superiority. After all, they believe that they are the *special ones* chosen by God to inherit heaven. This also tends to foster a strong sense of purpose and mission, for they are sure that they have been specifically selected by God to carry out His explicit will on earth, with their every word and deed expressly directed by Almighty God. Because of the widespread popularity of this doctrine, it is probable that there are some adherents to this predestination philosophy within the many professed Christians in the Bush Administration. Is it possible that some of the key *decision makers* inside the White House considered themselves to be predestined by their Christian God to invade Iraq?

Many Christian conservatives have publicly stated that George Bush was divinely placed in office to manage the events related to the terrorist strike against America. At times, comments made by Bush himself seem to imply that he considers himself to be called by God. He definitely exhibits a strong sense of purpose and mission, as well as an unwavering confidence that he is making the right decisions at all times. When asked on more than one occasion, he has only once been able to think of any specific mistakes that he has made during his entire presidency, and that admission was regarding the Hurricane Katrina catastrophe, where his real responsibility of mismanagement was summarily deflected toward others,. Katrina was, moreover, a natural disaster, an "act of God," thus one where his actions hadn't implemented it. Yet, of his own decisions directly responsible for the ongoing ordeal in the Middle East, he cannot remember making a single mistake.

These are notable earmarks of Christian Calvinists, because they believe that God has predestined *all* of their decisions. There is no doubt that the history of both Bush Presidencies and their mutual experiences with Iraq would certainly create a perfect Calvinistic predestination scenario. Did President Bush consider it to be his *divine calling* to invade Iraq and to complete the work begun by his father? Does he indeed believe that God has predestined the Bush Presidency, and that he is doing the predetermined work of God in his "war on terror," which mutated to his invasion of Iraq, as well as in his other executive decisions? If he adheres to a Calvinistic philosophy, this is unquestionably his view.

We can only hope that the Christian doctrine and philosophy of Calvinism had nothing to do with our nation's invasion of Iraq, but we can't deny the distinct possibility. It would be reprehensible if Calvinism motivated the Iraq war, because it is a repugnant dogma. In fact, when Calvinistic Predestination is combined with the other repulsive Christian doctrine of the eternal tormenting of lost sinners, the God of Christianity appears far more cruel and unjust than the gods of all other world religions. It would certainly be shameful if such an arrogant and unjust religious ideology had prompted any of our nation's political or military decisions.

It would indeed be interesting to ascertain the doctrinal beliefs of those within the "inner circle" of the Bush Administration. Are there key individuals who adhere to the Calvinistic Predestination dogma? If so, we can be sure that it influenced their decisions in a powerful and profound manner.

The Bush Presidency has been undeniably saturated with religious influence, remarks and policies. As mentioned, Bush's supporters are largely comprised of Christian conservatives who have attempted to implement their religious agenda within our secular culture and government. Unfortunately, it is overtly apparent that their religious, political activism is subject to hypocrisy and financial abuse.

In another effort to combine religion with government policy, Bush and his conservative Christian friends are spending a great deal of time and money trying to teach our secular society about the importance of marriage and family values. They act as though they are coming to the rescue of our culture with the wisdom of the "religious right"; yet recent surveys by the *"Barna Research Group"* reveal that Christians are experiencing the same family and marriage problems as non-Christians. As mentioned in chapter one, the divorce rate in the Christian Church is just as high as in the secular world, and in some sectors of the Church it is higher. Is it not hypocritical to pretend that you have the answers for our nation's marriage and family problems, when you have not been able to provide the answers for those same problems within the Church? Perhaps Bush and his religious colleagues should first attempt to apply their strategies within the Christian Church, before legislating them in the public sphere.

A similar Bush religious, public policy is his *faith-based initiative.* His channeling of government funds through religious institutions has been quite controversial. There are, of course, potential problems regarding separation of church and state. However, there is probably a much greater concern that dwarfs the church and state issue.

Can today's Christian churches and ministries in America be trusted with the federal funds dispensed to them? American Christianity has become very selfish and materialistic. The Church is already spending the vast majority of its funds upon *self-pampering projects*. If the Church is already misappropriating its own donated income, which will be clearly documented in later chapters, why should it be trusted with additional federal funds? Furthermore, the Church's questionable practice of employing _one-thousand-percent_ [1000%] markups on their gospel merchandise, as will be revealed in this book, should certainly cause concern that similar unethical tactics might also be conducted with any additional federal funds.

All of the above examples of merging religion with government policy during the Bush Presidency, clearly demonstrate that Bush's religion has indeed had a significant impact upon the affairs of our nation. It is even quite possible that religion was a major *co-catalyst* for the Iraq war, along with the incessant desire to establish a *foothold* in the "oil-rich" Middle East. In retrospect, it is certainly reasonable to wonder if Bush's religion and his politics proved to be a *deadly combination*. It definitely has produced *deadly results* for more than two thousand American soldiers, as well as thousands of Iraqi civilians caught in the crossfire.

I would be remiss if I did not at least touch on one of President Bush's most controversial government policies, the "Patriot Act." Bush claims that the Patriot Act is necessary in order to protect America's freedom. It is an interesting idea—*peculiar* and *contradictory*—for Bush to take away some of our liberties via the Patriot Act, so that we can be protected from enemies who would come in to take away those same liberties. Evidently, Bush just wants to make sure that we do it to ourselves, rather than allowing someone else to do it to us.

Bush claims that his Patriot Act, combined with his invasion of Iraq, has kept America free from terrorism since the September, 2001, attack. However, I must wholeheartedly disagree. I believe that we shall soon see that all of Bush's aggressive measures in Iraq and here in America with the Patriot Act, have not and will not stop the massive, nationwide attack that is coming. I am convinced that Bush's wiretapping of telephone and internet communications will prove to be futile, because our enemy is not stupid or naïve. They are fully aware that such methods of communication can be monitored, and are probably only using them as decoys to divert our attention from their real operational plans.

We must remember that the 2001 terrorist strike against our nation had been in the *planning stages* for years. Our enemy is very patient. Bush's claims are premature, to say the least. I suggest that our current respite from terrorism is not due to Bush's aggressive, anti-terrorism offensive in Iraq or his vaunted Patriot Act. In fact, his aggressive efforts on Islamic soil have probably only increased Al Qaeda's desire to bombard our nation and bring us to our knees, and, just recently, Osama bin Laden has threatened another catastrophic attack upon the United States as 'punishment' for Bush's war on Iraq.

I believe that the primary reason for our momentary respite from terrorist attacks in America is quite simply that our enemy is again patiently planning their attack; moreover, that their plans are much bigger and widespread than what we experienced in 2001, a prediction, which has now been validated by bin Laden's most recent threat. It is likely they are communicating and coordinating their plans via the slow but effective, *old-fashioned* method of "face to face" communications and hand-delivered messages, which is keeping their plans *under the radar* of Bush's vaunted Patriot Act's wiretapping.

I speculate that we are nearing an unprecedented, massive, nationwide terrorist strike on America that will prove that Bush's "war on terrorism" has failed miserably, and has only served to increase the hatred of our enemies toward us. I fear that the following scenario will take place in America in the near future. And again, per bin Laden, I am certain that the terrorists will continue to publicly proclaim that they have merely retaliated for Bush's attack on the Islamic people in Iraq and Afghanistan.

This nationwide attack may eventually be called "Black Sunday," when many of America's largest cities will concurrently come under attack by hundreds of radical, Islamic suicide bombers. I suspect that the terrorists will target busses, airline terminals, Amtrak terminals, hotels, restaurants, shopping malls, amusement parks, sports stadiums and *Christian mega-churches.* Sundays are huge attendance days for amusement parks, Major League Baseball and the National Football League, and are also the one day of the week when there are millions of Christians conveniently gathered tightly into mega-church buildings across America. Al Qaeda could not pick a better time to attack the religion and recreations of America.

Consider the impact of several hundred terrorists simultaneously detonating their "suicide bomb vests" in ten or twelve of America's largest cities, from the east coast to the west coast, including the normally peaceful cities in the central heartland. Furthermore, consider the impact of the wide array of venues being hit. People will not feel safe in hotels or restaurants, sports stadiums or amusement parks. They will not feel safe patronizing shopping malls or attending church. Moreover, they will realize their vulnerability when utilizing any method of mass-transit, whether bus, train or airplane. The all-encompassing scope of the attack will certainly produce a nationwide, perhaps, even *global* panic, as people will feel unsafe regardless of where they might reside, and regardless of whether they voted blue or red, they will carry the burden of a target mentality—even though George Bush's solution to their terror may be to exhort them once again to "go out and shop." Despite his simplistic exhortations, millions of Americans will simply stay at home, which will compound the devastating effect upon our economy. This nationwide panic, our crippled economy and hundreds of thousands of casualties throughout America, will force our government to bring our troops home to protect our own cities. America's "superpower" status will be gone.

I strongly believe that a scenario similar to the one that I've described will soon take place. Why hasn't there been one single suicide bombing in America, while they are happening regularly throughout the world? Could it not be because the terrorists do not want to "tip us off" in advance, so that we would be able to anticipate and prepare for such attacks? Is it not possible that they are waiting to deliver a surprise attack of monumental impact and repercussions, such as the one that I've described?

If I am correct, and I fear that I am, we will soon experience a "Black Sunday" in America that will eclipse every other national tragedy and disaster that our nation has ever experienced. In one fatal moment, Al Qaeda will deliver what they consider to be *payback* to George W. Bush and his supporters. There will then be an outcry across America for drastic changes in our national policies, but not until we have suffered an enormous loss.

We have seen how Bush's religion has influenced his political respon-sibilities. Shouldn't we take a look at the "flip-side" of that combination? How have his politics impacted his Christian religion? Regarding this issue, I would like to address some questions directly to our Christian president, George W. Bush. President Bush, why do you condone the use of torture during the interrogation of your enemies, while simulta-neously claiming to be a follower of Jesus? The Bible states that we are to "walk as He walked" (1John 2:6). Do you think that Jesus would tor-ture His enemies? In Matthew 5:44, Jesus said that we are to *love our* enemies and to *do good* to those who hate us. Mr. Bush, if you are truly a follower of Jesus, why are you allowing the torture of your enemies, instead of loving them and doing good to them? Has your "war on ter-ror" superseded your Christianity?

President Bush, you and your right-wing cohorts have apparently created a new version of Christianity that conveniently coincides with your government policies. You have told us that your invasion of Iraq was a necessary part of your war on terror. Many of your Christian, right-wing followers like to refer to it as being a "just war." Why is it a *just war*? Is a war defined as being *just* merely because it will eventually produce some "good results"? Does the *end* always justify the *means*? Does biblical Christianity embrace such a philosophy? Does it mandate "Christian leaders" to be policemen of the world, taking vengeance upon the unjust rulers of other nations?

President Bush, you and your supporters apparently need to spend a lot more time reading the New Testament. You obviously have a dis-torted view of biblical Christianity. Although it is true that God or-dained wars against evil nations in the Old Testament era, there is no such thing advocated anywhere in the New Testament for the Christian religion. In fact, the New Testament tells us not to repay *evil with evil,* and not to avenge ourselves, but rather to allow God Himself to do the *repaying* and the dispensing of *vengeance* (Romans 12:17-21). This coun-sel given in the book of *Romans* also reiterates Jesus' message about doing good to our enemies, by giving them food and water, <u>*not bombs and torture.*</u>

Jesus clearly stated the change in philosophy from Old Testament to

New Testament times, concerning our attitude toward our enemy, when He stated that, although the Old Testament said to *hate your enemy*, His New Testament command was to love them instead (Matthew 5:43, 44). President Bush, is bombing and torturing your enemies an expression of your love for them?

The Bible does not teach that the *end* justifies the *means*. In fact, the Bible addresses that type of philosophy in Romans 3:8. It asks if we should *do evil* so that "good" may result. It then states that people who would say such a thing, "their condemnation" is just. It would be wise for Christian conservatives who endorse this "just war" nonsense, to contemplate this message straight from the Bible. We know that all wars have a certain amount of "collateral damage" (civilian casualties). "Just war" proponents consider this to be an unfortunate, but *necessary evil* that accompanies war. However, aren't' these *just war* adherents doing exactly what was stated in the book of Romans? Are they not proclaiming that their war is just and their torture is just, merely because it will eventually bring about some good results, although the evil of civilian casualties will also occur? And, didn't the Bible state that those who say that it's alright to do evil if good results from it, deserve "just condemnation"? This is an extremely significant revelation. According to the New Testament, there are not "just wars," but there is *just condemnation* for those who declare that evil, such as the civilian casualties that always accompany war, is acceptable if it produces good results.

Whenever right-wing Christians discuss their "just war" doctrine, they always refer to World War II. This is because they are confident that any loyal American would have to agree that World War II was a *just war.* They often say that we would all be speaking German and eating *wiener schnitzel* if America had not entered into that "just war" against Hitler. Apparently, these Christian conservatives have forgotten that God is omnipotent. He is more than capable of solving this world's problems without the assistance of any particular nation, including America. My conservative Christian friends might only be able to think of one way to stop Hitler, yet I am confident that our omniscient, omnipotent God was able to stop him in numerous ways, *even without America.* The Bible states that God Himself removes kings and sets up kings (Dan. 2:21). Indeed, He has throughout biblical history via various supernatural interventions and other means.

Most right-wingers claim to trust in the authenticity and accuracy of the Bible, so I will remind them of a few of these miraculous, divine interventions, which stopped powerful armies and leaders of "world powers" in their tracks. The Bible records God's divine intervention into the life and reign of King Nebuchadnezzar of Babylon in Daniel chapter four, in which God brought insanity upon the king and he roamed the fields eating grass with the animals. In Isaiah, chapter thirty-seven, we're told how God sent an angel who supernaturally destroyed 185,000 Assyrian troops in one night, thus causing the army of the "then superpower" Assyria to return home. This event was followed by the assassination of Assyria's king, Sennacherib. There are, in fact, numerous assassinations recorded in the Bible, as God sovereignly overrides and overrules the affairs of kings and nations. The book of Exodus recounts how God supernaturally intervened to destroy the wealth and armies of Egypt, which was the *superpower* of that period in history. Once again, this was accomplished by miraculous, divine intervention, as God used plagues and natural phenomenon to humble the Egyptian empire. In Joshua, chapter ten, we're told how God cast down large hailstones from heaven to supernaturally destroy the majority of the Amorite army. The Bible also records that God sent swarms of hornets to attack the armies of the Hittites, Hivites, and Canaanites, thus causing them to retreat from their lands (Exodus 23:28; Joshua 24:11-12). Almighty God has an infinite arsenal of supernatural weapons at His disposal, and the Bible states that He does not change (Malachi 3:6). Therefore, He was fully capable of dealing with the Nazis just as He did with these other historic *superpowers*.

Right-wing Christians *downsize* the power of God when they make Him dependent upon America to dispense justice throughout the world. Just as Jesus told the religious leaders of His day that they were in error because they neither *knew* the Scriptures nor the "power of God," similarly He would likely tell contemporary right-wingers that their ignorance of scriptural truth and of His omnipotent power has caused their erroneous *just war* doctrine. Almighty God does not need George W. Bush and his comrades to help Him administer worldwide justice.

I have another question for our Christian president. President Bush, why do you disobey Jesus whenever you pray in public? Jesus plainly stated that we are to make our requests to God in His (Jesus') name (John 14:13-14; John 16:23-24). Why don't you, President Bush? Is it because you would be committing *political suicide?* If that is the case, is your powerful, political office more important to you than being faithful to Jesus? Perhaps you should not have run for political office if it requires you to disobey Jesus with every public prayer that you offer. President Bush, are you first and foremost a Christian or a politician? Jesus said that no man can serve two masters (Matthew 6:24). Are you, President Bush? It's time to stop *straddling the fence!* It's time to know where you clearly stand.

President Bush, do you believe in the Ten Commandments? Are you aware that the ninth commandment states that we are not to give a *false witness,* in other words, not to *lie.* Has your political office also caused you to often violate this Christian principle as well? Are you not aware that Satan was called the *"father of lies"* and that the Pharisees, who were the right-wing religious leaders of their day, were called liars and "children of the devil" by Jesus Himself? With this in mind, President Bush, why were so many of your statements related to Iraq found to be so consistently inaccurate and misleading? Why do you frequently "stretch the truth" as you exaggerate the progress that's been made during your presidency concerning the war on terror? Why did you claim during the 2004 presidential debates that seventy-five percent of Al Qaeda leaders had been brought to justice, when only three of the twenty-seven terrorists on your administration's "most wanted list" had been captured or killed at the time that you made that statement? What is more important to you, President Bush, honesty or political power?

President Bush, are you aware that the Bible states that Christians are not to keep company with, or eat with, other professed Christians who are sexually immoral (1 Cor. 5:9-11). Why do *you,* President Bush? Is it for the sake of political support? Why did you allow a pornography star, Mary Carey, and her pornographer boss, Mark Kulkis, to be invited to your "2005 President's Dinner and Salute to Freedom," which was hosted by the National Republican Congressional Committee? In spite of being a porn star, Mary Carey publicly claims to be a praying, Bible-reading Christian. Therefore, she certainly qualifies as being one of those professed Christians that the Bible tells you not to associate or eat with, because of their sexual immorality. Why did you disobey the Bible again, Mr. Bush? Does your desire for political support outweigh your Christian principles? Are you truly sure that you're a Christian, who just happens to also be a politician? Or, are you really a politician, who only claims to be a Christian?

Finally, President Bush, why do you, as a professed Christian, participate in idolatry? The Meiji Shrine in Tokyo, Japan was erected to house the spirits of the late emperor Meiji who revitalized Shintoism's emperor worship. Shinto worshippers clap to awaken the emperor's spirit and then bow in worship of him. Are you a Christian or a Shinto worshipper, Mr. Bush? If you're truly a Christian, why did you also clap to awaken the spirit of Meiji, and why did you bow to worship him? You may shrug it off as foreign diplomacy, but Christians in Japan called it public idol worship. And, because you are a professed Christian, the Bible that you so often quote, also declares your act to be idolatry.

There was a popular television program many years ago called, "To Tell the Truth." It is time for the real George W. Bush to stand up and tell the truth. President Bush, you've danced the *political/religious* "two-step" long enough. If you're really a Christian, then be faithful to Jesus and act like it. Stop bowing at Shinto temples. Stop telling lies and associating with porn stars, and pray in Jesus' name as He instructed you, or else don't pray at all, as each of your hypocritical actions and false statements prospers doubt in the non-Christian world as to the veracity and sincerity of the Christian faith. And, perhaps most importantly, stop cowering and bullying in the name of Christ and under the false pretense that you, and your administration, do not sanction, condone, or implement torture. To state you have had no hand in it, when you have others do it for you, would be nothing short of a "godfather" defense in a world court.

If being obedient to Jesus will result in "political suicide" for you and your cohorts, so be it. Is it not better to be a faithful and honest "political failure" than to be a successful *religious/political* hypocrite and deceiver? Once again, I must ask you, President Bush, are you first and foremost a Christian or a politician?

What's the conclusion? George Bush has managed to frustrate and alienate both his political opponents and supporters, while alienating the United States from the rest of the world. His "two-step" is not working. Unfortunately, we have two more years to watch him dance.

3

AN IMAGINARY MANDATE: "FUZZY MATH" PRODUCES *RIGHT WING* "LANDSLIDE"

O NE OF THE MORE memorable moments from the 2000 presidential debates occurred after Al Gore had challenged some of the economic numbers being presented by George Bush. In response to Gore's contradiction of his fiscal mathematics, Bush suggested that Gore was practicing "fuzzy math." It is indeed ironic that many of President Bush's "right-wing," religious supporters have also adopted their own version of *fuzzy math*, immediately following the 2004 election.

Religious conservatives claim that President Bush has received an overwhelming mandate in his victory over John Kerry. They present this supposed mandate in such a forceful and overbearing manner, that most people would probably assume that Bush's victory must have been by a landslide. Of course, this allegedly *huge* victory is seen as an ideal opportunity to further their conservative, religious agenda within our culture. Church leaders assert that the 2004 election results clearly demonstrate that our culture is rapidly moving away from a liberal, secular mindset. They are certain that American voters have decisively expressed their desire to move toward conservative, Christian values. The rhetoric emanating from right-wing pundits implies a victory of landslide proportions.

Unfortunately, my fellow conservatives are either self-deceived, downright dishonest, or simply ignorant of the dictionary's definition of the term, "landslide." A landslide is defined as being an *overwhelming victory*. Furthermore, the dictionary defines the word, "overwhelming," as *crushing* or *overpowering*. Is it accurate to describe the 2004 presidential election as a crushing and overpowering victory for President Bush? The actual facts seem to soundly contradict the *fuzzy math* of religious conservatives. There were approximately 115 million total votes cast for President Bush and John Kerry. Bush received about fifty-nine million votes, while Kerry received nearly fifty-six million. Is this a crushing and overpowering victory? If it is, then most modern presidential elections must also be considered as such, because most elections in recent history have been decided by a greater margin than Bush's three-million vote victory. This electoral *fuzzy math* being practiced by conservatives would require most presidential elections to be categorized as *landslides*. In fact, Bush's so-called mandate and landslide would be quite small by comparison.

It is noteworthy that right-wing pundits have employed obvious double standards within their analysis of the election results. Even as they were boasting that Bush's overwhelming victory had revealed a decisive turn toward religious values in our nation, they simultaneously claimed that this trend was even apparent in the heavily Democratic state of California. In their effort to demonstrate Bush's nationwide progress, right-wing spokesmen, Michael Medved and Hugh Hewitt, actually referred to the presidential election in California as having been *close* or "in-play." Kerry defeated Bush by more than ten percent in California! Isn't it contradictory and disingenuous to state that Bush's national margin of three percent was an overwhelming victory, while concurrently depicting Kerry's ten percent victory in California as being close?

Religious conservatives are also disingenuous in their depiction of an alleged trend toward Christian values, which they propound to have been clearly demonstrated in Bush's victory. However, an honest analysis of recent election results between similar candidates, actually reveals an entirely opposite trend.

The candidates in the 2004 election were unquestionably complete opposites. President Bush is generally viewed as being a staunch conservative, whereas Senator Kerry has been rated as the most liberal member in the senate. Probably the only other elections in modern history to have such *complete opposites* as candidates would be the 1972 and 1984 presidential races. In 1972 Richard Nixon and George McGovern certainly offered a stark contrast in political views, as did Ronald Reagan and Walter Mondale in 1984.

If religious conservatives are correct in their assertion that Bush's victory over Kerry revealed an obvious, decisive rejection of the liberal, secular and irreligious ideologies that were birthed in the *hippie days* of the late '60s and early '70s, then why do the election results from the aforementioned presidential races clearly reflect an obvious contrary trend? A comparison of the vote counts from the 1972, 1984 and 2004 elections, totally contradicts the rhetoric of right-wing pundits. In fact, the numbers actually reveal an indisputable and significant trend toward a liberal and secular agenda in America.

In 1972 there were seventy-six million votes cast for the Democratic and Republican candidates. Richard Nixon received forty-seven million, and George McGovern received twenty-nine million. Nixon's vote count equaled sixty-one percent of the total ballots cast for the presidency, whereas McGovern's total was only thirty-seven percent.

In 1984 the Democratic and Republican candidates received a total of ninety-two million votes. Ronald Reagan received over fifty-four million, and Walter Mondale received more than thirty-seven million. Reagan's total equaled fifty-nine percent of the presidential ballots, while Mondale's equaled forty-one percent.

An honest comparison of the numbers reveals that America has actually made a dramatic move toward a liberal and secular agenda over the past thirty years. As we compare the numerical results from the 1972, 1984 and 2004 elections, for the sake of brevity, I will refer to each of the Democratic candidates as "the liberal," and each of the Republican candidates will be referred to as "the conservative."

From 1972 to 1984, the liberal's vote count increased by nearly nine million votes, which was a twenty-nine percent increase. However, the conservative's increase of seven million votes, only reflected a sixteen percent increase in conservative ballots.

From 1984 to 2004, the liberal experienced an eighteen-million-vote increase, which reflected a growth of forty-eight percent. The conservative's vote count only grew by less than five million ballots, which was just an eight percent increase.

Therefore, from 1972 to 2004, the liberal candidate saw his vote total go up by twenty-six million votes, which was a ninety-one percent increase! On the other hand, the conservative's total only increased by twelve million, which reflects a comparatively meager growth of just twenty-five percent.

If the results of presidential elections between staunch conservatives and very liberal candidates during the past thirty years statistically prove that the liberal's vote count has increased by a whopping 91%, while the conservative candidate has only experienced a mere twenty-five percent gain, then we can be certain that the factual evidence clearly and indisputably contradicts the right-wing's assertion of a trend toward conservative, Christian values in America. In fact, the numbers reveal the complete opposite scenario. America is rapidly and markedly trending toward liberalization and secularization.

It is also noteworthy that polling done in public high schools across America has tended to reveal that the vast majority of students would vote for the liberal candidate. There are between two and three million high school graduates each year in our nation, who are also entering the American electorate. This means that there will be about an additional ten million voters potentially participating in the next presidential election, of which the overwhelming majority will probably vote for the liberal candidate. These additional voters coming out of our high schools throughout America will more than erase Bush's *three-million-vote* margin of victory.

All of the actual statistical evidence reveals that the "right-wing's" vision of an American trend toward a conservative value system is nothing more than wishful thinking. Their *fuzzy math* has produced an imaginary mandate that is pure fantasy. The reality is that Christian conservatives are *living on borrowed time*, regarding their presidential victories. They may not like it, but a close examination of the facts reveals that *the deck is stacked* against them in future elections.

I find it hard to believe that conservatives are not aware of the statistics that I've presented in this chapter. Are they hopelessly self-deceived concerning the reality of the situation, or are they intentionally misleading their audience in order to *rally the troops?* In either case their judgment and tactics should be called into question. It is certainly desirable for leaders to have a sound grasp on reality, as well as an inclination toward honest discourse.

4

THE NEW CHURCH
LEADERSHIP MODEL:
WORSHIPING *PROFITS* REPLACES
PROPHETS WORSHIPING

I T IS NO SECRET that Christian conservatives in America vote predominantly Republican, with the exception of racial minorities. It
is also no secret that one of the distinguishing platforms of the Republican Party is their opposition to *big government,* including various welfare and entitlement programs. I am not asserting that these conditions
are either right or wrong. It is a matter of each individual's personal
perspective. However, this situation does appear to create another serious double standard for today's conservative, Christian Church in
America.

In recent years Christian conservatives have become much more
vocal in the arena of politics. They openly speak out on a variety of
social and political issues, including the subject of *big government.* Of
course, they have the constitutional right to voice their opinion on issues. I am not suggesting that they should not be allowed this right.
What does concern me, however, is their inconsistency regarding this
issue. Church leaders have always stressed the importance of practicing

what you preach. Unfortunately, they've not followed their own advice. On one hand, Christian conservatives aggressively support the Republican Party's stance against *big government*, as well as its opposition to numerous welfare and entitlement programs; nonetheless, there is an interesting and contradictory trend simultaneously occurring within the Church itself. In recent years, while opposing big government, Christian leaders have been advocating and practicing "big church." The mega-church has become commonplace in America. Not only has the Church become big, but it has also become very affluent. Today's Christian Church in America is a gigantic business. Recent statistics from such sources as *The Yearbook of American and Canadian Churches*, and *The National Center for Charitable Statistics*, reveal that Christian churches and ministries in America have an annual income of about eighty billion dollars!

The amount of the Church's income is not the concern, but rather how the funds are being spent. Elaborate and extravagant church facilities with *state-of-the-art* equipment and luxurious furnishings are arising everywhere. More and more ministries are operating in expensive new buildings. Some of these ministries boast of flying to their meetings in their own private jets.

Of course, those in the Church who spend their donated funds on these things are quick to justify their actions. They remind us that the Jewish temple in the Old Testament was an extremely expensive and luxurious building. Unfortunately, their comparison and reasoning are both quite faulty. If they really want to compare their modern churches to the temple, the first thing they should do is to close down all their coffee shops, bookstores, arcade rooms and restaurants that they have included in their expensive church facilities. Why? Because Jesus cast the "sellers" and "money changers" out of the temple, and He said not to make His Father's house, a *house of merchandise* (John 2:16; Matthew 21:12). In other words, do not turn the temple into a shopping mall. Therefore, if today's church leaders want to compare their buildings with the temple, their profitable bookstores, restaurants and amusement rooms need to be eliminated. However, it is highly unlikely that you will be seeing this occur anytime soon. You see, the contemporary Church does not want to conduct itself like the Old Testament temple when it comes to reverence and sanctity, but only when it comes to expensive and luxurious adornment.

It is also noteworthy, that the Jewish temple housed the Shekinah Glory, the Ark of the Covenant, the tablets of stone with the Ten Commandments written by God, the "mercy seat" and other divinely appointed furniture and utensils. It was so holy that only the priests and Levites could enter it. In fact, only the high priest could enter the revered "Most Holy Place" of the temple, and just once each year.

On the other hand, in Jesus' day, there were numerous synagogues throughout the land, which the common people worshipped in on a regular basis; they were very ordinary structures. Those synagogues would be the equivalent of our churches today, and not the temple.

As previously stated, the leaders of today's wealthy, worldly and selfish churches want to compare their structures to the temple, in order to justify their elaborate buildings. Thus we are ending up with tens of thousands of *temples* throughout America, while the *commonplace synagogues* (churches) of worship are quickly vanishing from the American landscape.

Christian leaders have conveniently forgotten that there was only one temple in all of Israel, while there were numerous modest synagogues throughout the land. God didn't need thousands of temples in the land of Israel, and it is likely that He doesn't in America either.

There is, of course, nothing wrong with having a nice building. However, with thousands of homeless people in our cities, due to a shortage of clean, safe shelters, and with millions of children starving to death each year throughout the world, it is appropriate to ask if today's Christian Church in America has forgotten it's real mission and purpose.

One of the most common slogans in Christianity is, "what would Jesus do"? It would be a good idea for today's Church to ask itself this question. The Jesus we read about in the Bible spent His life ministering to people's needs, not ministering to Himself. I think it is reasonable to assume that He would ask His Church to follow His personal example, by also ministering to those in need, instead of ministering to itself. After all, Jesus taught in Matthew 25:31-46, that true Christianity is manifested in feeding the hungry, clothing the naked and ministry in general to those in need.

It is both astonishing and disturbing to realize what America's Christian churches and ministries could accomplish if they just dedicated a fraction of their annual income to _real ministry_. If they committed only twenty percent of their annual revenue to ministering to people in need, the following accomplishments could all be achieved in just _one year_. Twenty-million starving children could be fed three meals a day throughout the year; concurrently, five-thousand "million-dollar" homeless shelters could be built across our nation, with the capacity to house one-million homeless Americans; simultaneously, new Bibles could be printed and delivered to the five-hundred-million persecuted Christians worldwide, who are suffering for their faith without even having the comfort of having a Bible; moreover, one-million of America's inner-city children could be provided with tuition-paid scholarships to attend our Christian schools in a safe and edifying environment, instead of the drug-laden, gang-infested, inner-city school "war zones" that they are presently forced to attend.

In view of all of these _good things_ that could be accomplished in just one year, if our churches and ministries gave just twenty percent of their income, can there be any legitimate reason for not doing so? Can they not afford to give only one out of every five dollars to help those who are in such dire need?

Tens of billions of dollars are spent annually by America's Christian organizations on elaborate renovation and expansion projects, and on new, large, luxurious buildings for our numerous, wealthy mega-churches. However, just twenty percent of their income, only sixteen-billion dollars, would feed every starving child in the world three meals a day, house every homeless person in our nation, provide Bibles for the half-billion persecuted Christians who need them, and would offer our precious inner-city children the opportunity to attend safe schools with wholesome environments.

It literally sickens and angers me to see the selfishness, materialism and "luxurious living" within so much of the Christian Church in America, while millions of children die from starvation and the homeless live in cardboard boxes and eat out of garbage dumpsters. This is not _what Jesus would do!_ This is not biblical Christianity! This is the conducting of a profitable, religious "business enterprise," while masquerading it as a Christian ministry.

I'm offering the twenty percent challenge to all Christian churches and ministries in America. It's time to find out which ones are truly ministering organizations, and which ones are actually just religious "business enterprises." Anyone who has read the New Testament knows that Jesus loves and values people more than buildings and other material things. We've all heard the "_talk_" from America's Christian organizations. Now, it's about time to see the "_walk_."

I challenge the Church in America to put a "moratorium" on all building and expansion projects, until they have set aside the sixteen-billion dollars to provide for the desperate needs that I have mentioned. I think that most unbiased and reasonable people would agree that such a suggestion is appropriate. After all, they claim to be "ministering organizations." If they are not willing to do this, they should not even claim to be followers of Jesus. Jesus spent His life ministering to those in need; furthermore, the Bible states that if we see others in need, but do not help them, the love of God does not abide in us (1st John 3:17,18). It is time for the Church to practice what it preaches, or else to stop preaching. The Church's hypocrisy is surely an offense to God.

Another deplorable financial abuse being conducted within the Church is the _profiteering_ being practiced in the Church's marketing of the gospel. It is astounding to discover that the Church has _markups_ and profit margins much greater than those of most secular retail stores. It is common for churches and ministries to market their video and audio tapes at grossly inflated prices. For example, audio cassettes are purchased in large quantities for only forty or fifty cents each; furthermore, they can be labeled and mailed for about sixty or seventy cents. However, these same cassettes that have a total cost, including mailing expenses, of a little more than a dollar, are often sold for five, six or seven dollars. Another example of these huge _markups_ and profit margins is the sale of videotapes. Videotapes are purchased in large quantities for less than a dollar each; moreover, they can be labeled and mailed for slightly more than a dollar. However, these same videotapes that have a total cost, including mailing and processing expenses, of only about two dollars, are frequently sold for as much as fifteen to twenty dollars.

These are markups nearing <u>*one thousand percent!*</u> That is unquestionably a much greater profit margin than most expensive, secular, retail stores enjoy. Should churches and ministries be marketing Jesus' *free gospel of grace* with nearly 1000% markups? Jesus said, *"freely you have received, so freely give"* (Matthew 10:8). The apostle Paul said that he spoke the gospel *"free of charge"* or *"without charge,"* because he did not want to *abuse his authority* regarding the gospel (2nd Corinthians 11:7; 1st Corinthians 9:18). Considering the outlandish markups and profit margins on the gospel tapes being marketed by today's churches and ministries, would you conclude that they are certainly <u>not</u> presenting the gospel *freely,* and are certainly guilty of "abusing their authority" regarding the gospel? Is this not another disturbing example of the selfishness, materialism and financial abuse that has infected today's churches and ministries? And, if Jesus called the church hierarchy of His day, a *den of thieves,* because of their unethical practice of overcharging the people for their temple sacrifices and offerings (Matthew 21:13), then we can also be sure that today's one thousand percent *profiteering* schemes in the Church would surely be viewed as being *pure thievery* as well.

Perhaps the world would be more willing to listen to Christian conservatives if they truly practiced what they preached. If they want to condemn *big government,* with all of its extravagance, abuse and waste, then they should not be practicing "big church," with its own extravagance, abuse and waste. If they want to oppose numerous government welfare programs, then they should see to it that the Church starts spending more of its own massive wealth to supply the needs of the poor. Until Christian conservatives *put their money where their mouth is,* by getting the wealthy, American Christian churches and ministries to *step up to the plate* and provide the necessary funds to relieve the suffering of starving children and of the ever-increasing homeless population, it would be prudent for them to stop their harangue against *big government* and the various federal and state welfare programs currently being offered. It would certainly be pure hypocrisy for them to persist with their criticisms and accusations, while they concurrently tolerate and embrace the deplorable financial tactics and misappropriations within the Church.

5

TRADING UP,
A CROSS FOR A CADILLAC:
"QUID PRO QUO"
IN THE CHURCH

AFTER THE UNPRECEDENTED virtual tie in the presidential election race of 2000, many conservative church leaders began to focus on, what *they* considered to be, some disturbing results of exit poll surveys. It was discovered that African American Christians voted overwhelmingly Democrat to the same extent as non-Christian African Americans. This was an alarming and troublesome situation for Christian conservatives, who could not understand how professed Christians could support a political party whose stances on numerous moral issues were in direct conflict with fundamental, conservative, Christian views. I am not suggesting that conservative Christians' response to these poll results was either right or wrong. My concern is that the conclusions that they arrived at resulted in accusations against the Democratic Party that reveal serious inconsistencies and double standards within the Christian "right-wing."

The *disturbing* poll results prompted many conservative Christians to pursue a "cause and effect" analysis. They wondered what caused African American Christians to vote so heavily Democrat, while the vast majority of other Christians vote Republican. They quickly and easily arrived at their conclusion: African American Christians vote predominantly Democrat because the Democratic Party liberally dispenses entitlements and numerous welfare programs, and there is a larger percentage of African Americans who benefit from these programs. Therefore, the answer seemed obvious to Christian conservatives. They were convinced that African American Christians vote Democrat in order to receive continued government handouts.

Unfortunately, their conclusions prompted accusations concerning the motives of Democratic leaders. This is where the inconsistencies and double standards arise. Many conservatives have actually accused Democrats of intentionally using and manipulating African Americans, by promising them continued government handouts through a variety of social welfare programs, in order to guarantee their continued voting support. They imply a legal, but shady, type of "vote buying," by promising an endless supply of entitlements in return for receiving their votes.

What's the problem with these accusations? The Bible, which is supposed to be the inspired manual that guides the Church, states that man can only look on the outward appearance, and that God alone can see the heart. The Bible also states that we are not to judge others, or we will also be judged. Therefore, Christians should be the last ones to judge others' motives. The only one who knows the motives in the hearts of the Democratic leaders is God and the leaders themselves. Christian conservatives are violating their own belief system and transgressing the very Bible that they claim to espouse, whenever they engage in judging the motives of others. It is also interesting that the Bible declares in Romans 2:1, that those who judge others are guilty of the same things themselves. Could it be possible that this scripture applies to the Christian Church in America today? While accusing Democrats of giving *promises* to African American voters in exchange for their support, could many church leaders be practicing the same thing?

One of the most popular and fastest growing messages in today's Christian Church is the "prosperity message." What is it? Basically it promises Christians health and wealth for following Jesus. It teaches that when you have strong faith, the devil cannot harm you in any way.

This includes your health, finances and just about everything else. In other words, all Christians with strong faith will be healthy, wealthy and will prosper in every area of their lives.

It's too bad that these "prosperity preachers," with their great faith, are not able to go to many of the third world countries where impoverished Christians are being martyred daily for their faith. Evidently these poverty-stricken Christians, who are being maimed and killed for their faith in Jesus, must not have had the great faith of these American churches and ministries who proclaim the prosperity message. Also, the Apostle Paul, who wrote half of the New Testament, must not have had as great of faith as these modern preachers either, because he said that he was hungry, poorly clothed and homeless in 1st Corinthians 4:11. In fact, even Jesus must not have had a faith as great as theirs, because He said in Matthew 8:20, that even foxes and birds had homes, but He had no place to lay His head. If only today's prospering churches and ministries could have instructed Paul and Jesus, perhaps they could have lived their lives with greater faith and comfort. Of course, this is untrue and absurd, as is the prosperity gospel being preached today. However, this teaching is seductive, and churches and ministries who promote this doctrine are growing rapidly. With this teaching, you can have the best of both worlds. Now you can be a Christian, but not have to deny self anymore. Now you can be a Christian, but still enjoy all the things of the world. In fact, now being a Christian will guarantee you wealth!

It used to be that Christianity was known for the "cross" of self-sacrifice. Jesus told His disciples in Matthew 16:24, that anyone who wanted to follow Him would have to deny himself and take up his cross. However, much of today's Christian Church has come up with a *new and improved* tactic for recruiting disciples. They have decided to allow prospective disciples to *trade up* from a "cross" to a "Cadillac." Instead of asking for self-denial, as Jesus did, they promise the pampering of self with rewards of wealth for giving to God. Of course, the way that you give to God is by giving to their churches and ministries. Some have even gone so far as to promise donors a hundredfold return from God, on the donations made to their ministries.

Is it not inconsistent and contradictory for Christian conservatives to accuse and rebuke the Democratic party for supposedly manipulating African Americans, by making political promises to them in order to secure their support, while simultaneously much of the Church is caught up in it's own manipulation scheme, promising prospective members multiplied financial blessings from God if they give to their ministries? It appears that Christian conservatives have indeed fulfilled the scripture that I mentioned earlier (Romans 2:1), which states that those who judge others are guilty of the same things themselves.

6

THE CHURCH
MAKES SADDAM
LOOK GOOD

AMERICA'S MILITARY BROUGHT Saddam's dictatorship to an end, but there is a current dictator who is much worse than Saddam. He has been injecting infants with a chemical that has been proven to be abnormally abundant in the brain tissue of lifelong criminals. In fact, the presence of large amounts of this chemical has been discovered in the brain cells of every hardened criminal who has been tested. This sadistic dictator has successfully implemented a massive eugenics program that would make Saddam envious. He has pre-selected the offspring of designated *undesirable* families to be injected with this brain-altering chemical, while the offspring of *desirable* families are exempt from these injections. Everyone is familiar with this dictator and will recognize who he is, as soon as his name is revealed.

As part of his national *cleansing program* to purge his country of its inferior members, he has compounded his cruelty by implementing lifetime prison sentences in forced labor camps for every injected child who begins to demonstrate criminal behavior caused by the injections. His *free* incarcerated labor force is already filled with thousands of children whose only future is a lifetime of forced labor and torture in prison. It is not an exaggeration to say that this evil dictator makes Saddam look good by comparison. He has willfully and arbitrarily caused the criminal behavior of multitudes in his nation; then has sentenced them to lifelong punishment for the evil behavior *that he caused* by his injections!

Are you as indignant as I am? Are you ready to denounce this tyrant? Do you want to see him exposed and ousted from power? Who is this sadistic madman who practices such outrageous discrimination, injustice and cruel torture?

This despicable ruler will not be found among the Islamic nations. His dictatorship is not a part of the communist world. He is not a socialist, fascist or atheist. He is the god being heralded, taught and exalted by most Christian theologians. Actually, the god most Christian preachers are proclaiming is truly much worse than either Saddam or the other sadistic dictator whom I've described. Why? Many famous and respected Christian theologians teach that their *loving and just* Christian God, also willfully and arbitrarily predestines multitudes of people to lives of evil behavior; moreover, that He does not allow them the opportunity or freedom of choice to avoid their evil destiny. As mentioned in chapter two, they call this repulsive doctrine, " Calvinistic Predestination." According to this teaching, God has arbitrarily chosen who would go to heaven and who would go to hell before any of us were created; furthermore, that we have been preprogrammed accordingly and we are nothing more than *automatons* without the ability to choose. This doctrine becomes even more repugnant when you realize that the Bible states that the majority of people are going to hell, which means that God would be willfully creating most people for the sole purpose of torturing them in hell's flames.

Christian leaders then compound the abhorrence of their dogma, by teaching that the torture of this unfortunate, predestined, evil populous will continue forever throughout the trillions of years of eternity. That is certainly much more cruel and unjust than a lifetime prison sentence that has a maximum duration of sixty or seventy years. A human dictator who punishes people, whom he preprogrammed to do evil, for a life span of seventy years of torture, unquestionably is not as cruel as a god who punishes the people whom he predestined to do evil, for an eternity of trillions of years of pain and agony. One trillion years of torment in hell is _fourteen billion times longer_ than a painful prison sentence of seventy years. Therefore, even if punishment in hell was limited to one trillion years, the god proclaimed by most contemporary Christian leaders would be at least fourteen billion times more sadistic and evil than Saddam, Hitler, Stalin or any other tyrant who has ever existed. And, remember that these _loving Christian preachers_ teach that the torture does not end after a trillion years, but rather continues for trillions of trillions of years.

Wow! Aren't you impressed with their loving and just god? And, aren't you impressed with the compassion, wisdom, logic and _sense of equitable justice_ displayed by Christian leaders? I ask you, would it be wise to allow these individuals to assume the leadership of our government, so that they can also have the opportunity to display and implement that same compassion, wisdom and _sense of equitable justice_, as they write and enforce our nation's laws? If they teach and embrace such unjust and sadistic philosophies within the Church, will they not also endorse and embrace unjust and sadistic policies and practices in their positions of leadership within our government?

Fortunately, these sadistic doctrines being taught by Christian leaders do not reflect the teachings of the Bible. If they did, I would not be a Christian. The overwhelming weight of biblical evidence soundly contradicts these two sadistic dogmas of _Calvinistic Predestination_ and the eternal torment of human beings. I have thoroughly documented the massive biblical evidence that debunks these repulsive teachings in chapters eighteen and nineteen, "The Evidence: Part One" and "The Evidence: Part Two." However, the fact that so many preachers insist on teaching these two doctrines in spite of the volume of biblical evidence against them is very troubling. I ask you, why do most preachers stubbornly continue slandering the character of the God of Christianity? As mentioned, I have intentionally gone into great detail in the presentation of the "biblical evidence chapters," _dotting every "i" and crossing every "t,"_ in order to clearly reveal the blatant disregard and disobedience that Christian leaders display towards many clear and indisputable teachings in the Bible.

Why must these things be thoroughly documented? Due to the recent political activism by so many leaders in the Christian "right-wing," all Americans need to see the true character of these self-righteous men, for they desire to become leaders in our government. That is why I have compiled such a massive amount of biblical evidence: to prove their arrogant disobedience and disregard for the Bible and their God beyond the shadow of a doubt. Then, having demonstrated their infidelity within the Church, we can arrive at some very logical and significant conclusions. If Christian leaders can justify ignoring, disobeying and manipulating the teachings of the Bible, which they claim to honor and love, will they not also justify ignoring, disobeying and manipulating the noble principles set forth in our nation's constitution? If they have been unfaithful as leaders within the Church, will they not also be unfaithful as leaders in our government? If they have justified slandering the character of the God that they claim to revere and love, will they not also justify slandering the character of their political opponents? And, as previously mentioned, the basic judgment, logic and common sense of Christian leaders must be called into question, as they teach such cruel and sadistic doctrines that make their Christian God look worse than Saddam.

Ironically, since the fall of Saddam, these leaders are hoping for greater opportunities to *Christianize* Iraq. Are they planning to entice the people of Iraq to become Christians, by inviting them to submit to their *divine dictator* who tortures billions of times longer than Saddam? The people of Iraq do not need the sadistic teachings of modern Christian leaders who've slandered the God of Christianity by presenting Him as the worst tyrant in history. Christian preachers and teachers have disgraced their Christian God with their demented, unbiblical teachings. They're not blessing the people of Iraq by trying to *Christianize* them into a perverted religious system, which exalts a cruel and evil *divine dictator* whom Christian leaders have created within their own manmade doctrines. They would be doing a greater favor if they took their repulsive manmade doctrines and went home.

7

CHRISTIAN TERRORISM WILL SOON MURDER THOUSANDS: CHURCH LEADERS ACKNOWLEDGE FUTURE TRANSPORTATION INDUSTRY DISASTER

SINCE ISLAMIC TERRORISTS utilized our nation's transportation system to attack America, our way of life has been permanently changed. We analyze and judge things from a different perspective. We no longer feel safe and secluded from the horrors of terrorism and war. Our nation's borders have been invaded and plundered by religious terrorists, and we fear more attacks to come in the future.

The religion of Islam has, of course, been negatively impacted by these events. Many view the Islamic religion as a *breeding ground* for additional future terrorist strikes against America. Christian leaders maintain that Islamic terrorism has helped to clearly distinguish the superiority of Christianity over Islam. They remind us that we do not see Lutherans, Baptists or Catholics crashing airplanes filled with innocent passengers.

As a Christian, I also believe that "biblical Christianity" is the *true* religion. However, most contemporary Christian leaders do not represent "biblical Christianity." Modern, American Christianity itself has been *hijacked* by an unfaithful, disobedient, dishonest and arrogant *religious hierarchy*. Church leaders who are practicing and teaching the many contradictory, inconsistent, dishonest and hypocritical things that are exposed in this book, <u>do not represent</u> "biblical Christianity." Theirs is an adulterated, perverted, "manmade" religion that they try to *market* as Christianity.

Many of the same Christian leaders who remind us that the airplanes that crashed into our buildings were not piloted by Lutherans, Baptists or Catholics, astonishingly teach that there will be a future *Christian-related* disaster that will strike our entire worldwide transportation industry. These respected church leaders unabashedly profess that in one *simultaneous and fatal moment*, throughout the world numerous commercial airplanes, trains and busses that are piloted, engineered and driven by Christians, will be caused to *crash and burn* with thousands of unsuspecting passengers on board.

This worldwide catastrophe is sincerely believed and taught by many famous and respected church leaders within contemporary Christianity. It is commonly referred to as the "secret rapture" doctrine, and has been widely popularized by the phenomenally successful, *"Left Behind,"* Christian novel series. This doctrine teaches that Jesus will soon be "rapturing" Christians to heaven; furthermore, that this event will simultaneously occur worldwide, with all Christians instantly vanishing. Popular Christian books and movies have attempted to depict the confusion and hysteria caused by this event. They describe drivers, engineers and pilots vanishing from the controls of their commercial airplanes, trains and busses, thus resulting in a massive transportation industry disaster, as these vehicles full of unsuspecting passengers become doomed for horrific accidents, while the *raptured* Christian drivers, engineers and pilots are joyfully transported to heaven.

Although the scenario I've described probably sounds like a science fiction novel or movie, it is sincerely believed and eagerly anticipated by millions of Christians. And, church leaders who teach this *secret rapture* doctrine, offer no apologies for the horrific worldwide destruction and terror that will be caused by the *rapture* and disappearance of these Christians who were responsible for the safety of the passengers in their vehicles.

If it is terrorism for Islamic radicals to cause the death of passengers on our commercial airplanes, isn't it also a form of "Christian terrorism" to cause the death of passengers traveling in the planes and trains vacated by *raptured* Christian pilots and engineers? After all, if they truly believe that this *secret rapture* is a real event that will soon occur, shouldn't these Christian pilots and train engineers be resigning from their jobs, rather than causing the suffering and death of thousands of their passengers? If they feel certain that these things will happen, are they not guilty of willfully terrorizing the passengers who will be traveling on the planes and trains that they vacate when they are *raptured?* Their guilt becomes even more apparent when you understand that most of these *secret rapture* proponents also believe that there will be a "second chance" for people to be *saved* after the *rapture* has occurred. They believe that there will be a period of several years following this *secret rapture*, in which those who were not *raptured* can still place their faith in Jesus Christ and be *saved.* This "second chance" doctrine, however, seems to increase the measure of guilt for these Christian pilots, train engineers and bus drivers. Why? Because, by refusing to resign from their jobs, which include and mandate "passenger responsibility," they are not only willfully causing the death of their passengers who will perish when they are *raptured,* but in so doing, they are also eliminating any possibility of those passengers having access to that "second chance" of being *saved.*

If Islamic radicals are labeled as terrorists and murderers, because they intentionally cause the suffering and death of the passengers on the planes that they hijack, are not the Christian pilots and train engineers also terrorists and murderers when they willfully cause the death of their passengers, by insisting on continuing to pilot and engineer the commercial vehicles that they will vacate and abandon to destruction, and thereby also eliminating any possibility of their doomed passengers being able to be *saved* and enter heaven via the so-called "second chance"?

If their doctrine is correct, it is certainly a form of *Christian terrorism.* Fortunately, however, their doctrine is totally unbiblical, as is the case with many of the "sacred cow" teachings in today's Christian

Church. I completely disprove this doctrine in chapter twenty, "The Evidence-Part Three." Nonetheless, many Christian leaders persist in their proclamation, unashamed hope and eager expectation of this future event of "Christian terrorism," accompanied by its wake of worldwide destruction.

I will conclude this chapter with an admonition for proponents of this secret *rapture* doctrine. If secret *rapture* adherents are correct, Christian pilots, train engineers and bus drivers who refuse to resign from their positions of passenger responsibility and welfare, in spite of their knowledge that they will soon vanish from the controls of their commercial vehicles with multitudes of passengers in their care; then these Christian transit operators will soon be guilty of committing the greatest act of terrorism in history, as literally millions of people throughout the world will simultaneously perish in their vacated commercial vehicles.

If *secret rapture* adherents truly believe their doctrine, they have a moral responsibility to immediately resign from all positions that place the safety of passengers in their care. If they don't, they are freely choosing to become the greatest terrorists in history. That is, of course, unless they don't really believe their own doctrine. And, if that is the case, why are they espousing it?

I ask Tim LaHaye and Jerry Jenkins, who have become fabulously wealthy from their *secret rapture* based, *"Left Behind,"* Christian novel series, if they truly believe in this *secret rapture* event that they espouse in their books? If so, why haven't they encouraged all Christian pilots, train engineers and bus drivers to immediately resign from their positions? After all, those millions of passengers who will perish when the driverless planes, trains and busses crash, will not have an opportunity to be saved and to avoid hell during the so-called "second chance" for those who are *left behind.* Shouldn't these passengers, who will be doomed to perish and suffer in hell because of these Christian transit operators' refusal to resign their positions, also have been given that "second chance" opportunity to be saved? If LaHaye and Jenkins truly believe in this *secret rapture* and *left behind* scenario that they have written about and profited from handsomely, then moral integrity and compassion demand that they issue a statement advising all Christian transit operators to resign immediately before this *rapture* occurs. The only reason for not making such a statement is if they don't really believe their *secret rapture spiel* themselves, and if it has all just been a lucrative, money-making scheme. Mr. LaHaye and Mr. Jenkins, I await your response.

8

ARROGANT, ACTIVIST JUDGES WHO EXALT THEMSELVES (WHO ARE THEY? CONSERVATIVE, CHRISTIAN CHURCH LEADERS !)

ONE OF THE GREATEST CONCERNS of Christian conservatives and the *political right* in general, is something that they refer to as "judicial activism." Right-wing leaders claim that modern judges have exalted themselves above our constitution, as well as above the legislative and executive branches of our government. It is charged that our modern judiciary has become an *elite oligarchy*, with judges enforcing their own opinions and ideologies above the will of the people, legislated law and even above the constitution itself. The Church professes that our contemporary judicial branch of government has become a panel of arrogant, activist judges who have elevated themselves beyond the intentions of our *founding fathers*.

Fairly, one must admit that the Church may have some interesting and valid arguments. The primary problem (per nearly every situation discussed in this book) is the Church's hypocritical double standards.

Church leaders accuse modern judges of being an *elite oligarchy*, arrogantly exalting themselves and their personal opinions and ideologies. Perhaps Christian leaders are so cognizant of these particular characteristics because they are guilty of the same things themselves. When it comes to self-exaltation, contemporary church leaders can compete with anyone. And, just as these *arrogant, activist judges* allegedly ignore legislated laws and our nation's founding documents, in order to exalt themselves and their opinions; it is also certainly true that today's Christian leaders ignore and disobey their *founding document*, the Bible, in order to glorify themselves and to exalt their personal opinions within the Church.

Jesus stated in Matthew 23:8-12, that His followers are not to exalt themselves with *religious titles*, such as rabbi, teacher, father etc. He also gave the reason for His admonition. He declared that His followers are all *just brethren*. In other words, human followers of Jesus Christ are all *equal*. They are not to be elevated above one another through the use of self-exalting religious titles. Jesus clearly stated that such glorifying titles are reserved for God. He then concluded in verse twelve with the warning that those who exalt themselves with such titles will be abased or humbled by God.

Church leaders are fully aware of this admonition from Jesus, yet they willfully ignore and disobey it. Contemporary religious leaders love to be acknowledged and distinguished by such self-glorifying titles as father, reverend, rabbi, doctor, teacher and *best-selling author.* Those who have been honored with such titles within the Church are viewed as possessing superior knowledge and wisdom, thereby elevating the importance of their *personal opinions* and ideas even to the point of superseding clear and authoritative statements and commandments in the Bible, which is the Church's *founding document.*

As this book plainly reveals, modern Christian leaders are certainly guilty of their own form of *theological activism,* which has probably made more changes to the Bible, than have been made to the founding documents of our nation by activist judges. If there are judicial activists, there are certainly theological activists. If there are arrogant judges who are exalting themselves, there are definitely arrogant church leaders who are elevating and glorifying themselves. If there is an *elite judiciary* supplanting the wise, time-honored, tested truths of our constitution with the opinions and ideologies of contemporary judges, there is unquestionably an *elite church hierarchy* that is also supplanting the wise, time-honored, tested truths of the Bible with the opinions of contemporary, finite, human church leaders.

Once again, Christian leaders rise to the heights of hypocrisy, as they assail liberal judges with allegations of activist judicial behavior, while the same church leaders are obviously guilty of similar conduct within the Church. How can the Church continue to justify its aggressive assaults upon the judiciary, media and the *political left*, while such double standards, contradictions, inconsistencies and blatant hypocrisy reside within the church hierarchy?

You could accurately say that the Bible is the Church's constitution, so to speak. My advice to my right-wing comrades would be to clean up their own house first, before trying to clean up our nation's judiciary. It's time for them to cease from self-righteously chiding our federal judges for allegedly placing themselves above our constitution, until these *spiritual leaders* have ceased from exalting themselves above their *spiritual constitution* (the Bible). Until they have attended to this personal task, they have no credibility to speak to this issue.

9

"THE POT CALLS THE KETTLE BLACK": POLITICAL HYPOCRISY IN THE CHRISTIAN RIGHT

OR THOSE WHO have never heard this expression, a brief explanation should probably be given. This is a saying that has literally been around for generations. It goes back to a day when there was not a plethora of styles and colors available to choose from in pots and pans. Most pots and kettles were black. If pots could have talked, it would have been a self-condemning statement for the pot to call the kettle black in any derogatory manner, because the pot was also black. The pot would have been accusing the kettle of something that equally applied to the pot. This expression has lost some of its meaning today, because there are a variety of styles and colors from which to choose. It would probably also be fair to say that this phrase could be considered as being somewhat racially insensitive, although the original intent had nothing to do with skin color or racial issues. This expression was a way of telling someone that he was guilty of doing the same things that he was accusing others of having done. So, how does this apply to the Christian "right-wing" in America?

Many in today's conservative Christian Church lament the condition of our society in America. They decry the erosion of biblical, moral values. They point to the breakup of the traditional family and the high divorce rate. They also call attention to increasing drug, alcohol and sexual addiction trends. And, of course, many of their observations concerning these issues are correct. Furthermore, they have every right to address these issues.

The problem is, once again, the double standards practiced by the Church. For example, Christian conservatives accuse the *political left* of advocating and instituting a variety of liberal policies that have been eroding the sanctity of marriage and contributing to the high divorce rate, thus resulting in the breakup of the traditional family. They also decry the general sinful condition of our society, and associate it with the "cause and effect" of liberal, leftist ideology. The cause being liberal ideas such as situational ethics and the related notion that there is no such thing as *absolute truth*; thereby producing the effect of the erosion of morals and the creation of a sinful, wicked society.

The problem is not the positions or the conclusions arrived at by Christian conservatives regarding these issues. Their perspective has some merit. The problem goes back to our time-honored expression. It seems like the pot is calling the kettle black. Recent surveys of Christians done by the *"Barna Research Group,"* reveal that many of the sinful conditions that the Church denounces in the world are just as common in the Church. For example, the divorce rate among Christians is just as high as in our secular culture. In fact, there are areas in our nation where the Church's divorce rate is actually higher than the rate among non-Christians. These surveys also reveal that problems with family issues and various kinds of sinful behavior among Christians are similar to those in the world. Perhaps Christian conservatives should refocus their time and attention on getting their own house in order, before denouncing the same issues in the world.

It would probably also be beneficial for them to pursue the same "cause and effect" analysis of their own sin problem, as they do in judging the world's problems. They have concluded that the sinful condition in the world is the natural result of wrong, liberal ideology. Why isn't the same conclusion arrived at concerning the sinful condition in the Church? The *political left* does not have a monopoly on liberal ideology. As this book reveals, there is also plenty of liberal, theological ideology that has been adopted by the Church, even though it contradicts the Bible in many instances.

A good example of this liberal theology that applies to the "cause and effect" of the sin problem in today's Church in America, is the *"once saved always saved"* doctrine being taught in much of the Church. This doctrine teaches that once people have expressed faith in Jesus and accepted Him as their Savior, they are saved and have eternal life, regardless of how they choose to live in the future. In other words, they could choose to break every commandment in the Bible and live a life of total immorality and wickedness, yet still be assured of going to heaven! It should be noted that this teaching clearly contradicts the Bible, as is shown in chapter twenty-one, "The Evidence-Part Four." Why don't Christian conservatives apply the same principles of logic and analysis to arrive at the obvious answer to their sin problems within the Church, as they do in deducing the same conditions in our society? If the liberal ideologies of situational ethics and the rejection of *absolute truth* have obviously created the sinful behavior in our secular culture, as is argued by conservative Christians, isn't it also obvious that the liberal, theological ideology of the *"once saved always saved"* doctrine, has certainly contributed to the same sinful behavior in the Church? After all, in both scenarios there is a similar "anything goes" mentality. It seems quite hypocritical for Christian conservatives to be denouncing the sin in our secular society and declaring that these non-Christians must repent or they will go to hell, but then to tell Christians that they can commit the same sins and go to heaven, simply because they expressed faith in Jesus at some earlier time in their life. This type of hypocrisy does not pass the "common sense" test, and is certain not to pass the test of a righteous and just God. That being the case, it seems logical to also conclude that this duplicitous philosophy and poor judgment exhibited by Christian conservatives, does not *pass the test* for qualifying them to serve in positions of leadership within our government.

10

DO AS I SAY, NOT AS I DO:
MORE POLITICAL HYPOCRISY
IN THE CHRISTIAN RIGHT

A S THIS BOOK clearly documents, the conservative wing of the Christian Church in America has become quite outspoken concerning political issues in recent years. It is probably necessary to repeat that this is indeed a protected constitutional right, and that Christian conservatives should be welcome to exercise their freedom of speech in the public sector.

One area of major emphasis by right-wing Christianity has been to have the biblical Ten Commandments put back into our public schools and other public buildings. This issue received national attention when the Alabama chief justice, Roy Moore, was removed from his judicial position because of his refusal to remove the Ten Commandments from government property. The Church asserts that there is a direct connection between the moral decay in America and the removal of the Ten Commandments from our secular culture. Also of great concern to conservative Christians, as briefly mentioned in the previous chapter, is the rejection of "absolute truth" by those on the *political left*. According to the Church, this also has contributed significantly to the moral decline in our society. Of course, these two topics of *absolute truth* and the Ten Commandments are directly related, because Christian conservatives view *absolute truth* as being contained in the Bible, as are the Ten Commandments. In fact, they claim that, according to the Bible, God's *moral law* and *absolute truth* are basically synonymous.

The Christian right-wing has *drawn a line in the sand* on these issues, and it is willing to pursue all legal avenues to reinstate the Ten Commandments and *absolute truth* back into our culture. Conservative, religious, legal organizations, such as the *"American Center for Law and Justice"* and the *"Alliance Defense Fund,"* have fought, and are fighting, many legal battles on behalf of the Church in courts across America, regarding this Ten Commandment controversy. It is certainly true that conservative Christians have every right to pursue the legal remedies provided in our constitution. It is also true that they have some interesting and credible views on these issues. The problem is not their positions or their legal attempts to win these battles. The problem again is the hypocrisy and double standards, which make their legal efforts appear to be completely disingenuous and downright dishonest.

One would think that the conservative, Christian Church must certainly hold the Ten Commandments in high esteem and cherish them greatly, based on it's aggressive efforts to have them recognized in our public institutions. One would expect that the Church itself must be honoring, teaching and preaching these commandments. One would surmise that the importance of these commandments, and of obeying them, must be a major focus within the conservative, Christian Church. One would assume that the same Church that insists that the Ten Commandments should not have been removed from our public schools, would certainly never tolerate any attempt to remove them from the Church. It would be logical to assume and expect all of these things, yet this is not the case. This is a situation where right-wing Christianity's position is obviously, "do as I say, but not as I do."

A very common teaching throughout much of evangelical Christianity is that the Ten Commandments were nailed to the cross of Jesus and have been abolished. This doctrine is believed and taught by some of the leading biblical scholars in America, and it is accepted by millions of Christians in our nation. The same Christian Church that denounces the removal of the Ten Commandments from our public institutions, readily accepts the removal of the Ten Commandments from the Church. Most reasonable people would probably agree that this is inconsistent, contradictory and hypocritical. Why should our secular society want the commandments if the Church doesn't?

It is significant that the Bible states in Psalms 119:142 and 151, that all of God's laws and commandments are truth. This raises another question. Why should Christian conservatives rebuke the *political left* for rejecting *absolute truth*, while they have allowed the rejection of the *absolute truth* of God's law and commandments within the Church? Also significant, is the fact that they not only have embraced a glaring double standard, but are also in violation of the overwhelming weight of evidence presented in the "book" that they claim to love and honor, the Bible. This doctrine, espoused by a large percentage of the Christian Church, contradicts numerous biblical texts, as is clearly shown in Chapter 22, "The Evidence: Part Five."

If Christian conservatives want our secular society to recognize and honor the Ten Commandments, it would seem reasonable for the Church to do so first. It would also seem appropriate for these *supposedly* faithful Christians to bring their teachings into harmony with the overwhelming weight of biblical evidence. After all, they claim to cherish and honor the Bible, just as they claim to cherish and honor our nation and our Constitution.

It might be wise to close this chapter by stressing the significance of what Christian leaders are allowing and even endorsing, regarding the abolishing of the Ten Commandments within the Church. As I mentioned, the Bible is supposed to be a highly regarded and holy document to Christians, especially to religious conservatives who claim to regard it as the inerrant "Word of God." And, the Ten Commandments have been viewed as one of the most holy portions within the Bible, because they were written with the very finger of God.

If Christian conservatives can justify ignoring, disobeying and even abolishing the most holy portions of this divine book that they claim to revere and love, what will stop them from distorting, abusing and attempting to abolish portions of our nation's constitution? This is a realistic and justifiable concern that should alarm all freedom-loving Americans. Until these Christian leaders can prove to be faithful in their own *house*, the Church, why should we allow them to serve as leaders in the various *houses* of our government? Chapter 22, as well as all of the other "evidence chapters," clearly reveal that they have not been faithful in the Church or to the Bible, which they profess to honor and love. This should serve as a "wake-up" call to all who love our nation and its freedoms.

$\S$ 11 $\S$

THE GREAT LIE
AND COVER-UP IN
THE CHRISTIAN CHURCH

P ROBABLY ONE OF THE MOST effective and longest lasting lies
in the history of mankind is housed within the doctrines of
the Christian Church. This lie has been cherished and supported by the
vast majority of Christian leaders for centuries. The most famous and
respected Christian preachers and teachers in the contemporary
Church also embrace and espouse this great lie. Great efforts have been
made throughout recent church history to maintain the "cover-up" of
this cherished lie. The Christian Church in America has even united
with secular state, county and city governments at various times in our
nation's history, in order to legally enforce this lie.

What is the great lie and cover-up in the Christian Church to which
I am referring? It is the Church's revered tradition of Sunday obser-
vance and worship. This practice of honoring the first day of the week,
Sunday, is a tradition that dates back to early Christian Church history.
The exact date of origin varies between differing historical sources, but
it is safe to say that it probably began in the second or third century, if
not the end of the first century. This Christian tradition of honoring
Sunday is nearly a _2000-year-old lie and cover-up_.

Why is it a lie? What is the cover-up? How has the Church combined with secular government to legally enforce its religious tradition?

Throughout the history of America there have been "Sunday laws" enacted and enforced at different times and places across our nation. Even to this day there are many counties and cities in America that have Sunday laws in effect that require certain businesses to remain closed on the first day of the week because it is the Christian Church's day of worship.

Probably, most Americans assume this tradition of Sunday observance has its origin in the Bible via some specific commandments from God. It would be logical to assume that this is the case, in view of the Church's exaltation of the first day of the week. It will probably surprise most people, however, to discover that the Bible does not either command or encourage Sunday observance or worship. There is not one single text in the entire Bible that commands Christians to honor or worship on Sunday. There is not one single passage in the Bible that places any special blessing from God upon the first day of the week. Interestingly enough, the Bible does command us to honor and observe another day of the week, the seventh day. The Bible states clearly that God Himself has blessed and sanctified the seventh day, Saturday. In fact, there are over one hundred passages in the Bible that command, encourage or demonstrate observance of the seventh day.

It seems unusual and inappropriate that the Church should honor Sunday, a day that is not commanded or blessed once in all of Scripture, while simultaneously completely ignoring Saturday, a day which is endorsed over one hundred times in the Bible. Is it not dishonest for Christian preachers to be referring to the first day of the week as the Sabbath, when God plainly declared that the Sabbath was the seventh day of the week in the Ten Commandments? It also is disturbingly deceptive for Christian leaders to call Sunday the *"Lord's Day,"* when they know that Jesus Himself stated that He was Lord of the seventh-day Sabbath, Saturday, in Mark 2:28. Additionally, Church leaders' claim that observing and honoring Sunday is necessary to honor Jesus' resurrection, is certainly misleading as well, because there is not one single Bible verse that tells us to observe Sunday in order to honor the resurrection. What we have is a series of intentional lies by Church leaders to cover up their *great lie* that Sunday is the Sabbath.

This is not an insignificant issue. The observing and honoring of the seventh day of the week, Saturday, as the Sabbath, is one of God's Ten Commandments. It is included alongside God's commandments to not murder, steal, lie or commit adultery. How can the Christian Church chastise the secular culture for willfully breaking any of these other commandments, while the Church is in willful and constant violation of God's Sabbath commandment? The behavior of Church leaders becomes especially problematic when you consider the declaration by the apostle James in the New Testament, that when you violate one of the Ten Commandments you are guilty of violating all ten (James 2:10-11). Obviously God views His Ten Commandments as being a unit. The Bible is clear that you can't pick and choose which commandments you want to obey or disobey. Therefore, the Christian Church is just as guilty before God for its continual and intentional violation of God's Sabbath commandment, as is our secular society for its violation of any of the other commandments.

The Christian Church has been willfully endorsing a *great lie* in its tradition of honoring Sunday as the Sabbath, and has been practicing a massive cover-up by presenting a wide variety of deceptive and unbiblical excuses designed to maintain this lie. It is time for the Christian Church to confess and repent of this transgression and to become obedient to God's seventh-day Sabbath commandment, before reprimanding non-Christians for their disobedience to any of God's other commandments. It is time to put an end to this *great lie* and cover-up in the Christian Church.

Consider the Church's usage of government "Sunday-laws" to force compliance with their unbiblical Sunday doctrine. Christian leaders who have made use of government legislation in the past, in order to enforce compliance with religious beliefs, most probably will also engage in such activity in the future if they are given the opportunity. Remember, they succeeded in enforcing a religious dogma that is not even supported in the Bible! The overwhelming amount of biblical evidence that contradicts the Church's exaltation of Sunday is presented in Chapter 23, "The Evidence: Part Six."

12

DISTORTION, MANIPULATION, CENSORSHIP, AND BIAS

A RECENT BOOK that rocketed to the top of the bestseller list was well received in conservative Christian circles. The book, entitled *Bias,* accused the national media of leaning heavily to the left on most issues. It charged that the national media has been guilty of editorializing the news. The conservative, Christian Church has welcomed this book with open arms. The Church has made many of the same accusations against the press for the past several years. Church leaders maintain that today's media has become a wing of the Democratic Party.

They accuse the press of bias, distortion, manipulation of words, and even censorship. They claim that liberal agendas are always presented in a positive light, while conservative agendas are usually presented negatively. They accuse the media of "labeling" Christians as *conservatives, fundamentalists* or *right wing,* while not applying similar labels to liberals. They claim that today's media will even distort the facts if necessary, in order to advance their liberal ideas. The Church suggests that actual censorship often occurs, in order to prevent conservative, Christian views from being brought to the public.

The Church also accuses the Democratic Party of these same practices. It is alleged that words are often manipulated in historical documents by the *political left*, to create new policies that actually contradict the original intent of our founding fathers. Probably the best example of the Church's "manipulation charge," regards the issue of separation of church and state. The Church claims that the idea of there being a *wall of separation* between church and state in the constitution, is nothing more than a misleading manipulation of a personal letter written by Thomas Jefferson. The Church declares that this example and others mentioned in this book, reveal a dishonest and intentional pattern of behavior by the media and the *political left* designed to manipulate and distort the facts.

The Church's allegations are interesting and worthy of consideration. However, as before, there is a serious double standard engaged in by the Church. If the Church opposes the media editorializing the news by substituting liberal opinions in place of facts, shouldn't the Church also oppose substituting religious opinions for Bible facts? If the Church complains about the media "labeling" Christians as *conservatives* and *right wing*, shouldn't the Church refrain from labeling Christians who have different views? If the Church denounces the *political left* for distorting and manipulating words, in order to change the original intent of historical documents, shouldn't the Church also denounce the distortion and manipulation of words by theologians, in order to change the original content and intent of the Bible, which is the Church's "founding document? If the Church deplores the censorship of Christian views by the media, shouldn't the Church refrain from censorship?

Regarding the Church's substitution of religious opinions for Bible facts, and its manipulation of words to make changes in biblical doctrines, several examples could be given (some having been covered in previous chapters of this book). However, the best example is probably the Church's substitution of the Sabbath day, which we began discussing in the previous chapter. The Bible plainly declares in Genesis chapter two and Exodus chapter twenty that God established the seventh day of the week, Saturday, as the Sabbath. It also states that He blessed and sanctified the seventh day, and that He mandates us to keep it as one of His Ten Commandments. The Church, however, has chosen to observe the first day of the week, Sunday, instead of the seventh day. A variety of man-made opinions are given by the Church to justify changing the Bible facts concerning the Sabbath. A complete list of these *opinions/excuses* is supplied in Chapter 23, "The Evidence: Part Six." The bottom line, however, is that the Church has substituted its own opinions for Bible facts, which is the same practice it accuses the *political left* and the media of having done.

As mentioned in the previous chapter, the Church has manipulated words by calling Sunday the "Lord's Day," and by calling Saturday the *Jewish Sabbath.* Why is this manipulation? Because there is not one verse in the entire Bible that calls Sunday the *Lord's Day.* In fact, the Bible states that Jesus is Lord of the seventh-day Sabbath, Saturday. Also, there is not one verse in the entire Bible that calls Saturday the *Jewish Sabbath.* In fact, God established the Sabbath about 2000 years before the Jewish people existed. As you can see, the Church is guilty of the very same practice of distortion and manipulation that it accuses the media and the *political left* of conducting.

The Church also engages in the practice of *labeling* Christians. When sincere Christians confront the Church concerning the Sabbath issue, they are frequently labeled as *legalists* or as being *"cultistic,"* which is not a nice distinction in Christian circles. I have personally experienced this *religious labeling* from the so-called mainstream Church, and have also been denied access to Christian facilities that are available to others who comply with their "mainstream," though unbiblical, beliefs. I pastor a Christian church that observes the seventh-day Sabbath as commanded in the Bible. For several years we have been holding our worship services in a rented hotel conference room. We recently attempted to rent from another Christian church because we had heard that they were interested in renting out their facility in order to help them with their finances. I personally met with their pastor and their church board members. During subsequent conversations with their pastor I was told that our Sabbath belief, as well as our belief that God does not torture people forever in hell, was viewed as being *cultic* by some of their board members. And therefore, they had decided not to allow us to rent from them, although he admitted that they were intending to rent their facility to other Christian organizations. Why is it acceptable for the Church to label Christians who challenge its unbiblical positions, but when the media labels Christians it is wrong?

Finally, the same Church that accuses the media of censorship of Christian views, does it's own censorship of those Christians who confront its unbiblical stances. Once again, I have had first hand experience of being censored by the Church. Our church decided to run some radio ads on several Minneapolis radio stations to inform people about the Bible's teaching regarding the Sabbath. We ran ads on three major, secular radio stations, and they were happy to broadcast them for us. We also approached the Christian talk radio station, but they refused to broadcast our Bible ads.

Consider the irony of this situation. We attempt to run radio spots quoting Bible verses, and the secular "rock" radio stations agree to broadcast them, but the "Christian station" refuses! We have had a greater problem with censorship from the Church, than from the secular media. Should the Church complain about censorship from the media, while it is practicing the same censorship against those who challenge its unbiblical positions? Once again, the Church is guilty of the same conduct that it condemns in others.

It is appropriate to conclude this chapter by asking a few pertinent questions. If Christian leaders practice bias in the Church, will they not also practice bias within our government if given the opportunity? If they distort and manipulate words in order to mislead the Church, will they not also distort and manipulate laws and policies in order to mislead our nation? If they have employed censorship within the Church, will they not also attempt to censor their political opponents? Should we be so foolish as to assume that they would behave differently in our government than they have in the Church? The answer is obvious, and that is why I have sounded the alarm.

13

THE BLIND LEADING THE BLIND: THE CONSERVATIVE CHRISTIAN CHURCH'S FAVORITISM OF ISRAEL

ERHAPS THE MOST frequently covered subject in the news media today is the Middle East. It seems that new revelations of violence and atrocities are occurring daily. Radical Palestinian suicide bombers wreak havoc on innocent Israeli civilians. Israel's military promptly responds, but innocent Palestinian civilians often suffer in the process. The media is obliged to cover these events, while we watch and formulate our own opinions, as to who is right or wrong.

Recently, many Christian conservatives have become quite vocal about this issue, proclaiming Israel's cause as righteous, and that Christians should support Israel. They declare the media has allowed its liberal bias to influence its coverage of the Middle East situation. Conservatives assert that media coverage is usually slanted toward the Palestinian position. Most Christians who hold this view believe that the media's perceived bias is due to their ignorance of what the Bible has to say about Israel. They believe that people are "spiritually blind" without the gospel, and that this blindness produces ignorance.

Most Christian conservatives teach that the nation of Israel is still God's chosen people, and that God still favors them above all others. They refer to many Old Testament, biblical passages to make their case.

It is interesting that the same Christian leaders that reject the usage of Old Testament scriptures concerning other Bible doctrines, such as the Ten Commandments and the Sabbath, then resort almost exclusively to using Old Testament passages to justify their doctrinal position on Israel.

As previously stated, these conservative Christians propound that today's liberal media favors the Palestinian cause because of its biblical ignorance. However, numerous New Testament passages seem to indicate that these same Christians are also biblically ignorant concerning the subject of Israel. According to many New Testament scriptures, the term Israel, in the New Testament era, applies to all who accept the gospel of Jesus Christ. The New Testament replaces the significance of the literal nation of Israel, with the concept of a "Spiritual Israel." The Church has become Israel in the "gospel era." The New Testament clearly teaches that all distinctions between Jew and Gentile have been removed.

It is undeniable that part of the gospel message is indeed the good news that all ethnic, racial and social barriers have been eliminated. The New Testament specifically states that we have all become "one." Therefore, Christian conservatives' focus on the literal nation of Israel is biblically incorrect. In chapter twenty-four, "The Evidence-Part Seven," a thorough biblical analysis of the subject of Israel is presented. You will find the scriptural evidence to be clear and decisive. It will make you question, once again, the judgment and discernment of Christian, conservative leaders.

This biblical ignorance concerning Israel, on the part of Christian conservatives, has created a bias favoring Israel similar to their *perceived bias* of the media in favor of the Palestinians. And, of course, this bias naturally creates unfair and unjust judgments and standards when comparing the two sides. The best way to demonstrate this is by considering the most important teachings in Christianity. Those teachings would certainly be that Jesus Christ is the Son of God, that He died for our sins and rose from the grave, thus proving that He Himself was "Almighty God" manifest in the flesh. Keeping this in mind, Christian conservatives' claim that Islam worships a different god than Christians, because Islam rejects these doctrines concerning Jesus Christ. However, they proclaim that Jews do worship the same God as Christians, although Jews also reject these doctrines regarding Jesus Christ. Is this not an unjust double standard? In fact, Islam actually holds Jesus in higher esteem than does Judaism, because Islam regards Jesus as a great prophet of God, whereas Judaism only views Him as a good man and a teacher.

As previously mentioned, many conservative, Christian leaders feel that the media is *blind* concerning Israel, but it would be good for them to remember what Jesus said about the church leaders of His day in Matthew 5:14. Jesus stated that the church leaders themselves were blind. And, He said that when the blind lead the blind they both fall into the ditch. Could it be, therefore, that we have the same situation today? As many conservatives in the Church are trying to teach and correct the *blind media* concerning Israel, could it be a repeat of the scenario in Jesus' day? Are these contemporary, religious leaders also nothing more than the "blind leading the blind"?

The spiritual importance of Christian conservatives' erroneous ideas regarding Israel is covered in chapter 24. However, the importance for the purpose of the main theme of this book should be obvious. While they are casting accusations of bias at the media in regards to Israel, Christian conservatives are also guilty of much of the same bias themselves. While they accuse the media of biblical ignorance regarding Israel, they also reflect a similar ignorance, which is clearly revealed in chapter 24. This bias and ignorance displayed by many Christian conservatives should serve as another warning concerning their qualifications to wisely and justly govern our nation.

14

"DUMBING-DOWN" THE CHURCH:
IT'S NOT JUST A
PUBLIC SCHOOL PROBLEM

ANOTHER RECENT ACCUSATION of many Christian conservatives has been that the political, leftist elite has been intentionally "dumbing down" our schools, in order to produce a new generation that they can easily control. The charge is that today's public schools do not teach the basics like they once did. Many "right-wing" Christians claim that reading, writing and arithmetic have been replaced with a new network of classes having specific liberal, social, and sexual agendas.

These conservatives maintain that there is an obvious anti-Christian flavor in today's public schools, as well as an anti-American spirit being fostered within our children. According to them, this is a deliberate and carefully planned scheme intended to indoctrinate the next generation with *political leftist* ideology. Part of their accusation is that this "leftist elite" has literally been rewriting history in modern public school textbooks. They claim that new *politically correct* textbooks have replaced those studied by previous generations. They declare that much of our history's patriotic spirit has been watered down or eliminated completely in these textbooks.

According to conservatives in the Church, even our nation's constitution is being manipulated or else ignored completely in our public schools. They suggest that the overwhelming weight of evidence regarding our nation's patriotic spirit throughout history, and the noble truths and freedoms in our constitution, have been exchanged for inaccurate, modern, liberal, politically correct opinions and philosophies. Once again, Christian conservatives are entitled to their opinions and have the right to express them. Also, their views may have some merit. The problem for conservative Christian leaders repeatedly arises in the area of inconsistency and contradictory behavior.

They have accused our public educational system of neglecting the time-honored educational truths of the past, in favor of a new, liberalized, watered down, "touchy-feely" social agenda. However, they have watered down and liberalized their own doctrines as well, and the Church itself has also degenerated into a "touchy-feely" and *emotion-driven* organization throughout much of America. Some have labeled today's Church in America as being "church light." It tastes great to the senses and emotions, but is less spiritually and biblically filling. Much of America's Christianity has fallen to such a degree, that many church services could be correctly called selfish, "bless me" services.

While the Church is in a deplorable, materialistic, selfish and generally sinful state, it offers "feel good" services with *holy laughter*, people getting *drunk in the spirit*, and also being *slain in the spirit*. Translated into common secular terms, in many churches people are literally rolling on the church floors in laughter, falling down and slurring their words as if drunk from alcohol. It is indeed interesting that such *spirit-filled* Christians are still sinning at the same rate as non-Christians, according to recent Church surveys. It's also interesting that none of these Holy Spirit experiences in today's Church have any biblical precedent whatsoever. You could say that the Church is doing its own version of *dumbing down* the Church, by replacing plain Bible teaching, reverence and unselfish ministry to those in need, with "church light."

You could also say that modern church leaders are just as guilty of trying to rewrite the Bible, so to speak, as are those liberal educators of rewriting history and our constitution. How so? By changing God into a slot machine via the popular, perverted, prosperity message, where you put in a dollar to get a bunch of dollars back. Also, by twisting Bible texts, as is clearly demonstrated in chapters twenty-one and twenty-two, in order to create the erroneous doctrines of *once saved always saved* and the abolition of the Ten Commandments, thereby reproducing their own sinful generation within the Church, just as they claim is happening in our public school system. Furthermore, conservatives complain when the *political left* ignores the weight of evidence in order to advance its own agenda instead, yet they are guilty of doing the same thing with numerous doctrines within the Church, as is clearly revealed throughout this book.

Is our society being "dumbed-down"? This is a decision that each individual must make. However, one thing is certain. Christian conservatives should attend to their own "dumbing down" problems within the Church, before focusing on those in our secular society. The fact that they have not been able to remedy these issues in the Church, certainly disqualifies them from addressing them in the public sector.

₂ 15 ₂

THE CHURCH & EVOLUTION
(ANOTHER DOUBLE STANDARD)

CONSERVATIVE, FUNDAMENTALIST CHRISTIANS have long denounced the theory of evolution as being riddled with inconsistencies, lies and cover-ups. It is argued that the theory of evolution has no more factual basis than does the divine creation account presented in the Bible. The Church points out that actual frauds have been exposed and verified, in regards to supposed fossil evidence, and church leaders accuse the secular, scientific community of unethical and dishonest attempts to present their own unsubstantiated ideas and opinions as being factual.

The Church also bemoans the unfair exclusion of the creation theory from our public school system, while evolution is presented as being based on solid scientific evidence. It is argued that the creation theory should be given an equal opportunity to present its case. To be objective, one must admit that the Church's perspective on these issues is worthy of consideration. And, it is certainly the Church's prerogative to publicly address this subject by voicing its opinion.

As with all of the issues in the previous chapters, the problem is not the Church's views or its right to express them, but rather its own inconsistencies and contradictory behavior. It is interesting and significant that, while the Church asks our public schools to honor the divine creation account, the Church itself simultaneously continues to refuse to acknowledge and honor the "memorial" of God's creation, which God Himself established.

According to Genesis chapter two in the Bible, after God had completed the creation of the world in six days, He then rested on the seventh day, Saturday. As stated in chapters eleven and twelve, the Bible states that He also blessed and sanctified the seventh day. Moreover, in Exodus chapter twenty, the seventh-day (Saturday) Sabbath is included within the Ten Commandments. The commandment in Exodus repeats God's special blessing upon the seventh day, and then instructs His people to remember it and keep it holy. It also instructs them to refrain from their normal labor on that day. What is significant, however, is that the commandment also gives God's reason for honoring the seventh day and for commanding His people to honor it. What is that reason? According to the commandment, the Sabbath is to be kept in memory of God's creation of our world. In other words, honoring the seventh-day Sabbath represents a type of *memorial* of God's creative works. And, according to the Bible, God felt strongly enough about it, that He made it one of His Ten Commandments.

It is common knowledge, and has been previously mentioned, that the vast majority of the Christian Church has chosen to ignore and disobey God's commandment to honor the seventh-day Sabbath, and has instead substituted its own day to honor, Sunday. Why is the Church openly disobeying God's commandment concerning the seventh-day Sabbath? Knowing that this commandment honors and remembers God as being the creator of our world, why does the Church ignore this biblical memorial of His creation?

Why does the Church take the hypocritical position of asking our secular culture to honor God as creator, while the Church itself refuses to honor God's memorial of creation, by not keeping the seventh-day Sabbath as commanded in the Bible? Is it proper for the Church to accuse secular scientists of exalting their own opinions and ideas as fact, concerning the creation of the world, while the Church is also exalting its own ideas and opinions over God's specific commandment regarding the memorial of His creation?

Once again, there can be only one logical conclusion. The Church should practice what it preaches. If the Church expects the world to acknowledge God as creator, it should start by honoring Him as creator in the Church, by obeying the commandment that memorializes His creation. If church leaders are not willing to do this, they should cease harassing public school districts about presenting creationism ("intelligent design") as part of their science curriculum. To try to get our public schools to consider honoring God as Creator, while Christian leaders are not doing so, is pure hypocrisy.

16

DUMB DOGS
THAT DON'T BARK

WHAT WOULD BE your opinion of a crew of structural engineers who were hired to regularly check the structural integrity of the Hoover Dam by thoroughly inspecting it for any cracks, leaks or signs of wear and stress; nevertheless, who often neglected their duty and skipped their routine inspections?

How would you view them if they did not even bother to sound the alarm when they noticed a small crack or leak, because they thought it was small and insignificant; notwithstanding, there eventually were so many of these small cracks and leaks that the Hoover Dam collapsed and fell, and the flood destroyed multitudes?

You would probably agree that these engineers were irresponsible and unfaithful "watchmen," and were accountable for the deaths of all who perished in the flood. This chapter is not about floods, dams or structural engineers who keep watch over the dams. It is, however, about cowardly and unfaithful leaders who do not boldly and courageously stand for what is right, and proclaim the necessary warnings to alert and protect those who have been entrusted to their watchful care and oversight.

Many conservative Christians would be quick to apply this lesson to "dovish," liberal, Democratic leaders in our government. They've often charged them with appeasement and dereliction of duty in their approach to the *war on terror* and the protection of our nation.

It has been commonly stated by conservatives, that most Democrats do not understand the imminent danger and absolute evil posed by our radical Islamic enemies. It is maintained that liberals think that they can deal with terrorism as a normal law enforcement issue, rather than as an all-out war.

Christian conservatives assert that this philosophy endangers American citizens, because this lax and gullible attitude, allegedly possessed by Democratic leaders, fosters a much less aggressive approach to the war on terror. Conservative leaders in the Church and in the Republican Party suggest that the best *defense* against terrorism is to have a strong and aggressive *offense* against terrorism.

The conservative Christian Church largely believes that today's *terroristic* environment requires government leaders who are vigilant and faithful to boldly proclaim the necessary warnings, in order to alert and protect our citizens. Conservatives declare that liberal Democrats do not offer such vigilant and faithful leadership, and cannot be trusted to proclaim these necessary warnings. In the opinions of most conservative Christians, Democratic leaders are liable to produce the same deadly results as the unfaithful structural engineers in my illustration.

Each person must arrive at their own conclusion concerning the accuracy and validity of Christian conservatives' views on this issue. However, one thing is certain. Church leaders ought to take a look in the mirror before proceeding with their attacks against Democratic leaders. Why? Because, unfortunately, church leadership has had its own share of unfaithful leaders who have been clearly exposed in the Bible. Scripture reveals a long history of untrustworthy and disobedient priests, prophets, apostles, teachers and ministers throughout both Old and New Testament times; furthermore, we are told that this problem will continue to worsen as we approach the end of time.

Jesus called the Pharisees, who were church leaders of His day, *blind leaders* and *blind guides* (Matthew 15:12-14; Matthew 23:16-26). He also warned of false prophets down through the ages (Matthew 7:13-20; Matthew 24:11; Mathew 24:24).

The apostle Paul spoke of false apostles and ministers in 2nd Corinthians 11:13-15. We are also forewarned of false teachers by the apostle Peter (2nd Peter 2:1-3). And, in 2nd Timothy 3:13, we are admonished that "impostors" will grow worse and worse.

The prophet Jeremiah says that God's people became *lost sheep* because the "shepherds" led them astray (Jer. 50:6). He said that the prophets were guilty of giving false visions, prophecies and delusions, instead of revealing the people's iniquities or sins (Lam. 2:14). And, Ezekiel stated that the shepherds *fed themselves* instead of caring for the needs of the flock (Ezek. 34:2; Ezek. 34:6-10).

The prophet Isaiah accused the prophets and leaders of teaching lies, of causing God's people to err and thus also to be destroyed (Isaiah 9:14-16). In fact, Isaiah declared that *beasts* were able to devour the people because the watchmen were blind, and were like "dumb dogs" that don't bark to give the necessary warnings (Isaiah 56:9-11).

In summary, the Bible clearly chronicles a history of frequent unfaithfulness by church leaders in both Old and New Testament times. It speaks of *blind guides* and *blind watchmen* who lead the people astray. It tells of unfaithful leaders who teach lies and delusions, instead of revealing the people's sins. It refers to leaders who are like *dumb watchdogs* who don't bark to give the needed warnings.

However, even more concerning, the Bible tells us that these problems will intensify as time continues. Therefore, we can expect an even greater problem today with unfaithful leaders in the Church. As the apostle Paul told Timothy, imposters will grow continually worse. Additionally, in today's church, we do not have prophets and apostles such as Jeremiah, Isaiah, Ezekiel, Peter and Paul to faithfully and boldly sound the alarm, warning us of these deceptions and dangers. Nevertheless, we do have their warnings, as well as those of every other Bible writer including Jesus Himself, reliably recorded in the Bible. And, Christians need to thoroughly acquaint themselves with that divine book, if they are to guard against deception and error.

However, for our purposes in this chapter, it is once again obvious that the Church needs to attend to its own problem of unfaithful leaders who do not give the necessary warnings, before addressing this issue among liberal Democratic leaders. There are plenty of "dumb dogs" who are not *barking* the needed warnings within the church hierarchy. I suggest that Christian conservatives first focus their criticisms upon the unfaithful leaders within the Church who have failed to acknowledge and confess their biblical compromises, which are clearly documented in this book; moreover, who have also failed to proclaim the necessary warnings to a wayward Church. Once they have successfully addressed this problem within their own organization, their advice will seem more credible to those in the secular realm.

17

WHY I'M BLOWING
THE WHISTLE

THERE ARE TWO primary concerns that have prompted me to write this book. One concern is the recent trend of right-wing, Christian leaders trying to expand their sphere of influence into our government and secular culture. I am not suggesting that, because they are Christians, they should not be allowed to participate in our political process. My concern is that their hypocritical and dishonest behavior in the Church will be repeated on a much larger scale within our government.

Jesus stated that if people are unfaithful in small things, they will also be unfaithful in big things. Therefore, it is fair and biblical to ask the following questions.

If church leaders have justified *trampling* on the Bible, as will be clearly demonstrated in the eight following "Evidence Chapters," will they not also justify trampling on our constitution? If they have justified betraying their Church and their God, will they not also justify betraying their nation?

If church leaders have abused their positions of authority in the Church, will they not also abuse their leadership positions in our government? If they have marginalized, ostracized and censored those who disagree with them in the Church, will they not also employ such strategies within our government?

If church leaders have been unfaithful with the revenue donated to the Church (God's money), will they not also be unfaithful with our government's tax revenues? If they have embraced and promulgated cruel and sadistic philosophies within the Church, as will be clearly demonstrated in the next two chapters, will they not also embrace cruel and sadistic philosophies and practices in their course of governing our nation?

If Church leaders have participated in lies and cover-ups within the Church, will they not also participate in such activities in our government? Should we not expect them to repeat the same dishonest, hypocritical and abusive behavior within our government, which they have exhibited in their positions of authority in the Church?

They must not be allowed to expand their deceptive, dictatorial sphere of influence. They pose a unique and serious threat to our nation. Why? Because these are individuals who believe that they are called and guided by God, yet have simultaneously justified lies, manipulation, distortion and gross financial abuse while serving their God. Can you imagine a more dangerous scenario than having our nation ruled by a group of individuals who can justify such immoral and unethical behavior; moreover, believing that they are doing the will of God in the midst of their deception and hypocrisy?

My second primary concern is that the Church in America is misrepresenting the character of Jesus. Jesus is being given a *black eye* through the Church's inconsistencies, contradictions and double standards. The thing that Jesus seemed to detest most, according to the New Testament gospel accounts, was hypocrisy among His professed followers. Jesus' harshest language was used against the hypocritical church leaders of His day. He called them snakes and hypocrites. He said that the harlots would enter heaven before them. And, He asked them not to even call Him Lord, if they refused to do what He said. The Bible also states that Jesus is the same yesterday, today and forever. Therefore, Jesus detests the hypocrisy in today's Christian Church in America, just as much as He detested it in the Church of His day when He walked on this earth nearly two thousand years ago. If Jesus found it necessary to rebuke His Church back then, we can be sure that He would also rebuke His Church today for the same sins. The Church cannot be an effective witness to the world for Jesus, while it is practicing the contradictory behaviors discussed in this book. The Church needs to repent of it's own sins, before pointing the finger at the sins of the *political left.*

The Church's first step should be to publicly confess its hypocritical practices that have been revealed in this book. Then, the Church would be wise to do its own spiritual "house cleaning," before attempting to *clean* the liberal, political establishment. Jesus stated that you can't help remove the *speck* from another's eye, while you have a *log* in your own eye. It's time for the Church to remove the logs from its own eyes. After the Church has confessed, repented and reformed, it will be better prepared to address the problems in our nation.

I believe it appropriate to extend the Church *extra grace* concerning its stubbornness and disobedience regarding the seventh-day Sabbath commandment. The most well known religious group keeping the Sabbath has been the Seventh-Day-Adventist denomination. As a former Adventist, I left because of its legalism and its exalting itself as the one true "remnant church" of the Bible. It has numerous other doctrines that contradict the Bible, as well as claiming its own special "prophetess" named Ellen White, who has had numerous failed prophesies and contradictions of scripture. For these reasons, the Seventh-Day-Adventist Church has been viewed negatively in Christian circles. Unfortunately, because the seventh-day Sabbath has been primarily associated with their denomination in recent times, the Sabbath itself has also been viewed negatively. This has probably helped to produce a bad *aura* concerning the subject of the Sabbath in general.

However, this still does not excuse the Christian Church for taking the dishonest and duplicitous positions revealed in this book concerning the Sabbath and other biblical issues. The Church is guilty of serious double standards and blatant hypocrisy that must be exposed in order to force the Church to confront, confess and repent of its sins. Its misrepresentation of Jesus and the Bible must be stopped. The whistle needed to be blown. My hope is that the Church will not try to hide or excuse its compromises and sins, but that it will acknowledge and deal with them.

§ THE EVIDENCE §

18

THE EVIDENCE—PART ONE: DOES GOD PUNISH SINNERS ETERNALLY?

I T'S TIME TO EMBARK UPON an investigation of the biblical evidence that will clearly reveal compromises, manipulation of Bible texts, distortion of clear biblical passages, as well as overt disobedience to authoritative commands in the *book* that church leaders claim to revere and love. We will begin our first "evidence chapter" with a couple of illustrations.

What would be your impression of a nation whose justice system gave everyone the same sentence regardless of his or her crime? Would you consider it to be unfair and unjust for a brutal serial killer who tortured women and children, to receive the same length of punishment as a poor, unemployed man who stole bread and milk from a grocery store to feed his family?

How would you view a parent who always punished his children for five months whenever they were disobedient for five seconds? Could you possibly be convinced that this parent was a kind, merciful, just and loving parent, despite numerous reasons given?

The answer to these questions is obvious. All would agree that the punishment in both scenarios was completely unjust and inappropriate. All would agree that the excessive response by the parent to his children's disobedience, clearly revealed the parent to be unkind, unmerciful, unjust and unloving.

Yet, the Christian Church expects the world to accept and embrace a God who the church claims is kind, merciful, just and loving, while simultaneously declaring that their God will punish sinners for billions of years without end, in return for living disobedient lives for seventy years on earth.

The Church expects the world to view their God as fair and just, while Adolph Hitler, who tortured and killed millions including women and children, receives the same eternal hell fire punishment as the poor, unemployed, grocery store thief who stole bread and milk for his family.

If we would reject and denounce any nation or parent who practiced such forms of inequitable justice, why would we expect others to accept and embrace a God who conducts Himself the same way?

Any unbiased reader must agree it is a major contradiction to call the nation and the parent unjust and unfair, while maintaining that their God is fair and just, even as He does the same things. A just nation practices equitable justice. Loving parents show kindness, mercy and love toward their children. Thus, a loving and just God reflects love and equitable justice in all of His dealings with His children.

However, although this seems to be a reasonable and logical conclusion to arrive at, the most important thing is what the Bible says regarding this subject. And, it will probably surprise you to discover that the weight of biblical evidence overwhelmingly contradicts the widespread teaching that God punishes sinners forever. It will be proven beyond the shadow of a doubt, that our loving and just God does not torment people in hell for eternity.

The Bible clearly states that there is an everlasting or eternal hell fire; in fact, it is mentioned several times. It is interesting, though, that the subject of sinners' living forever in torment in that fire, is not referred to several times. There is *not one* text in the entire Bible that specifically states that people will suffer in pain and agony for endless ages. There are a few passages which seem to imply the eternal tormenting of sinners, but none that specifically state that this is the case.

Yet, there are numerous scriptures that directly contradict the few vague texts being used to support the eternal torment doctrine.

It is necessary to mention that the hell fire will be a real experience for unrepentant sinners; for them it will be a place of indescribable pain, agony and torment. Jesus described it as a place of wailing and gnashing of teeth (Matthew 13:42-50). I am not denying the reality of hell, but I am declaring that the weight of biblical evidence does not support the idea of sinners' living in torment there forever. The devil and his angels who caused this "nightmare" sin experiment with all of its suffering and heartache for billions of people, will indeed be tormented there forever, and rightly so. God does justly distinguish between the author of evil, the devil and his evil angels, and people whom they have deceived. The devil and his angels, tormenting billions of people over thousands of years, are responsible for billions not receiving eternal life in heaven. No one should question the justice of eternal punishment for the devil and his angels. Their case is uniquely different from the case of those whom they have deceived.

Now, what does the Bible say about the hell fire and sinners' punishment in it? Jesus said that it is an everlasting fire (Matthew 18:8; Matthew 25:41). The Bible also states that it is a fire that will never be quenched (Isaiah 66:24; Luke 3:17; Mark 9:43-48). Also, according to scripture, this everlasting hell fire was prepared for the devil and his angels, and he will be tormented there forever along with the "beast" and "false prophet" described in the book of Revelation (Matthew 25:41; Revelation 20:10).

From these scriptures it is clear that there is an eternal hell fire; it is also clear that the devil, his angels, and the *beast* and *false prophet* will be tormented forever in that fire. However, thus far, we have had no specific reference to people living in eternal torment in hell.

Before I list the numerous scriptures that completely disprove and refute this eternal torment dogma, we will examine the few passages used to support this doctrine. You will find a "common thread" running through all of these texts. They all share the usage of the words *everlasting, forever* or *eternal.* However, you will soon see that not one of them specifically states that people suffer in pain and agony eternally. They will refer to the fire itself as burning forever, to the devil being tormented forever, to smoke ascending forever, and to worms not dying, but not one of these texts clearly and unequivocally states that people are suffering pain and torment throughout eternity. Let's examine each verse individually.

Proponents of eternal torment refer to Matthew 18:8, but this passage simply warns about being thrown into the everlasting fire. It does not say you will suffer there eternally. They mention Matthew 25:41, but this text simply states that the wicked will be put into the everlasting fire. It does not declare that they will agonize in it forever.

Eternal torment advocates also cite Isaiah 66:24 and Mark 9:43-48, which speak of the wicked being cast into a fire that will not be quenched, and these also mention worms or maggots that will not die. As with the other passages, these verses do not state that the wicked will be in painful torment within that fire forever. These texts also do not say that the wicked people themselves do not die, but rather that the worms and maggots don't die. In fact, the wicked people are referred to as corpses or carcasses. The Hebrew word used is *peger*, which literally means corpse, carcass or dead body. Therefore, this scripture contrasts, not compares, the people with the worms or maggots. The worms are alive, but the people are dead! A more detailed explanation of this text and its proper interpretation is presented later in this chapter.

Another text used to support the eternal torment doctrine is Revelation 14:9-11. It states that the wicked will be tormented with fire and brimstone, and the smoke will ascend forever. Notice that it does not specifically state that the torment will last forever, but rather that the smoke resulting from that torment will ascend forever. Once again, we still have no direct, unequivocal statement of people suffering in pain and agony forever. And, later in this chapter, this passage will also be explained in a more detailed manner, which also accords with Scripture.

Eternal torment proponents also refer to Daniel 12:1-2 in their effort to support this doctrine. They point out that the wicked receive everlasting contempt. Is everlasting contempt the same as suffering in pain and agony throughout endless ages? Of course not! As with all of the previously mentioned texts, this passage does not specifically refer to the eternal torment of sinners. Also, the original Hebrew word that is translated as *everlasting* in this passage, is used in numerous other biblical texts throughout the Old Testament to describe other *everlast-*

ing things, events or practices that have ceased long ago. Therefore, it becomes obvious in Scripture that the term everlasting does not always necessarily describe a process that goes on forever throughout the trillions of years of eternity. This original Hebrew word is used at times to describe something that will continue until it has fulfilled its purpose, or to describe something that produces everlasting results. However, in this particular passage, the exact interpretation of the intended usage of *everlasting* is insignificant, because this specific text does not even mention anything concerning the subject of suffering painful torment. The fact that eternal torment advocates even try to make use of this text reveals how few biblical passages they have that are even remotely connected to their disgusting doctrine. Therefore, they will grab anything that even comes remotely close to their dogma, and try to make use of it.

Advocates of this doctrine also mention verses six and seven in the book of Jude. Verse six describes the fallen angels who are in everlasting chains. It does not say that wicked people are in everlasting chains. Verse seven states that Sodom and Gomorrah are an example for us of God's vengeance, as they suffered eternal fire. If they are an example of God's vengeance, what can we learn from this? Is the "eternal" fire that destroyed Sodom and Gomorrah still burning? No! Have the wicked inhabitants of those cities continued to live on in agonizing torment down through the centuries in that fire? No! They died in that fire, and the Bible states that this is an example of God's vengeance. Therefore, this passage actually contradicts the eternal torment dogma.

Sometimes verse thirteen in the book of Jude is also cited to support this doctrine. It states that the blackness of darkness is forever reserved for the wicked men described in this passage. Does this text specifically declare that these men will be tortured throughout eternity? No! It says that darkness is reserved for them. And, it is interesting that Job also refers to the grave, or place of the dead, as a place of darkness (Job 17:13). Therefore, this passage is probably referring to the darkness of eternal death, which awaits the wicked. It certainly does not state anything about suffering pain and agony throughout eternity.

Matthew 25:46 is another text often mentioned by those who teach this doctrine. This verse proclaims that the wicked will receive everlasting punishment. Does that necessarily mean they will be tormented in the hell fire forever? Couldn't it simply be referring to a punishment that produces everlasting results? Isn't the eternal death of the wicked an everlasting punishment? The wicked perish forever! It is significant that the destruction of the wicked is also called a *sudden destruction* in 1st Thessalonians 5:3; furthermore it is described as a *swift destruction* in 2nd Peter 2:1. How can it be sudden, everlasting and swift? There is only one logical and reasonable explanation. It is sudden because it comes unexpectedly and takes the wicked by surprise. It is swift because it is accomplished in a short period of time when compared to eternity. It is everlasting because it produces everlasting results. The wicked are destroyed and gone forever.

The other passage used by those who espouse the eternal torment doctrine is found in Revelation chapter twenty. They point out that verse ten says that the devil is cast into the lake of fire where the "beast" and "false prophet" are, and that they are tormented there forever. And, I completely agree that this will be the fate of the devil, *beast* and *false prophet*. However, it does not say that this is also the fate of wicked people in general. In fact, in verse nine, it says that the wicked are *devoured* in the fire! The Bible clearly states that while the devil is tortured forever in the fire, the wicked are simply *devoured* by the fire. The Greek word for devour is *katesthio*. This word is never used one single time in all of Scripture to describe an eternally ongoing process. It always describes something that is consumed and gone. Also noteworthy, is the fact that *katesthio* is never used to describe the devil's or antichrist's fate in the fire. Why? Because they will suffer forever as the Bible plainly states, and they will never be consumed and gone. But, *katesthio* is used for wicked people because they do not suffer forever, but rather are consumed by the fire and perish. In a "last-ditch" attempt to support this hideous doctrine, some will declare that the fire that devours the wicked in verse nine, is a different fire than the one they're cast into in verse fifteen. If that is true, the wicked dead would have two resurrections, because they would be raised after the millennium and destroyed by God in the fire described in verse nine, only to be resurrected a second time and thrown back in the fire again in verse fifteen. This is both absurd, and contradicts scripture. Hebrews 9:27

clearly states that men die once, and then they face the judgment; not that they die twice before the judgment. The death which the wicked experience, mentioned in verse fifteen, is called their *second* death; but, if their death experience referred to in verse fifteen is in addition to the one mentioned in verse nine, then their death told of in verse fifteen would be their *third* death. They would have died their *first death* before the millennium. They would have died their *second death*, as described in verse nine, after the millennium. Therefore, if their verse fifteen death is in addition to their verse nine death, the verse fifteen death would be their *third death*. This, of course, would also contradict the Bible. I find it amazing that preachers and theologians will even contradict other scriptures in order to maintain this dubious doctrine that portrays God as a vindictive, cruel tyrant. Obviously the fire of verse fifteen is the same fire that destroys the wicked in verse nine, and is simply "replayed" in John's new vision beginning in verse eleven when he states: *"Then I saw."* This wording often begins a new vision for John in the book of Revelation, and his visions frequently overlap and restate previous scenes. It should also be noted that the wicked's experience in the fire is called a second *death*. It is not called an everlasting torment. It is certainly not a coincidence that the devil's ultimate fate is never referred to as death, whereas the final fate of wicked people is called death. It is highly significant that this passage in Revelation chapter twenty clearly differentiates between the devil and wicked people, when describing their experience and fate in the hell fire. The devil's fate in the fire is described as torment forever (Rev. 20:10), whereas the fate of wicked people is referred to as death and being devoured (Rev. 20:9; Rev. 20:15). When you study this passage in Revelation closely, you find that it actually contradicts the eternal torment doctrine.

We have covered all of the texts used to substantiate this hideous eternal torment doctrine that maligns the character of our gracious, merciful, kind and loving God. Although some of these passages could imply the eternal tormenting of people, there is not one that specifically and unequivocally states that this is the case! When you put these few vague and inconclusive references up against the massive, solid Bible evidence which I am about to present, it is difficult to understand why so many theologians still insist on misrepresenting our fair and just God. They insist that you must believe that our merciful and loving Jesus, who the Bible states "has no pleasure in the death of the wicked" (Ezekiel 33:11), will torture them for the equivalent of nearly 30,000 years for each and every single minute that they lived on this Earth. That equals fourteen billion *"units"* of punishment as recompense for every single *"unit"* of disobedience! And, this is based on spending just one trillion years in hell. Our "kind and merciful" Christian preachers tell us that lost souls will be tormented there for trillions of trillions of years! This would eventually equal millions of years of pain and agony as supposed *just punishment* for each and every second that they lived on this Earth. Any reasonable and unbiased person should certainly agree that this is pure *sadism.*

In view of the fact that they have no actual, clear and unequivocal Bible texts that specifically state that lost sinners will suffer pain and agony in hell throughout eternity, proponents of this sadistic doctrine attempt to resort to a couple of feeble arguments of supposed logic. They ask why God would throw sinners into an everlasting fire if they are not going to suffer in it forever; moreover, they question why the Bible repeatedly refers to the hell fire as being eternal or everlasting, if sinners experience only a limited time of suffering in it.

I will answer their *questions of logic* with biblical and *logical* answers. This frequent emphasis on the fact that the hell fire is never going to be extinguished, gives sinners the clear and forceful message that they are *doomed to perish* in this fire. "This fire is not going out, so they are not getting out alive." However, undoubtedly the main reason that the Bible repeatedly refers to the hell fire as being eternal is because <u>that is the accurate description of the fire.</u> It is an eternal fire! God is accurately describing the hell fire's duration. Do eternal torment advocates want God to use different, deceptive language to describe it? It is certainly not God's fault that sadistic human beings have taken the duration of the hell fire, and then applied that duration to everything that is thrown into the fire.

Just because things are thrown into a particular fire does not necessitate that the items themselves will continue to burn for the entire duration of that fire. If you have told your friends to come to your home to enjoy an all-day bonfire in your backyard roasting hotdogs and marshmallows on a *crisp* autumn day, does that mean that everything thrown into your bonfire will burn all day long, just because you're making an all-day fire? Absolutely not! During the course of the day you will probably throw in some small twigs and branches that are consumed in minutes. You might also throw in some paper or plastic plates and cups from your meal, which will literally be consumed in seconds. And, there will be logs in your fire that will burn for hours before being totally consumed. You told your friends the truth when you said that it would be an all-day fire, but that did not mean that everything put into the fire would burn all day long! The various items put into your all-day fire actually burned for varying durations of time before eventually being consumed and gone. How long each item burned was determined by the *composition* of each item. Do you understand the significance of the point that I'm making? God is making an eternal fire, but that does not mean that everyone put into that fire will burn eternally. As with my all-day bonfire example, their duration of time in the fire before being totally consumed and gone, will be determined by their "sinful composition." The more sin that is present, the longer they will burn.

This brings us back to the other supposedly logical question asked by eternal torment advocates. As I previously mentioned, they ask why God would throw sinners into the same everlasting fire that He uses for the devil if they are not also going to suffer in it eternally. I have a very logical answer to their logical question. How many hell fires should God kindle to handle the various durations of punishment? Should He have a one-day fire for some; a one-week fire for others with more guilt; a one-month fire for those with even more sin; a one-year fire for those who had an abundance of sin throughout their lives; a ten-year fire for those who committed heinous sins against numerous people; and finally a seventy-year fire for those who are in a class by themselves, spending their entire lives murdering and torturing, such as Hitler and Stalin? I think God's plan is much better. He uses the same fire to deal with all of the varying durations of punishment. And, He makes it eternal so that it can justly continue to torment the devil and his evil angels throughout eternity, because they were the ones who originated sin on this planet and are responsible for billions of people losing their opportunity to have eternal life in heaven. Therefore, it is perfectly just for them to receive an eternal sentence in hell.

Eternal torment proponents remind us that the overwhelming majority of Christians espouse the eternal torment doctrine, and that it is only a very small percentage of believers who disagree with this teaching. If adherents to this doctrine think that such an argument increases the likeliness that their position must be correct, they have a faulty sense of biblical history. The majority of people have been wrong the majority of the time throughout history. There were only eight people who went aboard Noah's ark. There were only seven thousand in all of Israel who had not participated in idol worship of Baal, which was probably *less than one percent* of the population. There were only 120 disciples in the "upper room" before Pentecost; this was after three and a half years of tireless ministry by the greatest preacher, teacher and prophet in history, Jesus Christ. Jesus Himself said that only *few* would enter into eternal life, whereas *many* would travel the path to destruction (Matthew 7:13-14). Therefore, to base the correctness of your doctrinal positions upon whether the majority of people are in agreement with your position, is a dangerous and *slippery slope* that biblical history suggests will probably result in embracing doctrinal errors.

Eternal torment advocates are also quick to remind us that the respected *"church fathers"* of past centuries also espoused the eternal torment doctrine. So what? The respected *"church fathers"* of the Old Testament era committed polygamy, but that did not make polygamy acceptable. There has always been error within the Church, so we must not base our doctrines upon the *"church fathers,"* but solely upon the Bible! We must not forget that the Bible records that Abraham lied, Noah got drunk, and David committed adultery and murder. Just because these respected "Old Testament" *church fathers* committed these sins, does not make these sins acceptable. It just stresses the importance of basing our doctrines solely upon the Bible, not upon the *church fathers*. It should also be remembered that even the precious doctrine of *justification by faith* had been ignored and contradicted by *church fathers* for a thousand years, until courageous *reformers* stood up and challenged the erring church hierarchy of their day during the Protestant Reformation. For many centuries church leaders had misrepresented God's loving and gracious character regarding *justification by faith*, just as they've also continued to misrepresent His loving and just character down through the centuries by promulgating their eternal torment dogma.

I believe that many church leaders will find themselves being rebuked by God as Job's friends were in Job 42:7, when God told them that His anger was aroused against them because they had not spoken of God correctly. They had maligned God's character, and so have the proponents of this eternal torment dogma!

What is the final fate of the wicked, according to the overwhelming weight of biblical evidence? The Bible declares that the soul who sins shall die, not that he will be tortured forever (Ezekiel 18:4; Ezekiel 18:20). It also states that the wages of sin is death, not eternal torment (Romans 6:23). The prophet Malachi declares that the day is coming when the wicked will be burned like stubble, and they will be reduced to ashes under our feet (Malachi 4:1-3). If they have become ashes that returned to the earth under our feet, how can they still be burning? The book of Psalms tells us that the wicked will be destroyed, perish and have no future, and that they *will be no more* (Psalm 145:20; Psalm 37:37,38; Psalm 37:10; Psalm 37:20). I will comment in more detail on these texts a little later.

Although we have already laid a strong foundation for supporting the annihilation of the wicked, rather than their eternal torment, we have only just begun to dismantle and eradicate this horrid doctrine. The scriptures that follow will put the final "nail in the coffin" to this repugnant teaching.

All the scriptures that I am about to cite have two things in common. They discuss the ultimate fate of the wicked, and they utilize the Greek word, "apollumi," to describe that final fate. This is significant because Scripture always uses this Greek word to mean destruction, perish, kill, die or fully destroy. The only exception to this rule is in several instances when *apollumi* is translated as *lose* or *lost*, describing things that are lost and can be found, such as sheep, coins and people. However, it is __never__ used to depict eternal torment or suffering.

Before I list the verses that use this Greek term to describe the wicked's final fate, I will cite numerous other texts that also utilize the Greek word *apollumi*. Although these passages are not referring to the ultimate fate of the wicked, they conclusively show that this Greek word means being destroyed, perished, killed or caused to die. Not one time in all of scripture does it imply being tortured eternally.

In Matthew 2:13 we're told that Herod tried to *apollumi*, or destroy, the baby Jesus. Herod was not trying to torture Jesus forever, but rather to kill Him.

In Matthew 8:25 and Mark 4:38 the disciples warned Jesus that they were about to *apollumi*, or perish, in the storm. The disciples were not saying that the storm was going to punish them forever, but that it was going to kill them.

The Bible tells us that the pharisees and priests plotted to *apollumi*, or destroy, Jesus (Matthew 12:14; Mark 3:6; Mark 11:18; Luke 19:47). These religious leaders were not plotting to torture Jesus forever, but to kill Him.

In Jesus' parable about the wicked vinedressers who beat and killed the servants sent by the owner of the vineyard, He said that the owner would *apollumi*, or destroy, the wicked vinedressers (Matthew 21:41; Mark 12:9; Luke 20:16). Jesus was not saying that the owner would torture them forever, but rather that he would kill them.

In Matthew 26:52 Jesus proclaimed that all who take the sword will *apollumi*, or perish, by the sword. Once again, Jesus was not suggesting that those who use a sword would be tortured with a sword forever, but that they would be killed with a sword.

In Matthew 27:20 we're told that the priests influenced the multitude to ask for Barabbas to be released, and for Jesus to be *apollumi*, or destroyed. They were not suggesting that Pilate should torment Jesus forever, but that he should kill Him.

In Luke 13:33 Jesus stated that a prophet can't *apollumi*, or perish, out of Jerusalem. He was not saying that a prophet could not be punished eternally outside of Jerusalem, but rather that a prophet could not be killed outside of Jerusalem.

Acts 5:37 states that Judas of Galilee rose up in the days of the census and drew many people after him, but later he *apollumi*, or perished. This does not mean that he was tortured eternally, but that he died.

The Bible states that those who tempted Christ and those who complained against Him in the days of Israel's wandering in the wilderness, were *apollumi*, or destroyed (1 Corinthians 10:9-10). They were not eternally tormented; rather, they were killed.

In verse five of the book of Jude, we're told that some of those who had been saved out of Egypt did not believe and were later *apollumi*, or destroyed. They were not punished forever, but were killed. Verse eleven compares the evil men referred to in the book of Jude, to those who *apollumi*, or perished, in the Old Testament rebellion of Korah. Those who participated in that rebellion were not tortured forever, but were killed.

In Luke 17:27-30 Jesus said that the wicked in the days of Noah and Lot were *apollumi*, or destroyed. Of course we know that in both instances the wicked were not inflicted with painful suffering forever, but were killed. It is also significant that Jesus said it will be the same scenario when He returns. In other words, once again the wicked will be *apollumi*, or killed, not subjected to eternal torture.

Finally, in 2 Peter 3:5-9 we're told that the floodwaters in the days of Noah caused the wicked to *apollumi*, or perish. Did the floodwaters torture the wicked forever? No! They killed the wicked by drowning them. Then Peter goes on to compare that destruction of the wicked with the destruction that will occur in the hell fire. He uses the same word *apollumi* in verse nine for those who will perish in the hell fire, as he did for those who perished in the flood in verse six. Thus, the wicked destroyed in the hell fire will experience the same fate as the wicked in the flood, which was death rather than eternal torment. Do you recognize the pattern? The Greek word *apollumi* means to perish, be destroyed, die or be killed. It is _never_ used to depict eternal torment!

Now we can get back to those other verses I mentioned earlier, which use the Greek word *apollumi* to refer to the ultimate fate of the wicked. Remember, we already know that this Greek word means to perish, be destroyed, die or be killed. In fact, we've already examined one of these *apollumi* verses regarding the final fate of the wicked in 2 Peter 3:9. That passage said that if they don't repent, they will *apollumi*, or perish, not suffer eternal torment, and compared it to what happened to those who died in the flood. They did not drown forever in the flood; neither will the wicked suffer forever in the fire.

A similar scripture is found in Luke 13:3-5, where Jesus proclaims that all who don't repent will *apollumi*, or perish, not suffer eternally.

Jesus told Nicodemus, as recorded in John 3:16, that all who believe in Him will have everlasting life, and will not *apollumi*, or perish. The two options Jesus gave were life or death, not life or eternal torment.

In 2 Corinthians 2:15-16, the apostle Paul declares that we are the fragrance of Christ to God. He goes on to say that it is the aroma of death to those who *apollumi*, or perish. Once again, the two options given by Paul were life or death, not life or eternal torment. The Bible plainly states in 2 Thessalonians 2:10 that those deceived by the Antichrist will *apollumi*, or perish—*not continue living* in eternal agony.

Finally, Jesus eliminates all doubt in Matthew 10:28. After telling us not to fear men who can only kill the body, He tells us instead to fear God, who will *apollumi*, or destroy, both soul and body in hell! Remember, we've already established that *apollumi* means to perish, be destroyed, kill or caused to die. It is never used to describe eternal torment! Therefore, Jesus is unequivocally stating that both body and soul will be destroyed, killed or caused to die in hell, not suffer throughout endless ages.

Although I have already presented an immense amount of evidence refuting this unjust and sadistic doctrine, we will now apply some "frosting" to the biblical cake that we've baked, actually several indisputable layers of frosting. It is noteworthy that the Greek words *katargeo* and *luo* are used to describe the destruction of the devil and his works in Hebrews 2:14 and in 1st John 3:8; furthermore, *katargeo* is also used in 2nd Thessalonians 2:8 to describe how the antichrist or "beast" is destroyed. However, *katargeo* and *luo* are never used in all of Scripture to describe the destruction of the wicked. Obviously the devil's fate in the hell fire, as well as that of the antichrist or *beast* of the book of Revelation, is different than the fate of lost people.

It is also significant that the Bible clearly states that <u>*only God*</u> possesses immortality (1st Timothy 6:16). Man does not possess immortality apart from the "new birth" experience in Christ. Without that *new birth* experience, there is no immortality for man. Lost people, of course, have not become *born again* in Christ; consequently they have no immortal soul to live on forever in hell. These are not my words, but rather are precisely what the Bible teaches. As I previously stated, the Bible declares that <u>*only God*</u> has immortality (1st Timothy 6:16). Because man does not have it on his own, the Bible states that he must seek for it in Christ (Romans 2:7). The apostle Paul plainly states that immortality for human beings is only "brought to light" (made available) through the gospel of Christ (2nd Timothy 1:10). In other words, only those who place their faith in Jesus Christ have access to immortality. Therefore, according to the Bible, it is impossible for people without Christ to possess immortality and live forever! In fact, this becomes obvious immediately after *man's fall* as recorded in Genesis chapter three. God found it necessary to ban Adam and Eve from the Garden of Eden, and also to station angels to keep them from accessing the "tree of life." The Bible clearly states that God did this so that they could not eat from the *tree of life* and live forever (Genesis 3:22-24). Therefore, the now sinful couple obviously had become mortal beings as a consequence of their sin, and God did not want sinful beings to become immortalized by eating from this supernatural *tree of life*. It is clear from this text, as well as many others that I've cited, that there was no immortal nature inherent within human beings after they had fallen into sin. And, according to the Bible, it is also apparent that the only means to receive immortality was by eating from the *tree of life* or by faith in Christ. Of course, the Bible records that God immediately cut off access to the supernatural tree, which left only one means to receive immortality, *faith in Christ*. The Bible plainly teaches that without faith in Christ there is nothing immortal within mankind.

This is, of course, in agreement with the rest of Scripture. Throughout the entire Bible the choice that is given to mankind is life or death, not life or eternal torture. The Bible clearly teaches that eternal life is only for those who accept Jesus Christ as their Savior and Lord. However, according to the "eternal torment" doctrine, the wicked also have eternal life. Their eternal life is terrible and painful, but it is still eternal life. This is a blatant contradiction of Scripture!

Now we will go back to those passages in the book of Psalms that I said we would return to later. In Psalm 145:20 God states that He preserves all who love Him, but that He will *destroy* the wicked. The Hebrew word used for destroy in this text is *shamad*. This word, *shamad*, is also used in Psalm 37:37 and 38, where God declares that a wonderful "future" awaits the honest and good, but He also states that the wicked will be *destroyed* ("shamad"), and will have *no future*. According to the *"Strong's Expanded Exhaustive Concordance,"* *shamad* means to utterly be brought to naught, perish or *annihilate*. It goes on to emphasize that *shamad* <u>always</u> expresses complete destruction or *annihilation*. Therefore, the precise rendering of these two passages in Psalm 145:20 and Psalm 37:37 and 38, is proclaiming that the honest and good people who love God will be preserved and will have a wonderful future, whereas the wicked will be completely destroyed and *annihilated*, and will have no future whatsoever! They do not live on forever in torment. They are destroyed, annihilated and gone! As it also states in Psalm 37:20, "they are no more." In view of the Bible's usage of the Hebrew word *shamad* to describe the *annihilation* of the wicked, it is interesting and even humorous that these arrogant *eternal torment* preachers often refer to people such as myself, who do not accept their eternal torment dogma, as *annihilationists*. Are we labeled as such because, based on the enormous amount of biblical evidence that supports our position, we maintain that God does not torture people forever, but rather that He does indeed *annihilate* them in the hell fire? After all, we have just seen that this is exactly what God teaches us in the Bible. Therefore, I have "good company" in my belief, because God Himself is also an *annihilationist*. I think it would be fair play for me to also come up with a descriptive title for all of the preachers who cherish proclaiming this *lovely* eternal torment doctrine. I accept the *annihilationist* title that they have given to me, because it accords with what the Bible teaches. I believe that an honest and accurate title for my opponents would be *eternal tormentors* or *everlasting torturists*. Unfortunately for them, however, the Bible clearly reveals that God does not keep company with them in their distorted belief.

There is no comparison between the voluminous weight of biblical evidence which clearly and specifically states that the ultimate fate of the wicked is to be utterly destroyed and die; this is far more than the few vague texts used to support the eternal torment dogma which refer to worms not dying and smoke ascending forever. To hold on to this eternal torment doctrine, one must intentionally choose to ignore a mountain of solid biblical evidence, in exchange for a few vague passages. Why would anyone want to do that, just so they can continue to portray God as a vindictive, cruel tyrant who enjoys torturing people forever? One day God will ask preachers and theologians why they insisted on misrepresenting His merciful, just and loving character.

To suggest that God's torturing people forever is more loving than destroying them in the hell fire, though ridiculous, is an easy assertion to make until you or your loved one is the one actually experiencing the perpetual torture. Any family who has watched a loved one suffer during the final days of an excruciatingly painful and terminal disease, knows that, out of love for the dying person, they want the suffering to stop. Although they will miss their loved one, they tell them it's ok to stop fighting and to pass into the sleep of death. The family's love causes them to do this because they don't want to have their loved one suffer for additional days and weeks when there is no hope of getting well. Now, remember that the torment in hell is not for days and weeks, but for the billions of years of eternity, according to the eternal torment advocates. If true love causes a family to desire death for their loved one rather than having them suffer for more days or weeks, wouldn't true love also desire the *"lost"* to die in the hell fire rather than suffer in it for billions of years? Any reasonable person knows that death is preferable to living in pain, misery, torment and suffering every day and night, year after year, decade after decade, century after century, millennium after millennium, through a ceaseless eternity. It is an insult to God to suggest that He demonstrates His love to *"lost sinners"* by torturing them forever!

A final important point to be considered is that the Bible teaches that we will be rewarded according to our works, both for those who have done good, and for those who have done evil (Matthew 16:27; Revelation 22:12; 2nd Corinthians 5:10). In fact, the Bible specifically states that God will reveal His wrath towards the wicked on the *day of judgment,* by rendering to each one according to his deeds (Romans 2:5,6). If God is going to render to those who have done evil, according to their deeds, would He punish them for lives of seventy years of disobedience, with pain and torment for billions of years without end? That would not be punishment based upon people's works, but would be billion-fold and trillion-fold punishment. That would be far more extreme than the illustration I used of the parent who punished his children for five months when they disobeyed for five seconds.

Obviously, if we are rewarded or punished according to our works, then the rewards and punishments must necessarily vary based upon those works. Adolph Hitler and the grocery store thief, who robbed to feed his family in my illustration, cannot receive the same sentence in hell if they are to be justly punished according to their works.

In Luke 12:42-49 Jesus Himself illustrated this principle. He clearly states that unfaithful servants are punished differently according to their personal measure of guilt. Some will be beaten with few *stripes*, whereas others will receive many *stripes*. After stating this, Jesus immediately refers to the "fire" He will send on the earth. Is this a coincidence? Probably not, because it is in that fire where the wicked will receive their punishment, or *stripes*. Some will receive a few, and others will receive many. However, it is interesting to note that none of them will be beaten forever. In fact, that is exactly what David says in Psalm 28:4 when he tells God to measure out punishment in proportion to their wickedness.

Now you can see why there is not one Bible verse that specifically and unequivocally states that people are tortured with pain and agony throughout eternity. Because if there were such a verse, it would contradict numerous other passages of scripture, and we know that God does not contradict Himself. The Bible does clearly state that the hell fire itself burns forever, and that the devil, his angels, the beast, and the false prophet will be tormented in that fire forever. However, there is not one verse in the entire Bible that specifically states that this is also the fate for wicked people in general. The closest references to such an assertion are the two texts which state that the *worms* or *maggots* do not die in the fire, and the passage which says the smoke resulting from the torment of the wicked ascends forever. When you stop to think about it, even these few texts are in perfect harmony with the enormous amount of biblical evidence I have presented. Bodies are not eaten by maggots while they are alive. The maggots appear after the body dies and is decaying. The maggots are the result of dead bodies. Do you understand? The maggots are the result, and in this case, concerning the final destruction of the wicked, the result is eternal death. The wicked are killed and have perished forever. Therefore, the maggots do not die, because they represent that eternal result. This explanation also applies to the text that speaks of smoke ascending forever. Smoke is the result of a fire. Long after many fires are extinguished, the smoke continues to billow and rise. Once again, the smoke is the result of the fire, and in this case concerning the final destruction of the wicked, the result is eternal. Therefore, the smoke is said to ascend eternally.

It is much easier and more logical to find such a reasonable explanation for the few vague eternal torment verses, than to blindly and stubbornly ignore the multitude of texts that unequivocally disprove this hideous doctrine.

The real choice presented to people throughout the Bible is not eternal life versus eternal torture, but eternal life versus eternal death. From beginning to end, the Bible presents the choice of life or death.

Why is this issue of great importance? I believe it is extremely important if you truly love God. You would never allow the character of someone you truly loved, to be unfairly and falsely portrayed. If you had a kind and loving earthly father, but people were saying untrue and unkind things about him; wouldn't you come to his defense and set the record straight? You know you would! How much more so, should we defend the wonderful character of our Heavenly Father, and be willing to make a stand for Him, and set the record straight concerning His gracious, kind, just, merciful and loving character?

Only God knows how many millions of people have chosen to reject Christ because of this hideous teaching that portrays the God of Christianity as a vindictive, cruel and unjust tyrant. Those who choose to continue teaching this ugly and false doctrine, will one day stand before Jesus Christ, the righteous Judge, to give an answer for what they have done. Remember that Jesus said it is better to have a millstone hung around your neck, and be thrown into the sea, than to cause someone else to stumble. Only God knows how many have been caused to stumble and reject Christianity because of this ugly and distorted teaching. Romans 2:4 states that it is God's *goodness* that leads people to repentance. Would the average person, who has not been previously indoctrinated with the Christian eternal torment doctrine, consider it to be a revelation of God's goodness for Him to punish every minute of disobedience with *thirty thousand years* of painful torment and agony?

I ask you to honestly ask yourself the following questions, and try to answer them from an unbiased perspective. If you had been raised in an environment with no Christian influence or teaching whatsoever, and someone told you that their God punished people fourteen-billion-fold, would you view their God as being loving and just?

If you heard about some parents who locked their children in a hot dark room for six months each time they had been disobedient; furthermore, that once each day they placed their children's hands on a hot stove during the entire six months of punishment; could anyone convince you that the punishment was justifiable, because the parents said that rebellion and disobedience were so offensive and repulsive in their sight? Absolutely not, and you know it! Yet, Christian preachers present a *Heavenly Parent* (God) who supposedly punishes *billions of months* for each act of disobedience; moreover, this *Heavenly Parent* doesn't just burn the hands once each day, but He burns the entire body *non-stop*, every second of every minute of every hour of every day throughout the trillions of years of eternity!

If your child, spouse or sibling was caught shoplifting a few DVD's, and was brought before a judge who gave your loved one the same lifetime prison sentence that he gave to brutal murderers; would you accept the judge's argument that all violations of the law are deserving of the same punishment, because they all reflect the same selfish and disobedient spirit? You know that you would consider such a judicial decision and declaration to be ludicrous, and you would denounce the judge's sentence as being grossly unjust. Yet Christian preachers present a *Heavenly Judge* (God) who gives your lost loved ones the same sentence of eternal torment in hell that He gives to genocidal maniacs like Hitler and Stalin. Wailing and gnashing of teeth throughout eternity shall be the fate of your lost child, sibling or spouse, just as it shall be for these mass-murderers, according to most Christian preachers.

The feeble argument presented by these preachers, that God views all sin in the same manner, is not only ridiculous, but also contradicts the Bible. God does **not** view all sin as being the same. Jesus told Pilate that the sin of the religious leaders was *greater* than Pilate's sin (John 19:11). Paul told the Corinthians that they were tolerating a sexual sin in their church that was worse than the gentiles would allow (1st Corinthians 5:1). And, it is common knowledge to any good Bible student that there were many varying penalties for many different sins recorded in the Old Testament. Some sins bore the death penalty, but not all. Some sins were classified as being abominations, but not all. The Apostle John states that there are sins *not onto death*, and that there is sin that *is onto death* (1st John 5:16-17). Anyone who contends that God views all sin in the same manner is either dishonest or seriously lacking in biblical knowledge.

It should be obvious that this eternal torment *spiel*, being promulgated by most Christian preachers, depicts greater injustice than any parent, ruler or government has practiced throughout human history. Anyone who would attempt to characterize the administering of thirty thousand years of torture, as being equitable recompense for each and every minute of disobedience, has certainly flunked the "common sense" and *sound reasoning* test.

At this point, eternal torment advocates will often suggest that you can't apply human *reasoning* to things that deal with God's purposes and doctrines. Unfortunately, those who make this claim find themselves, once again, contradicting Scripture. God has told us to come and *reason* together with Him (Isaiah 1:18). We're told that Jesus had been *reasoning* with the Sadducees and Pharisees concerning their doctrines (Mark 12:28). The Bible states that on numerous occasions Paul *reasoned* with Jews and Gentiles, as well as with the Roman ruler, Felix (Acts 17:2; Acts 17:17; Acts 18:4; Acts 18:19; Acts 24:25). The Bible does not discourage the use of *sound reasoning*, but rather endorses it. In fact, it is when we forget to use "common sense" and *sound reasoning* that we get into trouble. God gave us brains and He expects us to use them! And, it is readily apparent that *sound reasoning* demands that we reject the grossly unreasonable, inequitable and unjust doctrine of the eternal torment of human beings. God does **not** practice that kind of unrighteous and inequitable justice. To the contrary, the Bible states that God judges with righteousness and *equity* (Psalm 98:9).

It is time for the Church to repent for teaching such a heinous doctrine that maligns the character of God. The kind of God most preachers have been presenting has a system of justice that they would denounce if used by any parent, ruler or government. Such a system of justice that repays every second of disobedience with the equivalent of fifty or sixty years of punishment, would be considered an outrage if employed anywhere on this planet; yet the Church has insisted on attributing to our Lord and Savior, Jesus Christ, a system of justice that allegedly repays every second of disobedience with millions of years of punishment! Can't you just feel the justice, mercy and love that these eternal torment preachers embrace and teach?

The Bible says that God has no pleasure in the death of the wicked, and that He asks them why they will die (Ezekiel 33:11). The kind of God who takes no pleasure in the death of the wicked, does not punish them through billions of years of eternity, as justice for a life of seventy years of disobedience. It is also significant that God asks them why they will "die" in this passage. He does not ask them why they will suffer torment forever.

You now have the biblical evidence, and it is obvious that it overwhelmingly contradicts and refutes the eternal torment doctrine. If preachers choose to reject the overwhelming evidence that I've presented, their argument is not with me, but with God Himself. I will not be the one calling them to account for misrepresenting and maligning God's character. They will stand before Jesus Christ Himself, the *Righteous Judge*, to explain why they have insisted on portraying His character in such an offensive and repulsive manner.

I challenge the Church to abandon this vindictive doctrine that presents a *God of torture* instead of a God of love. If the Church refuses to do so, the rebuke spoken to Job's friends for misrepresenting God's character, will also be spoken to today's Church. God declared that His anger was aroused against them, because they had not spoken what was right about Him (Job 42:7). Proponents of the eternal torment dogma should seriously consider these relevant words of admonition spoken by God.

The fact that church leaders have continued to embrace and proclaim such a cruel, unjust and sadistic philosophy, notwithstanding the enormous amount of biblical evidence that contradicts their doctrine, should serve as a warning to our nation. If these arrogant men can justify slandering their God, rather than humbly confessing their error, will they not also justify slandering their political opponents? If they can justify misleading their Church, will they not also justify misleading our nation? If they willingly embrace and promulgate such a cruel, unjust and sadistic philosophy within their Church, will they not also embrace and promote unjust and sadistic philosophies and practices within our government? Their unfaithful past history in the Church foretells an equally unfaithful future serving our nation. Until they are willing to humbly confess and renounce their sadistic philosophies revealed in this chapter and in the following chapter, they should be rejected from consideration for serving in any leadership capacities.

19

THE EVIDENCE—PART TWO: CALVINISTIC PREDESTINATION

THIS SECOND "EVIDENCE" CHAPTER explores the Church's Calvinistic predestination doctrine. Once again, I will begin with an illustration.

What would you think of the ruler of a nation who made the arbitrary decree that all people with the AIDS disease must be killed; furthermore, that same ruler, forced all the nurses, doctors and hospital staff throughout his nation to inject multitudes of predetermined babies with the AIDS virus? How would you view that ruler years later, as he put every child to death who developed AIDS from the injections that he had given them?

I am sure that all would agree that this ruler was a cruel and evil man. After all, how could he punish people for something he had caused, and which they could not change or avoid? There would certainly be unanimous agreement, that those who were killed for contracting AIDS were actually victims of a cruel experiment for the sadistic pleasure of an evil monarch.

It would be unthinkable for anyone to come to the defense of the depraved and wicked ruler in the previous illustration. No one would dare to suggest that he was a good, kind and loving leader. Such an assertion would be ridiculous and absurd.

Nevertheless, there is a large segment of the Christian Church that is actually portraying God in a similar manner, and making similar assertions. How? It is happening through the teaching of the Calvinistic predestination "TULIP" doctrine.

What is this "TULIP" doctrine? It uses the five letters in the word tulip as an acronym to convey the following teaching:

T - Total Depravity of Man
U - Unconditional Election by God
L - Limited Atonement
I - Irresistible Grace
P - Perseverance

What does it all mean? Calvinism teaches that man is totally depraved. It also declares that God predestines individuals for heaven or hell through an unconditional election process. In other words, God chooses to create some people to go to heaven, and He chooses to create some people to go to hell; moreover, that people themselves have no choice in the matter.

Calvinism also teaches that Jesus only provided a *limited atonement*, because He did not die for everyone, but only for those He had predestined for heaven. And, Calvinism professes that God has "irresistible grace." Therefore, if God chose you for heaven, you are going whether you like it or not. Once again, you have no freedom of choice in the matter, because you are *preprogrammed*. Additionally, Calvinism says that you must *persevere*, and you will if you were predestined.

Calvinism turns God into an evil ruler similar to the one in my illustration. The evil ruler said that all with AIDS must die; then he injected chosen ones with the disease, and put them to death as they manifested the disease. Calvinism presents God as choosing to create and preprogram some with hellish desires, interests, inclinations and behavior, then to sentence them to the hell fire when they manifest these hellish characteristics and behavior. Should we be surprised that so many reject God, when He is presented in such a manner?

Some Calvinists try to make their predestination doctrine seem less offensive by restating their position in a more tactful and palatable manner. They point out that all men are evil to begin with because of Adam's original sin. Therefore, they assert that all men are destined for hell already. Because of this, they then conclude that God does not actually predestine them for hell, because they are already going on their own. These "milder" and "gentler" Calvinists suggest that God simply chooses to intervene on behalf of certain *chosen ones*. They say that He arbitrarily chooses which ones He will save from their destiny in hell, and then supernaturally intervenes in their lives and opens their hearts to receive the gospel. These *chosen ones* are then predestined for heaven, while the rest of humanity continues on its path to hell, with no hope or opportunity to be saved.

Although this may sound slightly better than "hard core" Calvinism, the end result is still the same. God is still picking and choosing favorites. After all, He could choose to intervene on behalf of all people, open all of their hearts to the gospel, and then predestine all to be saved. Therefore, the bottom line is, God is still intentionally choosing to not even allow multitudes of people to have the option to be saved. And, when we consider that God knows "the end from the beginning," that means that before He ever creates them, He is fully aware that multitudes of these "*unchosen ones*" will have no hope or opportunity to be saved; He knows in advance that He is creating these people with only one possible destiny, *hell!*

This "TULIP" predestination doctrine becomes even more repulsive when you realize that, according to Jesus Himself, the vast majority of people will be going to hell. He said in Mathew 7:13-14 that only a *few* would go through the narrow gate leading to life, whereas *many* would go through the wide gate leading to destruction. Therefore, Calvinists are teaching that God predestines the vast majority of people that He creates, to go to hell.

According to Calvinists, He does this in order to demonstrate His justice to those "chosen ones" who will be saved. Isn't that special! The Calvinists' *loving God* tortures the vast majority of people, so that a small minority can see His justice. Anyone who tortures large numbers of people who have no opportunity to avoid the torture, in order to demonstrate something to a small group of people, is not demonstrating justice, but rather injustice.

The Calvinist "TULIP" doctrine presents God as a Divine Ruler with attributes that we would denounce and condemn in any earthly monarch; yet this doctrine is widely accepted in today's Christian

Church. This is illogical and unreasonable.

Even more important than the lack of logic and common sense, is the fact that the weight of biblical evidence contradicts this doctrine. There are references to predestination in the Bible, but not in the sense in which Calvinism portrays it.

God has predestined or predetermined the *method of salvation.* There is only one way to be saved and to enter heaven, and that is through faith in Jesus Christ. Jesus said that no one could come to the Father, except through Him (John 14:6). The Bible says that there is no other name under heaven, given among men, whereby we can be saved (Acts 4:12). Jesus is the only way. That is the only method of salvation and entrance into heaven, and has been predestined or predetermined by God Himself. Therefore, all who will accept Jesus Christ as their Savior and Lord, and put their faith in Him, are predestined to receive salvation, eternal life and entrance into heaven.

As you can see, there is a vast difference between this kind of pre-destination, and the kind presented in the Calvinist "TULIP" doctrine. In the predestination that I've just described, God still allows people the freedom of choice. They can choose whether or not they wish to accept God's predetermined method of salvation. Therefore, every individual is responsible for their own eternal destiny, because they are allowed to make their own decision. They choose either to accept Jesus or reject Him; and in so doing, have chosen heaven or hell. Remember, in Calvin-ist predestination, God makes the decisions for you before you are born. You are nothing more than a type of robot doing what you've been pre-programmed to do, and for many their programming destines them to be tormented in hell.

Calvinists are quick to declare that God's sovereignty must apply to every sphere of His dealings with mankind, including His grace. Are Calvinists suggesting that God's sovereignty requires Him to only offer grace to some? Are Calvinists putting God *"in a box,"* by saying that He cannot offer grace to everyone if His grace is to be sovereign? God does not need Calvinists to tell Him that His sovereignty requires Him to offer selective grace only to a *chosen few.* God is fully capable of offer-ing grace to every person He has created, while still maintaining His sovereignty.

As with the eternal torment advocates discussed in the preceding chapter, TULIP predestination proponents point out that many of the respected *church fathers* down through the centuries also supported the TULIP doctrine. My answer to this assertion remains the same: So what? As stated in the last chapter, the respected heroes and *church fathers* of the Old Testament era committed polygamy, but that did not make polygamy acceptable. There has always been error within the Church, so we must not base our doctrines upon the *church fathers*, but solely upon the Bible.

Many Calvinists try to convince us that their TULIP predestination doctrine actually demonstrates God's love in a more profound and perfect manner. They say that His act of choosing certain people to be saved before they were born—*without having deserved or earned their special selection by God*—is a revelation of God's infinite love that would not be seen without Calvinism's TULIP doctrine. That sounds good if you're one of those predestined for heaven. However, if you are one of those predestined for hell, you would certainly have a different opinion. We must remember that according to Jesus Himself, many more people are going to hell than to heaven. He said that the gate to heaven is narrow and only a *few* go through it, whereas the gate to hell is wide and *many* go through it. Therefore, according to the Calvinists, God will be demonstrating His love to the vast majority of people He creates by predestining them to an eternal existence of torment, suffering and agony. I'm sure those multitudes will appreciate that kind of love!

I would like to ask a TULIP Calvinist to look at one of his precious children or grandchildren and ponder their destiny. What if that precious young child is one of those predestined for eternal torture in hell, as is consistent with his doctrine? Because there will be many more people going to hell than to heaven, as stated in Matthew 7:13-14, there is actually a better chance that your precious *little one* is predestined for hell, according to your TULIP doctrine. Remember that you believe God has decided their destiny before they were born and there is nothing, including your prayers, that can be done to change that destiny. If you have a family with five children, there is a good chance that three or four of them are predestined for hell. Can you picture them tormented and tortured throughout eternity without having had any opportunity to avoid their horrid fate? Can you feel the *warm love* taught by the TU-LIP doctrine as you ponder your children's future in hell? If the TU-LIP doctrine were correct, most loving parents would not bring any more children into this sinful world because the majority of them would be predestined to eternal torture in hell. Any reasonable Christian who knows Jesus intimately should be fully aware that He is <u>not</u> the author of the TULIP doctrine. This teaching comes straight from the pit of hell and slanders the character of our kind and loving God.

Where does this hideous TULIP doctrine come from, that turns God into some kind of mad scientist conducting a cruel experiment on His creatures? Are there any scriptures that imply such a teaching?

In fact, there are several scriptures that Calvinists use to support this doctrine. And, to be fair, I do admit that a few isolated texts could be viewed as supporting this teaching, if it were not for the multitude of scriptures that clearly contradict this doctrine. And, as with the isolated verses used to support the eternal torment dogma, which we debunked in the previous chapter, there are also reasonable explanations for each verse used to promote the Calvinist "TULIP" doctrine.

Calvinists point out that when Paul and Barnabas preached the gospel in Antioch, the Bible states that those who were "appointed" or "ordained" to eternal life were the ones who believed (Acts 13:46-48). They also refer to Romans 8:28-30, where Paul declares that those who God *foreknew*, He "predestined" to be conformed into the image of His Son; then He called those whom He had predestined. Calvinists remind us that Paul said God "chose us" in Christ before the foundation of the world to be holy and without blame, and also predestined us to be adopted to Himself by or through Jesus Christ; thereby also predestining us to obtain our inheritance (Ephesians 1:3-5,11).

Proponents of Calvinism direct our attention to 1st Thessalonians 1:4-5, where Paul states that he knew of the Thessalonians' *election* by God, for he had presented a gospel message to them that was not in word only, but also in power. Calvinists also allude to Paul's proclamation in 2nd Thessalonians 2:13, in which he declared that God, *from the beginning*, had chosen the Thessalonians for salvation through sanctification by the Spirit and belief in the truth. Advocates of Calvinism usually refer to Isaiah 6:9-10 as well, where God tells Isaiah to *make* the people's ears heavy, and also to *shut their eyes.*

Calvinists insist that their doctrine is additionally supported by the following passages that make reference to Jesus having *chosen* certain people. In Matthew's gospel account, it is recorded that Jesus twice stated that, while *many* are *called,* only *few* are *chosen* (Matthew 22:14; Matthew 20:16). And, the Apostle John documents that Jesus stated that He had *chosen* His disciples (John 15:16; John 6:70).

Adherents to Calvinist predestination also assert that their doctrine is advanced in chapter six of John's gospel. They remind us that Jesus said that it is the ones that the Father *gives to Him,* who will come to Him; moreover, that no one can come to Him unless the Father draws them (John 6:37; John 6:44).

To support their "limited atonement" claim, Calvinists refer to two statements made by Jesus, which are recorded in Mark's gospel account. They point out that Jesus only shed His blood for *many,* and that He also only gave His life as a ransom for *many* (Mark: 14:24; Mark 10:45). Calvinists believe that these references offer proof that Jesus did not shed His blood and offer His life for *all.*

Before we examine the final major text used by Calvinists, we'll take a closer look at the ones just mentioned. Upon close examination, and comparison with numerous others scriptures which refute Calvinism, it is apparent that these texts do not necessitate the kind of interpretation employed by the "TULIP" doctrine.

As previously stated, God has predestined the method of salvation, by predetermining that faith in Jesus Christ is the only way to come to God and be saved (John 14:6; Acts 4:12). The apostle Paul also declares that God has appointed the method of salvation to be through Jesus Christ (1 Thessalonians 5:9). Therefore, all who will choose to accept Jesus Christ have been predestined to obtain salvation and an inheritance in heaven.

Keeping this in mind, let's review these *supposed* Calvinist scriptures that I have listed. The reference in the book of Acts simply stated that those who believed had been "appointed" or "ordained" to eternal life. And, the text in the book of Romans, merely said that God predestined those He *foreknew,* to be conformed into the image of Jesus, and then He called them.

These two texts do not need to be interpreted in accordance with the Calvinist "TULIP" doctrine. These scriptures simply reaffirm God's chosen "method of salvation" form of predestination. God has predetermined that all who accept and believe in Jesus, will have eternal life. Therefore, in the book of Acts, as people chose to believe, they became part of God's predetermined or appointed group. In the book of Romans, it said that God predestined and called those He *foreknew*. God has foreknowledge. He knows the end from the beginning. He knows beforehand who will accept Jesus Christ. Therefore, this text simply says that God predestines those that He knows will accept Jesus, to be changed into His image, and that He also calls these predestined ones that He knew beforehand. Neither of these scriptures actually says that people have no freedom of choice in the matter, or that God has preprogrammed them for heaven or hell.

The scripture used by Calvinists from the book of Ephesians also does not necessarily imply what they say it does. It merely states that God "chose" us "in Christ" before the world began, and predestined us to be adopted as His children through Jesus Christ, and to receive an inheritance. This is actually more in accordance with "method of salvation" predestination, than it is with the "TULIP" doctrine. Before the world began, God chose the method of salvation to be "in Christ"; He predetermined that all who would choose to accept Jesus would become part of His *chosen group*, and be adopted into God's family. Therefore, all who are willing to choose Jesus are indeed predestined for adoption, salvation and a heavenly inheritance. This scripture does not literally say that people have no freedom of choice in this matter, or that God has preprogrammed them for heaven or hell.

The passage in 1st Thessalonians merely states that Paul knew of the Thessalonians' *election* by God. It apparently was obvious from their noble lives that they had experienced salvation and were part of God's *elect group*. This passage does not say that they had no freedom of choice in this process, nor does it state that God had preprogrammed them for heaven. In fact, it is clear in this text that their *election* was directly related to their having believed the powerful gospel that Paul had proclaimed. The words *elect* and *election* have been thoroughly distorted and abused by Calvinists in order to bolster their weak doctrinal position. The apostle Peter plainly states that being considered as part of God's *elect* is based upon God's "foreknowledge" (1st Peter 1:1,2). The elect are those who God, through His omniscient foreknowledge, knows will place their faith in Christ. Once again, this is a prime example of *method of salvation* predestination.

The text in 2nd Thessalonians simply declares that God, from the beginning, had chosen the Thessalonians for salvation through sanctification by the Spirit and belief in the *truth*. As with all of the previous passages, this text does not proclaim that they had no freedom of choice in this operation. This scripture just states the required criteria that God had chosen for their (and our) salvation; that criteria being experiencing sanctification by God's Spirit, and also believing in the *truth*, which the Bible defines as being Jesus Himself (John 14:6). This is, in fact, another classic example of *method of salvation* predestination. God has chosen or predestined that all who will place their faith in Jesus Christ and receive His sanctifying Spirit, will receive salvation.

The verses in Isaiah do appear to be more challenging and difficult on the surface. They stated that God instructed Isaiah to *make* the people's ears heavy, and also to *shut their eyes*. This does, on the surface, seem to be saying that God had shut their eyes and ears for them, without allowing them the freedom of choice to decide whether or not to have them shut. However, when Jesus quotes this specific passage in Isaiah, He expounds and elaborates on its proper meaning and intent, by clarifying that it was the people themselves who had closed their eyes and ears (Matthew 13:14,15). According to Jesus, they were indeed allowed to exercise their freedom of choice in this matter. Jesus obviously did not believe that Isaiah was espousing a doctrine similar to Calvinism, and neither should we.

The passages in Matthew that recorded Jesus' statement that *many* are *called*, but only *few* are *chosen*, actually offer no support for Calvinist predestination when examined closely. In Matthew chapter 22, the *call* to attend the marriage feast went out to *many*, but only those *few* who responded to the invitation and dressed in the appropriate wedding garment, were *chosen* to participate in the feast. Their "chosen status" was based upon their decisions to respond and to wear the appropriate attire. This text actually contradicts Calvinism. The related statement in

Matthew chapter twenty has nothing whatsoever to do with election to salvation. The context clearly deals with being called and chosen to work in God's vineyard in various capacities, and receiving the appropriate rewards for that labor. It is an obvious manipulation of Scripture to attempt to use either of these passages to support Calvinism's claim concerning unconditional election to salvation.

The two texts from John's gospel, which stated that the disciples had been *chosen* by Jesus, also have nothing whatsoever to do with election to salvation. In John 15:16, Jesus did indeed state that He had *chosen* His disciples. The fact that Jesus chooses who will serve Him in various capacities is universally accepted in Christian doctrine, and has nothing to do with Calvinistic predestination to salvation. In fact, the second passage in John 6:70, actually proves that this *choosing* by Jesus is **not** related to salvation. Why? Because the twelve that Jesus stated that He had *chosen* included Judas, whom Jesus referred to as a *devil*. The Bible clearly reveals that Judas is not saved, and yet Jesus stated that He had *chosen* Judas, because Judas was one of the twelve. Therefore, Jesus' *choosing* of His disciples obviously does not refer to salvation. Once again, Calvinists fail in their attempt to biblically justify their doctrine.

Although the texts from John chapter six may appear at first glance to be supportive of Calvinism, upon closer scrutiny they also fail to advance the Calvinist dogma. In John 6:37, Jesus does say that the ones that come to Him are the ones that the Father *gives to Him*. Who are those ones that the Father *gives to Him*? John 6:39 states that they are the ones that Jesus will *raise up at the last day*. There is something else that is also true concerning these ones that Jesus will *raise up at the last day*. John 6:40 reveals that they are also the ones who *believe in Jesus*. Therefore, you could say that we have a biblical equation. We've all had a math teacher tell us that if "A" equals "B," and "C" equals "B," then "A" also equals "C." As pertains to our biblical equation, if the ones who *believe in Jesus* equal the ones who He will *raise up at the last day*, and if the ones who the Father *gives to Jesus* equal the ones who He will *raise up at the last day*, then the ones who *believe in Jesus* also equal the ones who the Father *gives to Jesus*. In other words, the ones who choose to place their faith in Jesus are the ones that the Father gives to Jesus. This is not Calvinistic, unconditional election to salvation, but rather is simply salvation through faith in Jesus Christ. And, it also accords with numerous other scriptures regarding salvation via faith in Jesus, which also contradict Calvinism. The bottom line is that there is no support for Calvinism found in this text.

The other text mentioned in John chapter six stated that no one can come to Jesus unless the Father draws him (John 6:44). Does this passage support Calvinism? Does it say that God only draws a few elect ones? No! In fact, in John 12:32, Jesus clearly states that His being *lifted up* (on the cross), draws *all* people to Himself. Therefore, *all* are drawn, not just a few elect ones. Consequently, Calvinists again fail in their attempt to support their doctrine.

Finally, the two verses from Mark's gospel account that Calvinists use to justify their "limited atonement" teaching, also fail to offer any true support for their dubious doctrine. Do Jesus' statements that His blood and life were offered for *many*, automatically also mean that they were not offered for *all?* Although it is true that *many* may not always equal *all,* it is also true that *all* can and does often equal *many.* If Jesus did die for *all* of the people in our world, that would certainly be a number that could be accurately referred to as being *many.* Consequently, His statements about dying for *many* do not contradict Him also having died for *all.* Elsewhere in Scripture the words *many* and *all* are used synonymously or interchangeably. For example, in Romans 5:19 Paul states that Adam's disobedience made *many* to become sinners. Of course, the Bible clearly teaches that *all* were made sinners as a result of Adam's disobedience. Nonetheless, this text in Romans chooses to refer to the *all* as being *many.* The same usage is obviously intended in these two texts from Mark's gospel, because otherwise it would contradict numerous other passages that plainly state that Jesus did indeed die for *all.* These scriptures will be listed later. However, for now, we can confidently say that Calvinism *comes up empty* once again.

The truth of the matter is, the Calvinist "TULIP" predestination doctrine stands upon the foundation of only one true, supportive Bible text. This text, if interpreted the way Calvinists do, clearly contradicts a multitude of other scriptures. First, let's examine this one individual text. Then, we'll debunk the Calvinist interpretation of this text, through the use of numerous other scriptures. The weight of evidence will be overwhelming. It will make you wonder why the Christian Church even tolerates this hideous doctrine to be taught.

The Calvinist "ringer text" I am referring to is found in Romans 9:10-23. The first portion of this passage deals with Esau and Jacob. It states that God *elected* the older brother to serve the younger brother before they were born. It points out that neither child had committed good or evil when this *election* by God occurred. Calvinists frequently refer to these verses about Esau and Jacob as an example of TULIP predestination. However, they have committed a serious and obvious contextual error. Why? Because Jacob's and Esau's individual salvation and eternal destiny is not being discussed here. This reference is a direct quotation from Genesis 25:21-23. Proper biblical analysis requires the examination of the text in Genesis that has been quoted, before you can ascertain the correct biblical context in Romans. Genesis 25:23 clearly presents the context. The focus is not upon Esau and Jacob as individuals, but rather upon the nations of people that would descend from them. God told Rebecca that she had two *nations* in her womb and that two *peoples* would proceed from her body, with one being stronger than the other. After clarifying those points, God then told her that the older would serve the younger. In other words, the nation of the Edomite people, who descended from the older brother, Esau, would serve the nation of the stronger Israelite people who descended from Jacob. Therefore, the proper context in Romans concerning the *election* of Esau and Jacob is not dealing with their personal salvation, but rather with their callings related to the nations that would descend from them. God had elected to call Jacob to be the progenitor of His chosen people of Israel instead of Esau. Why? Because God's omniscient foreknowledge allowed Him to know in advance who would be the better choice for this important calling. And, of course, Esau's descendants did serve Jacob's descendants because Israel did become the stronger nation. The prophecy in Genesis 25:21-23 was precisely fulfilled through the nations of Israel and Edom. It should also be noted, however, that if this text referred to Esau and Jacob individually, as many Calvinists suggest, then the prophecy would have been unfulfilled and untrue, because there is no biblical reference to Esau's ever personally being in servitude to Jacob during his lifetime. Nevertheless, we know from the context established in Genesis that the focus was on their descendant nations, thereby fulfilling this prophecy. It should be obvious to any good Bible student that the first part of this Romans text does not offer any support for the Calvinist TULIP doctrine.

The second portion of this passage in Romans states that God "wills" or "chooses" to have mercy on some, and to harden some. The specific example used is of Pharaoh when he refused to listen to Moses and let Israel go.

It is interesting that the hardening of Pharaoh's heart is referred to many times in the Exodus account, and that about half the time the Bible says that God hardened his heart, and about half the references say Pharaoh hardened his own heart. Which is it? Obviously, they are being used interchangeably.

Also, note the account of Job. The Bible makes it clear that Satan is the one who attacked Job's property, livestock and family, and finally Job's own body as well, after receiving permission from God to do so (Job chapter 1 and 2). And yet, in Job 2:3 it says that God Himself had been incited against Job to destroy him. The verse-by-verse account makes it clear that Satan was the one who did it after God chose to allow it, but God is still given credit for it, as if He had done it.

In scripture it appears, at times, that God is given credit for doing things which He simply *allows to happen*, or does not prevent from happening. That is why the scriptures can say that Pharaoh hardened his own heart in one verse, and then say God hardened Pharaoh's heart a few verses later; because God is "said to have done" those things which He *allows*, or does not prevent from happening. When Pharaoh chooses to harden his heart and reject God, he is allowed to do so. God does not force Pharaoh to obey Him. However, because God is omnipotent and could have forced Pharaoh to obey, and yet chose not to do so; God is given credit for having done it. Of course, the reason God didn't force Pharaoh to obey, was because He respected Pharaoh's *freedom of choice*, just as He respects ours. This is a reasonable explanation to the second part of this *Romans text*, which also is in accordance with scripture.

The third portion of this passage in Romans compares God to a potter who makes clay vessels. It states that some vessels are made for honor, while some are made for dishonor. The vessels made for dishonor are referred to as *vessels of wrath prepared for destruction*. As always, thoughtful consideration of the biblical context is essential.

Paul, as he often does, is referring back to an Old Testament scripture in Jeremiah 18:1-11, which compares God's dealings with people to a potter making clay vessels. This is important to remember because the previous passage in Jeremiah helps to establish the proper context for Paul's related reference in Romans chapter nine, because Paul would not be contradicting Jeremiah. What was Jeremiah's context regarding the comparison of a potter making clay vessels, and God's dealings with people? Does Jeremiah imply that people are predestined by God to be obedient or disobedient, and that they cannot change because the *Divine Potter* predestined them? Absolutely not! In fact, Jeremiah teaches us the exact opposite. According to Jeremiah, the "human vessels" have the capability to turn from disobedience to obedience, or from obedience to disobedience; he also states that their decision will cause God to refrain either from punishing them or blessing them. In other words, the future of the vessels depends upon their obedience or disobedience. It is not an arbitrary, predetermined choice by God. Having this proper contextual understanding as a foundation for correctly comprehending Paul's related reference to the *Divine Potter* in Romans chapter nine is essential. As previously stated, Paul would not be contradicting Jeremiah. Paul was a Bible scholar and was certainly aware of Jeremiah's previous usage of this concept. Therefore, we can be sure that Paul's message is consistent with Jeremiah 18:1-11. Some human vessels are indeed made for honor, while some are made for dishonor. However, as clearly stated in Jeremiah, it is the choices of the human vessels to obey or disobey that determines their destiny and valuation as being honorable or dishonorable. It is true that, because of God's omniscient foreknowledge, He knows in advance who will be obedient and disobedient, and therefore, who will be an honorable or dishonorable vessel. However, God's foreknowledge of His vessels' choices does not force them to make those choices! He simply knows what they are going to do before they do it. With this proper understanding, which also accords with Jeremiah 18:1-11, we can now correctly comprehend Paul's statement concerning the *potter* in Romans. As previously stated, because of God's foreknowledge, He is already aware of the entire lifetime of choices and the final destiny of every human vessel He creates at the very moment He creates them. Therefore, He is aware at the instant of creation whether He is creating an honorable or dishonorable vessel. That is why Paul can state, from God's omniscient perspective, that He is creating vessels for honor or dishonor. God knows in advance which vessels are going to heaven and which ones are going to hell, but that does not mean He has preprogrammed them to go to heaven or hell. Nevertheless, because He knows in advance before He creates each vessel, the Bible can correctly state that He is making an *"honorable heaven-bound vessel,"* or a *"dishonorable hell-bound vessel of wrath prepared for destruction,"* without indicating that God arbitrarily predestined them for their final destination, and without suggesting that the vessels had no freedom of choice pertaining to their destiny. When studied in this proper biblical context with the similar passage in Jeremiah, we simply have another revelation of God's omniscient foreknowledge. There is no need to interpret this text in Romans as the Calvinists do. Their interpretation maligns the character of God and contradicts numerous other scriptures that plainly teach that we have "free will." However, as you can see, the proper biblical contextual understanding requires us to reject the Calvinist interpretation of this passage in Romans. Consequently, even the one supposed "ringer text" used by Calvinists has been debunked.

The Bible does not contradict itself. There is a reasonable and biblical explanation for each one of the Calvinist texts used to support their false TULIP doctrine.

Let us remember that Calvinism's "TULIP" doctrine teaches unconditional election by God. God predestines and preprograms everyone, and there is no "free will" or freedom of choice. However, this contradicts many Bible verses such as the following texts.

The prophets Ezekiel and Joel told the Israelites to repent, turn away from idols, and to return to the Lord (Ezekiel 14:6; Joel 2:13). The prophets Jeremiah, Zechariah and Malachi also told the people to return to God, and that He would take them back and likewise return to them (Jeremiah 3:14; Jeremiah 18:11; Zechariah 1:3,4; Malachi 3:7). They were telling the people to "make choices" to repent and return to God. Why would they do that if they had no freedom of choice?

The prophets Hosea, Nehemiah, Zechariah, Ezekiel and Jeremiah accused the people of refusing to repent, obey and heed God's judgments, words and correction (Hosea 11:5; Nehemiah 9:17; Zechariah 7:11; Ezekiel 5:6; Jeremiah 13:10; Jeremiah 5:23). Why would they chide them for refusing if they had no freedom of choice?

The apostle Paul admonished the people to "turn" from their old ways, and also said that God commands men to repent (Acts 14:15; Acts 17:30). Ezekiel, John the Baptist, Jesus and Peter also told the people that they needed to repent (Ezekiel 18:30; Matthew 3:2; Matthew 4:17; Acts 2:38). Why would God command people to make choices to turn and repent, if they had no free will to do so?

Both Joshua and the prophet Elijah challenged the Israelites to *choose* between serving the God of heaven or false idol-gods such as Baal (Joshua 24:15; 1st Kings 18:21). Moses told the people to *choose* life so that they and their descendants could live (Deuteronomy 30:19). Why would they have told them to make these choices, if it were not possible to do so?

The deacon Stephen accused the religious leaders of his day, and their ancestors, of always "resisting" the Holy Spirit (Acts 7:51). If they were rebuked for resisting the Holy Spirit, they obviously had the power of choice to do so. Also, the Bible instructs all people to *resist* the devil (James 4:7). Therefore, it is apparent that we all have the freedom of choice to do so! Furthermore, Luke states that the Pharisees and lawyers had *rejected* the will of God for themselves because they had not been baptized by John the Baptist (Luke 7:30). Once again, the Scriptures clearly state that people have the freedom and ability to *reject* or *resist* God's will for them.

In Ezekiel 33:11 God tells the wicked that He doesn't want them to die, and asks them to "turn" from their evil ways. Why would God ask them to do something they were not able to do?

The prophet Joel stated that multitudes are in the *valley of decision* (Joel 3:14). And, the book of Acts says that the people on the island of Malta *changed their minds* (Acts 28:6). If we do not have a "free will" with the power to choose, how did these people *change their minds*, furthermore, how can multitudes be in the *valley of decision* if they have no "free will" to *choose* or *decide* with?

The Lord Jesus Christ told the Jews of His day that He had wanted to gather them to Him as a mother hen gathers her chicks under her wings, but they "were not willing" (Matthew 23:37). According to Jesus Himself, these people had *free will*, and chose not to come to Him.

Also, note all of the following texts that unquestionably teach that people have *free will*. Hosea proclaimed that the people of Ephraim were oppressed because they had *willingly* walked by human precept (Hosea 5:11). Nehemiah recorded that the people blessed all of the men who had *willingly* offered to dwell at Jerusalem (Nehemiah 11:2). In Judges 5:9, the Bible states that there were rulers in Israel who offered themselves *willingly* to the Lord. The Bible records in Exodus 35:29, and in numerous other passages, that the children of Israel brought *free will* offerings to the Lord. The Apostle Paul declared that the Macedonian believers had been *freely willing* to minister to the needs of the saints (2nd Corinthians 8:3-4). In Hebrews 10:26, the Bible states that if we sin *willfully* after we've received knowledge of the truth, then there no longer remains a sacrifice for our sins. The Apostle Peter proclaimed that scoffers *willfully* forget that God is the Creator (2nd Peter 3:5). All of these texts, as well as many others that could also be cited, clearly and unequivocally teach that people have a *free will* with the ability to make their own choices.

There is truly a massive amount of biblical evidence that totally refutes Calvinism's "unconditional election" doctrine. But, remember, the "TULIP" predestination doctrine also teaches that Jesus only provided a "limited atonement" that was not meant for everyone, but just for those whom He had predestined for heaven. Once again, this contradicts numerous scriptures.

Jesus Christ said He would draw "all people" to Himself, and "whoever" believed in Him would have eternal life (John 12:32; John 3:16). The apostle John declared that Jesus offered Himself for the sins of the *whole world*, and is Savior of the "*world*" (1John 2:2; 1John 4:14).

The apostle Paul clearly states that God wants "all" to be saved, and that Jesus gave Himself as a ransom for "all" (1st Timothy 2:3-6). The apostle Peter agrees by saying that God wants "all" to come to repentance, because He is not willing for any to perish (2 Peter 3:9). Additionally, Hebrews 2:9 tells us that Jesus tasted death for *everyone.*

Do these verses describe a limited atonement, where the benefits and rewards from Jesus' sacrifice are only for a select few chosen beforehand by God? Absolutely not! In fact, you have to intentionally choose to totally ignore these scriptures and _many_ more that could be listed, in order to believe in Calvinism's _limited atonement._ Why would you want to do that?

It would seem much wiser to reject Calvinism's insulting "TULIP" doctrine, rather than a multitude of other scriptures. The Bible clearly teaches that God loves all of us and that Jesus died for all of us; furthermore, that He doesn't want any to perish, but rather that all would be saved. Additionally, there are numerous references where God encourages us to choose Him so that we can be saved.

The "TULIP" doctrine contradicts the Bible and maligns God's character by making Him the author of evil, because He is allegedly the one preprogramming people to do their evil deeds. This "TULIP" is not a pretty flower. It is also a very dangerous doctrine. Why?

According to this doctrine, everything is decided ahead of time, and we have no "free will" or choice in the matter. God has already predetermined who goes to heaven and hell, and has preprogrammed them accordingly. Therefore, we can't change anything. Certain people are going to heaven or hell regardless of what they or we do. Consequently, this teaching discourages evangelism because our evangelistic efforts are indeed meaningless. Every case is predetermined and we can't change it.

This teaching requires us to change the name of our message. How can we call it the gospel or good news, when it is actually bad news for the majority of people in the world, because it tells them that they have a one-way ticket to hell?

This teaching diminishes the beauty and importance of Christ's sacrifice, because He is no longer unselfishly dying for sins that we chose to commit, and which He had nothing to do with, but rather, He's simply dying for the very sins that He Himself had caused us to do when He preprogrammed us.

If any of my Calvinist friends think that I am exaggerating or unfairly describing their Calvinist predestination doctrine, I ask them to read and consider the following statements made by the _father of Cal-_

vinism, John Calvin himself. I forewarn you that the following statements made by John Calvin are both alarming and repulsive.

"By predestination we mean the eternal decree of God, by which he determined with himself whatever he wished to happen with regard to every man. All are not created on equal terms, but some are preordained to eternal life, others to eternal damnation; and, accordingly, as each has been created for one or other of those ends, we say that he has been predestined to life or death."

[John Calvin, Institutes of the Christian Religion," iii, xxi, sec. 5, p. 1030-1031]

"...Since the arrangement of all things is in the hand of God, since to him belongs the disposal of life and death, he arranges all things by his sovereign counsel, in such a way that *individuals are born, who are doomed from the womb to certain death, and are to glorify him by their destruction.*" (EMPHASIS ADDED)

[John Calvin, "Institutes of the Christian Religion," iii, xxiii, sec. 6, p. 231]

"There is no random power, or agency, or motion in the creatures, who are so governed by the secret counsel of God, that *nothing happens but what he has knowingly and willingly decreed* ... the counsels and wills of men are so governed as to move exactly in the course which he has destined." (EMPHASIS ADDED)

[John Calvin, "Institutes of the Christian Religion," iii, xxiii, secs. 3 & 8, p. 175 & 179]

"God not only foresaw the fall of the first man, and in him the ruin of his posterity; but also *at his own pleasure arranged it.*" (EMPHASIS ADDED)

[John Calvin, "Institutes of the Christian Religion," iii, xxiii, sec. 7, p. 1063]

"The word hardens, when applied to God in Scripture, means not only permission, (as some washy moderators would have it,) but also the operation of the wrath of God: for all those external things, which lead to the blinding of the reprobate, are the instruments of his wrath; *and Satan himself,* who works inwardly with great power, is so far his minister, that he *acts not, but by his (God's) command....* Paul teaches us, that the ruin of the wicked is not only foreseen by the Lord, but also ordained by his counsel and his will ... not only the destruction of the wicked is foreknown, but that *the wicked themselves have been created for this very end; that they may perish.*" (EMPHASIS ADDED)

[John Calvin, "Calvin's New Testament Commentaries," (Romans 9:18)]

Because John Calvin's teachings about predestination are often so blunt, abrasive, unjust and downright sadistic, many modern Calvinists go to great lengths to "explain them away." However, Calvin's own personal statements speak for themselves.

Calvin specifically stated that we are not all created on equal terms. He plainly declared that some are preordained for eternal life, and others for eternal damnation. John Calvin does not need "contemporary translators" to try to *soften* his cruel doctrine. Calvin made certain that all could clearly understand the *intent* and *extent* of his teaching when he declared that individuals were *doomed from the womb*; furthermore, that God was glorified by their destruction! I must remind you that the majority of people are going to hell, according to Scripture. Therefore, the inevitable "bottom line" is that John Calvin taught that God is glorified by eternally torturing the majority of people that He creates, in hell. And, remember that Calvin also taught that these eternally tormented multitudes had been arbitrarily *doomed from the womb*, with no ability or opportunity to avoid their horrid fate! That is true, original and authentic Calvinism *straight from the horse's mouth*, before having been "doctored up" by modern Calvinist proponents who attempt to *soften the blow* of hardcore, genuine Calvinism.

As you read these quotes from John Calvin, I'm sure you noticed that Calvin stated that _nothing happens_ without God having *knowingly* and *willingly* decreed its occurrence. I ask you to consider the ramifications of that statement. According to John Calvin, everything that has happened in our world has been decreed to occur in accordance with God's knowledge and will. _God has willed every event_ that has taken place, according to Calvin. Therefore, God is responsible for the 9-11 terrorist attack on America. God willed for thousands of people to die in that inferno. God also willed every human genocide that has been conducted by men like Hitler, Stalin, and Saddam Hussein. God has also willed every child abduction, molestation, rape and murder. All of the evil men that committed these horrific acts were mere *pawns* or *stooges* whom the God of Christianity used and manipulated to accomplish His will. They were mere *puppets* helplessly and totally controlled and directed in accordance with the specific will of the "Divine Puppeteer." This is the "bottom line" and *end result* of true, original Calvinism as taught by John Calvin himself.

Calvinism results in God being ultimately responsible for every evil deed throughout human history. In fact, God is not only responsible, but it actually was His will for sin and evil to exist, according to Calvin. John Calvin stated that God not only foresaw the "fall of man," but that He actually *found pleasure* in arranging it! In fact, according to Calvin, even Satan's despicable actions are commanded by God! Thus, the devil himself is also just a helpless puppet whose detestable deeds have been totally controlled by the "Divine Puppeteer." True, original Calvinism, as taught by its founder, literally turns God into the devil. The doctrine of Calvinistic predestination is an indictment of our God, and should be an offense to all sincere Christians.

Finally, as previously stated, Calvinism maligns the character of our gracious, kind and loving God. To begin with, Calvinism presents God as someone who is biased and practices favoritism by arbitrarily choosing *favorites* to be saved, while allowing everyone else to go to hell. This clearly contradicts numerous Bible texts, and also results in Calvinists presenting their God as being a hypocrite and a liar. Why? The Bible repeatedly states that God is not a "respecter of persons" and does not practice *partiality* or *favoritism* (2nd Chronicles 19:7; Acts 10:34; Romans 2:11; Ephesians 6:9). It also declares that God's wisdom that comes from above is *without partiality* (James 3:17). Therefore, if Calvinists' teaching is correct, that God does favor only certain individuals to be saved from hell, then God would have lied in all of the passages where He stated that He does not practice favoritism or partiality. Calvinists are presenting God as being a liar. They also present Him as being a hypocrite. Why? The Bible tells us that we should not do anything with partiality or favoritism; moreover, that showing "respect of persons" and practicing partiality or favoritism is not good; furthermore, that such conduct is *sin* (1st Timothy 5:21; Proverbs 28:21; James 2:9). Therefore, when Calvinists state that God does favor only certain individuals to be saved from hell, while He simultaneously tells us that we must not practice such favoritism ourselves because it is not good to do so and is sinful; then Calvinists are certainly presenting their God as being a hypocrite! The Calvinist God says, "Do as I say, not as I do." The God of Christianity is **not** a liar or a hypocrite! Calvinists must stop this outrageous slandering of our Christian God. If they do not do so, they should cease to be recognized as part of the Christian community. It is time for the Church to rise up and denounce this Calvinist "TULIP" predestination doctrine, declaring it to be an abomination.

I ask you to ponder the following scenario. The owner of a large youth recreation center, located in a remote and picturesque country area, was widely proclaimed to be a kind, just and loving man by those who knew him. He offered his center to be used by a large group of "troubled teens," numbering about two hundred. The teens ignored the numerous signs that forbid smoking, and started a fire that quickly engulfed the building and blocked all of the exits. The building was several stories high, and had a door that led to the roof, but due to the height of the building and the concrete parking lot that surrounded it, any attempt to jump from the roof would lead to certain death. As the two hundred teens gathered on the roof to avoid the heat and smoke as long as possible, their only hope was an air rescue by this reportedly kind and loving man. The remote country location made it impossible for the nearest city's fire department to arrive in time, but this wealthy owner had a fleet of five helicopters that he used for another "scenic tour" business, and he kept these helicopters in a hanger just blocks from the youth center. The owner and his four sons were all qualified pilots who lived on the property. As soon as the fire alarms sounded and it was apparent that they would not be able to rescue the teens via the fire exits, the owner and his sons prepared the helicopters to perform an airlift rescue from the roof. Because the helicopters were located just minutes away and were each capable of carrying ten passengers, there was plenty of time to make the four trips to the rooftop necessary to safely rescue all of the two hundred teens. However, after the first trip had been completed and fifty of the teens were safely on the ground, the owner and his sons parked the helicopters and ceased all rescue operations, leaving the remaining 150 teens to suffer and perish in the fire. When asked why he had only rescued fifty when he was fully capable of rescuing them all, the owner gave the following reasons. First, he said that the teens that perished got what they deserved for being disobedient to his signs that forbid smoking. Second, he said that by choosing to save just a small elect group he would be more profoundly demonstrating his love to the teens whom he had saved, than if he had saved everyone. This way the rescued teens would feel even more loved, chosen and special. Third, he said that intentionally leaving the 150 teens to perish enabled him to demonstrate his justice to the ones that he had saved. After all, the doomed teens had received their just punishment for their disobedience, and, in the process, the saved teens were allowed to behold the righteous justice of the owner.

Would there be any reasonable and sane person who would agree with this owner's tactics, and who would still declare him to be a kind, just and loving man? Absolutely not! In fact, most people would proclaim him to be a sadistic, unjust and evil tyrant.

However, the scenario that I've just presented is an accurate representation of how Calvinism presents the God of Christianity. Yet, Calvinists expect us to view their God as being kind, just and loving, in spite of His unjust, unloving and sadistic behavior, which actually dwarfs the evil conduct of the owner in my illustration. The owner in my story was leaving the teens to die in the smoke and fire, which would only take a period of several minutes. The Calvinist God tortures them relentlessly throughout the trillions of years of eternity. The teens in my illustration had chosen to smoke and endanger themselves, but the Calvinist God causes them to smoke, according to John Calvin. The Calvinist God, in effect, was the one who started the fire, because, as John Calvin taught, everything that happens was decreed by God in accordance with His will. Therefore, if the owner in my story is evil, unjust and sadistic, then the Calvinist God is far more evil, unjust and sadistic. It is completely disingenuous, dishonest and hypocritical to condemn the actions of the owner in my illustration, while simultaneously approving of the actions of the Calvinist God. Hopefully this illustration will have helped to demonstrate and accentuate the injustice and sadistic cruelty that permeates the Calvinist predestination dogma.

I'll conclude by offering a more appropriate definition for "TULIP." .

Teaching that
Undermines the character of a
Loving God,
Indicting Him for the
Problems in this sinful world, because He would be guilty of pre-

destining everything, including all the evil that was ever done by wicked sinners. And, indicting God for the agonizing eternal torment, as Calvinists believe, of billions of people whom He had created and predestined for hell. After analyzing the evidence, it is obvious to any unbiased reader that the Church's "Calvinistic predestination" dogma is not in harmony with the overwhelming weight of biblical evidence. Those who teach this despicable doctrine are clearly slandering God! As I've previously mentioned, when this Calvinistic predestination doctrine is combined with the eternal torment doctrine, the God of Christianity is being presented as being more cruel, unjust and sadistic than that of any other religion; moreover, than any earthly tyrant such as Hitler or Stalin.

If Christian leaders can unashamedly embrace such a God as they describe, and unabashedly proclaim that this obviously vindictive and sadistic divine monarch, whom these hideous doctrines reveal, is still somehow a merciful, good, just and loving potentate; this should serve as a strong warning that their sense of character and justice is extremely flawed; that they view cruelty and injustice as being good; furthermore, that they will also be likely to conduct and approve of such unjust and sadistic leadership within our government if they are given the opportunity to serve in leadership positions. Until they can demonstrate better judgment within the Church, why would we want them to lead our nation?

Because many contemporary Calvinist proponents have learned to deceptively "cloak" and restate their despicable doctrine in language that confuses and misleads many sincere Christians into accepting their dogma, I am concluding this chapter by listing the names of some of today's prominent Calvinist teachers who promote this hideous doctrine, and who have excelled in concealing the true, original, God-slandering nature of historic, authentic Calvinism. Well-known, modern teachers of contemporary "cloaked" Calvinism include: John MacArthur, John Piper, James White, R. C. Sproul, D. James Kennedy and R. Scott Clark.

§ 20 §

THE EVIDENCE—PART THREE:
THE SECRET RAPTURE

THE FINAL DAYS of American involvement in the Vietnam War were hectic ones. The North Vietnamese army was about to overrun Saigon, and our nation was quickly evacuating all American personnel before this occurred. Any Americans left behind were certain to be tortured or killed.

What would have been your impression of our military leaders, if they had told the remaining Americans that they could either board the evacuation planes currently there, or they could catch other ones coming later; notwithstanding, that no other evacuation planes had actually been promised by the "Commander and Chief"? You would probably agree that the military leaders had created the false impression that there would be a *second chance* to escape the coming destruction; thereby having diminished the urgency of the situation, which caused some to procrastinate and eventually be destroyed.

Fortunately, our military leaders did not dispense such misinformation during those climactic days in Vietnam when people's lives were literally at stake. However, many church leaders are guilty of dispensing similar misinformation concerning the climactic days of earth's history, which is giving millions the false impression that they will have a second chance to be saved after Jesus has *raptured* faithful Christians to heaven.

This misinformation is the popular *secret rapture* doctrine being taught by many church leaders. As mentioned in chapter seven, this doctrine has gained worldwide attention due to the phenomenal success of the *"Left Behind"* Christian novel series. Millions are being told that they truly will have a second chance to be saved after Jesus has *raptured* His Church. Therefore, there is no urgency to surrender your life to Jesus now, because you can catch Him *on the rebound.*

What do I mean by that? The secret rapture theory presented in the *"Left Behind"* series, teaches that Jesus will soon be conducting a "secret rapture" of His saints in which they will simply disappear from this world. They will vanish into *thin air*, and all that will be left is their clothing. If they were driving a car at the moment of their rapture, the car will proceed without a driver, crashing into whatever is in the way. If a Christian was piloting a commercial airplane, the pilot will vanish and the plane full of passengers will crash and burn.

However, according to these books, all of the people who are *left behind* after this secret rapture will have a second chance to be saved by Jesus after going through a traumatic tribulation period. Many other church leaders, in addition to the authors of the *"Left Behind"* series, also teach this "second chance" version of the secret rapture doctrine. According to all of these teachers, this secret rapture of the church could literally happen any day.

I find it extremely interesting that these teachers think that today's Christian Church in America is ready to be raptured home to heaven. I ask you to think about it. The same disobedient, selfish, worldly, materialistic, sin-filled Church, which has broken and abolished God's law; accused God of creating evil via Calvinistic predestination; changed the gospel into a "get rich scheme"; maligned God's character by presenting Him as an unjust and unfair judge who punishes a billion fold; moreover has twisted and manipulated God's Word to foster an "anything goes" attitude, which has produced a Church just as sinful as the world; according to these secret rapture preachers, is ready to be raptured home to heaven. I don't think so! Today's Church in America is more deserving of *judgment* than *rapture.*

Where does this "secret rapture" doctrine come from? That's an intriguing question. There is little or no biblical support for this doctrine. In fact, they've chosen a good name for this teaching, calling it the *secret rapture*. Why? Because it's so secret, you can't even find it in the Bible!

It takes a vivid imagination to produce today's secret rapture concept based solely upon scripture. Bible verses are stretched and embellished in an attempt to create a biblical foundation for this teaching.

Proponents of this dogma refer to Revelation 4:1 where the apostle John is told by God to *come up here*. John is then allowed to view the throne in heaven where God was seated. How does this text support the disappearance of the Church via a secret rapture during the last days? This verse is addressing the apostle John to *personally* "come up here," so that he can view the things God wants him to write about. It makes no reference whatsoever to a rapture of all believers.

Probably the main text used by proponents of the secret rapture is Luke 17:30-36, where it says that one will be *taken* and the other will be *left* when Jesus returns. Does this text necessarily portray the scenario being presented by modern preachers, where people are vanishing into "thin air" with no one seeing what happened to them? Not at all! It simply says that some will be taken by Jesus, while some will be left. It does not say that the ones left will not be able to see or know what happened to the ones who are taken. And, it certainly does not say that the ones left will get a *second chance* to be taken later! These verses simply tell us that there will be two types of people when Jesus returns. Some will be ready and will be taken by Him; some will not be ready, and will be left behind to perish. It is also obvious that it will not matter what your job is, what your physical location is or what you're doing at the time; those who are ready will be taken and those who are not ready will be left, regardless of any of these things.

More important than the lack of biblical support for this doctrine, is the presence of numerous scriptures that clearly contradict this teaching. Remember, the secret rapture is presented as being a quiet, invisible, mysterious event to those who are left behind. They will not have seen, heard or understood what happened to all of these missing people, according to this doctrine. The following scriptures disprove this modern secret rapture scenario, beyond the shadow of a doubt.

When Jesus returns to take His faithful followers home, it will be

anything but secret, quiet or invisible. The Bible states that He will return in the same manner in which He ascended to Heaven, which was
"visibly" in the clouds; that all the tribes of the earth, and every eye will
see Him return (Acts 1:9-11; Matthew 24:30; Revelation 1:7). The Bible
also declares that His return will be quite audible. It says there will be
the "great sound of a trumpet" and a shout; that there will be "great
noise" (Matthew 24:29-31; 1 Thessalonians 4:16-17; 2 Peter 3:9-10). It
is interesting to note that Jesus said that it is the "false christs" who will
appear *secretly* in the desert or "inner rooms"; furthermore, that His return will be as visible as lightning flashing from the east to west
(Matthew 24:24-27). Therefore, according to scripture, proponents of
the secret rapture theory are unwittingly describing and anticipating
the appearance of *false christs*.

Advocates of the secret rapture hasten to point out that they espouse two returns of Jesus. They teach that His first return will be the
quiet, invisible, secret one to rapture His saints, but His second return
will be the loud and visible one in which He will destroy the wicked.

Unfortunately, their teachings are in direct contradiction of scripture. The Bible proclaims that Jesus came to earth once to bear our sins,
and that He will return a "second" time to save those who are eagerly
waiting for Him (Hebrews 9:27-28). According to the secret rapture,
Jesus comes to earth three times, because He came the first time to bear
our sins, but then will yet return two more times, for the secret rapture
and the final, audible, visible return when He destroys the wicked.
There is no biblical support for this "triple coming" of Jesus. The Bible
speaks of His second coming, but not a third.

Secret rapture proponents also contradict the Bible when they teach
that the rapture of the saints and the destruction of the wicked occur
during two separate returns of Jesus. The Bible clearly states that the
same return of Jesus, which makes all the wicked tribes of the earth
mourn by bringing destruction upon them, also gathers the "elect
saints" to Jesus and gives them rest as they are caught up to meet the
Lord in the air (Matthew 24:29-31; 2 Thessalonians 1:6-10; 1 Thessalonians 4:16-17 and 5:1-4). Also, in Matthew 25:31-46, Jesus makes clear
that He will simultaneously separate the wicked from the righteous and
give them their rewards when He returns with His angels. Once again,

the same return of Jesus that punishes the wicked, also brings the inheritance of the kingdom to the saints.

As you can see, the secret rapture doctrine is a concoction of men with vivid imaginations who have stretched and manipulated a couple of Bible verses. The weight of biblical evidence strongly contradicts this teaching.

In fact, even their assertion that the saints are raptured before the appearance of the antichrist and the great tribulation period is yet another contradiction of scripture. The Bible clearly declares that we will not be gathered together to Jesus until after the antichrist arises with all power, signs and lying wonders (2 Thessalonians 2:1-10). And, Jesus plainly stated that the sounding of the great trumpet gathering the saints from the earth happens "after" the great tribulation events, such as the sun being darkened, the moon not giving light, the stars falling from heaven, the powers of the heavens being shaken, the sea and waves roaring, the distress of nations and men's hearts failing for fear (Matthew 24:29-33; Luke 21:25-31).

It would be wise to return to the Bible and abandon this doctrine, which contradicts so many Bible texts. Also, with the current spiritual lethargy prevailing in our society, the last thing we need to tell people is that they'll have a second chance to accept Jesus after this supposed supernatural secret rapture. Not only is it untrue, but it also encourages even greater procrastination and spiritual lethargy.

Our military leaders would never have told the remaining American personnel in Saigon that they could catch a second evacuation plane, unless the leaders were absolutely certain, beyond the shadow of a doubt, that the second plane was coming. Why? Because the stakes were too high. There are certainly even higher stakes at risk concerning the return of Jesus Christ. Eternal life and eternal death are the stakes! Therefore, it would be wise for today's preachers who proclaim this secret rapture message, to reconsider what they are preaching. It is even more important for them to be absolutely certain, beyond the shadow of a doubt, that there will indeed be a *second chance* to be *evacuated* by Jesus Christ. If there is not such a *second chance*, and people are eternally lost because they had procrastinated making their decision for Jesus based upon the incorrect information that they had received from these *secret rapture* preachers, I will not be the one they will have to answer to, but rather to God Himself! They ought to remember that Jesus said that it is better to have a millstone hung around your neck and for you to be thrown into the midst of the sea, rather than to cause someone else to stumble and perish.

Upon examination of the evidence regarding the Church's secret rapture teaching, it is clear that this doctrine is totally unbiblical. As with so many other teachings being proclaimed within the Church, a massive and indisputable amount of biblical evidence is being intentionally ignored and completely disregarded, while today's theologians teach and exalt manmade theories and opinions.

To reiterate, if secret rapture proponents are correct, Christian pilots, train engineers and bus drivers who refuse to resign from their positions of passenger responsibility and welfare, despite their knowledge that they will soon vanish from the controls of their commercial vehicles with multitudes of passengers in their care, then these Christian transit operators will be guilty of committing the greatest act of terrorism in history, as literally millions of people throughout the world will simultaneously perish in their vacated commercial vehicles.

If secret rapture adherents truly believe their doctrine, they have a moral responsibility to immediately resign from all positions that place the safety of passengers in their care. If they don't, they are freely choosing to become the greatest terrorists in history. That is, of course, unless they don't really believe their own doctrine. And, if that is the case, why are they teaching it?

Once again, I ask Tim LaHaye and Jerry Jenkins, who have become fabulously wealthy from their *secret rapture* based, "*Left Behind,*" Christian novel series, if they truly believe in this secret rapture event that they espouse in their books? If so, why haven't they encouraged all Christian pilots, train engineers and bus drivers to immediately resign from their positions? After all, those millions of passengers who will perish when the driverless planes, trains and busses crash, will not have an opportunity to be saved and to avoid hell during the so-called "second chance" for those who are *left behind.* Shouldn't these passengers, who will be doomed to perish and suffer in hell because of these Christian transit operators' refusal to resign their positions, also have been given that "second chance" opportunity to be saved? If LaHaye and Jenkins truly believe in this *secret rapture* and *left behind* scenario that they have written about and profited from handsomely; then moral integrity and compassion demand that they issue a statement advising all Christian transit operators to resign immediately before this rapture occurs. The only reason for not making such a statement is if they don't really believe this *secret rapture spiel* themselves, and if it has all just been a lucrative money-making scheme. Mr. LaHaye and Mr. Jenkins, I await your response.

21

THE EVIDENCE—PART FOUR:
"ONCE SAVED, ALWAYS SAVED"

THIS CHAPTER DOCUMENTS the biblical evidence regarding the "once saved always saved" teaching. There are several primary texts that are used by those who teach this doctrine. A list of these verses and what they say follows. Afterward, this "manmade doctrine" will be subjected to detailed, analytical, biblical scrutiny, which will expose the manipulation and deception of its proponents. Here are the verses used by the "once saved always saved" advocates.

[John 5:24] Jesus said that the one who believes in Him has everlasting life and shall not come into judgment, but has passed from death to life.

[John 6:37] Jesus said anyone who comes to Him, He will not cast out.

[John 10:28-29] Jesus said He gives them eternal life and they shall never perish, and no one is able to snatch them out of His hand.

[Romans 8:38-39] The Bible states that nothing can separate us from the love of God.

[2nd Corinthians 1:21-22] The Bible states that God has anointed us, sealed us and given us His Spirit as a guarantee.

[Philippians 1:6] The Bible states that He who began a good work in us, will be faithful to complete it.

[1 John 2:19] John said that they (the antichrists) went out from us, manifesting that they were never of us.

[1 John 3:6-9] John said whoever abides in Him does not sin. And, whoever sins has not known or seen Him, because whoever is born of God does not sin, because His seed is in him.

The above verses indeed give us assurance of salvation. They tell us that God loves us, accepts us, changes us and saves us. They assure us that no one can separate us from that love and that no one can take our salvation away from us. We can be sure of our salvation! But, is that the same as "once saved, always saved"?

Does God take our freedom of choice away when we're saved, so that we can't choose to depart from Him if we want to? If God takes our freedom of choice away, why didn't He do that in the beginning with Adam and Eve, thereby avoiding all the misery that sin has caused? Also, the Bible says that God does not change (Malachi 3:6), so if He allowed Adam and Eve to choose to depart from Him when they were "perfect," why wouldn't He allow us to depart from Him? Do we with our sinful, corruptible natures have greater strength to resist departing from God than Adam and Eve did with their sinless, incorruptible natures?

Yet, the answer is obvious. The doctrine of "once saved, always saved" is illogical and unbiblical, as shall be demonstrated. It is comforting and assuring to know that no person, demon, power, circumstance or even the devil himself can take away our salvation that Christ has given us. But, if we choose to give it up ourselves by departing from Jesus, God will respect our choice, just as He did with Adam and Eve. The following scriptures clearly show that it is possible to "fall away" or depart from God; there are conditions to remain in your *saved state.*

[1 Timothy 4:1] Paul said, "Some will depart from the faith." (You can depart.)

[1 Timothy 6:9-10] Paul said, "Some *stray from the faith*." (You can stray.)

[1 Corinthians 10:12] Paul said, "Take heed lest you fall!" (You can fall.)

[2 Peter 3:17] Peter said, "Beware lest you fall and be led away with the error of the wicked." (You can fall.)

[2 Peter 2:20-22] Peter said, "You can turn away from Jesus, and if you do, you're worse off than before you accepted Him." (That would be lost!)

[Galatians 5:2-4] The Bible says it's possible to *fall from grace* and be estranged or separated from Christ. (That's being lost.)

[1 Corinthians 8:8-11] The Bible says it's possible for a "brother" to violate his conscience and perish! (A "brother" can still perish.)

[1 Thessalonians 3:4-5] Paul said it's possible to be *tempted away*, and our previous faith to have been in vain. (We can be tempted away.)

[Hebrews 2:1-3] The Bible says it's possible to *drift away* if we're not careful, and if we do, how shall we escape for neglecting so great a salvation? (We can drift away from our salvation.)

[Ezekiel 33:18] Ezekiel said if the righteous turns to iniquity, he will die. (A righteous man can turn to iniquity and die.)

[Hebrews 6:3-6] The Bible says it's possible for someone who was *really close* to Jesus and "filled with His power," to fall away: it's impossible to bring them to repentance again! (They're lost.)

[Hebrews 10:26-29] The Bible says it's possible for someone who "was sanctified" to turn away from Jesus and turn back to a life of sin, and therefore be *devoured by the fire*. (Previously sanctified people can turn away and be devoured by the hell fire.)

[James 5:19-20] James said it's possible to *wander away* from the truth, and if you do, someone needs to turn you back from your error to save your soul from death. (It's possible to wander away and to need to be saved again.)

[Colossians 1:21-23] Paul said we must "continue in the faith" to remain reconciled.

[1 Corinthians 15:1-2] The Bible says we're saved, *if* we "hold fast" to the gospel, otherwise we'll have believed in vain. (We must hold fast to the gospel to remain saved.)

[Romans 11:17-22] Paul said if we don't *continue in the faith*, we will be broken off from God's olive tree. (As branches in God's "Church tree," we can be broken off.)

[Hebrews 10:35-39] The Bible says we must "endure" to receive the promise; you can "draw back" or "fall away," resulting in your perdition or destruction. (You can "draw back" and be destroyed.)

[Hebrews 3:12-14] The Bible says we are "partakers of Christ," if we *hold fast* until the end. And, according to this scripture, it is possible to depart from the living God.

[Revelation 3:5] The Bible states that those in the Church who overcome will not have their names blotted out of the Book of Life. (Therefore, it obviously is possible to have your name removed from God's Book of Life, which completely contradicts the *once saved always saved* doctrine.)

[2 Timothy 2:12] Paul states that we will reign with Christ *if* we endure, but he also says that He will deny us *if* we deny Him! (Paul is writing to Christians, so it is possible to *"not endure,"* to *deny* Jesus, and thus resulting in His justly denying us.)

In fact, according to 1 Corinthians 9:27, even the apostle Paul knew that it was possible for him to be rejected and become a *castaway* or *reprobate* if he was not spiritually disciplined. And, don't let any modern "seeker sensitive" preachers deceive you concerning what Paul meant here, by telling you that he was not referring to the loss of his salvation, but only to losing extra rewards in heaven. The Greek word used by Paul is *adokimos*. He said he disciplined himself lest he should become *adokimos*. What is "adokimos"? It means rejected, unapproved, disqualified, *worthless, a castaway or a reprobate.* A reprobate is defined in modern dictionaries as being a wicked, immoral, depraved or corrupt person. Paul said he disciplined himself so he would not become like that.

The original Greek word makes it clear that Paul realized that even he could fall into the depraved, immoral, corrupt and wicked condition of a *reprobate.*

Think about it. If the Bible states that this could even happen to the apostle Paul, couldn't it also happen to modern Christians? And, do you think that wicked, corrupt, depraved, immoral reprobates are still "saved" people who will enter heaven? Of course not! This text alone refutes the "once saved, always saved" dogma.

It is also highly significant that the same Greek word, *adokimos,* which Paul said that he could become if he were not disciplined, was the word he used to describe the list of rejected sinners in the last days that we are to turn away from or avoid (2 Timothy 3:1-8). He said in verse eight that these people were *adokimos* ("reprobate"-KJV, "rejected"-NIV, "disapproved"-NKJV) concerning the faith. In other words, they were reprobates who were rejected and worthless. Remember, Paul admitted that he also could become *adokimos* just as these rejected sinners. Are the *adokimos* sinners listed in 2nd Timothy 3:1-8 still saved? Of course not! This is a description of people who are lost; Paul said that even he could also become like them if he were not disciplined.

Furthermore, in Romans 1:28, Paul states that the sinners that he lists, including fornicators, murderers, idolaters and *haters of God,* had forsaken God and developed an *adokimos* ("reprobate"-KJV, "depraved"-NIV, "debased"-NKJV) mind. Their minds, thoughts, attitudes and purposes had become depraved, immoral, corrupt and wicked as those of a *reprobate.* These *adokimos* minded sinners in Romans chapter one, were *not* saved people. They are presented as rebellious, wicked and rejected by God; Paul uses that same word, *adokimos,* to describe what he could become if he were not spiritually disciplined. Even Paul could become like them. Even Paul could fall into such a state of depravity and wickedness, thereby resulting in him being rejected as a reprobate.

This Greek word, *adokimos,* is only used eight times in the entire New Testament. Every single time, _without exception,_ it describes people or things that are wicked, depraved, debased, worthless, rejected, disapproved, disqualified, reprobate etc. It _never_ depicts anything good or of *saving value.* We have already looked at three of these *adokimos* texts. Let's examine the other five passages.

Titus 1:16 mentions a group of people who had denied Christ, and as being abominable, disobedient and *adokimos* ("reprobate"-KJV, "disqualified"-NKJV, "unfit"-NIV) for every good work. Remember, the Apostle Paul said that, if he was not disciplined, he could also become *adokimos* like the people described in Titus.

Hebrews 6:4-8 describes people who forsake Christ, comparing them to land that drinks in God's blessings of rain, then bears only useless thorns and briers. It then declares that land to be *adokimos* ("rejected"-KJV and NKJV, "worthless"-NIV), and whose *end* is to be *burned.* Remember that the Apostle Paul stated that he could also become *adokimos* like that land if he did not discipline himself.

In 2 Corinthians 13:5-7, Paul uses *adokimos* three times. In verse five he states that Jesus Christ is *in you,* unless you are *adokimos* ("reprobate"-KJV, "disqualified"-NKJV, "failed the test"-NIV). He then said in verse six that he trusted that the Corinthians knew that he and his companions were not *adokimos.* And, in verse seven, he prayed that the Corinthians would avoid evil and live honorably, whether or not they viewed him as being *adokimos.* Of course, the key verse in this passage is verse five. Paul clearly stated that Jesus Christ is *in you,* unless you are "adokimos." In other words, to be *adokimos* is to *not* have Jesus within you! As before, remember that Paul declared that he could also become *adokimos,* not have Jesus within himself, if he did not maintain spiritual discipline.

That's why Paul said that he disciplined himself. He did not allow himself to have a careless or lazy spiritual attitude. Paul did not believe in *once saved, always saved,* and neither should we.

It is also certainly not a coincidence that, immediately after Paul admits the possibility for himself to become *adokimos,* he uses the example of Old Testament Israel to teach us not to repeat their sinful compromises (1 Corinthians 10:1-12). He reminds us that many of the Israelites who had been "baptized" *in the sea,* eaten the spiritual food (manna), and drank the spiritual drink from the "Rock" (Christ), nonetheless, later perished through various sinful compromises with lust, idolatry, sexual immorality and complaining. He concludes by saying, "therefore let him who thinks he stands take heed lest he fall."

Paul's message is clear, and it should be a *wakeup call* for today's unbiblical, "once saved, always saved" preachers! Immediately after Paul admits the possibility for himself to become *adokimos* in 1 Corinthians 9:27, he then shares examples of how many of God's "Old Testament Church" (Israel) fell into sin and perished, after initially having been delivered from Egypt. He concludes his point by stating that these things were recorded as examples for our admonition; moreover, that we, therefore, who think that we'll stand, should take heed lest we fall (1 Corinthians 10:11-12).

In summary of these verses in 1st Corinthians, Paul's message is certainly powerful and clear. He reminds us that even he, the powerful and inspired apostle, could fall into the depraved, wicked and *lost* condition of a "reprobate," if he did not keep himself spiritually disciplined. He additionally reminds us that many Old Testament Israelites who had initially been delivered from the *sins of Egypt*, did later fall into sin and perish. He then instructs us to be admonished and to learn from their example, lest we fall due to our arrogance! It is undeniably obvious to any honest and unbiased person that this passage unequivocally refutes the Church's *once saved, always saved* dogma.

The Bible is clear on this issue. A "righteous" or "saved" person can choose to *depart from the faith* (1 Timothy 4:1), *perish* (1 Corinthians 8:8-11), have his previous faith to have *been in vain* (1 Thessalonians 3:4-5; 1 Corinthians 15:1-2), and thereby resulting in him being *devoured by the fire* and dying (Hebrews 10:26-29; Ezekiel 33:13). That's why the Bible warns us in these verses to: "hold fast to the gospel," "continue in the faith," *endure, beware* and to *not depart from God*. Why would God give us numerous warnings not to "depart" or "turn away" from Him, unless it can happen?

You have seen the biblical proof. It is obvious that the Church's "once saved, always saved" doctrine contradicts the overwhelming weight of biblical evidence. I would advise Christian leaders to come down from their self-righteous *judgment seats*, from which they rebuke and condemn non-Christians regarding the liberal philosophies and policies being advanced in our secular culture. As long as they embrace and proclaim their own liberal, unbiblical, doctrinal philosophies within the Church, which are producing similar sinful results, they are in no position to sit in judgment of others.

§ 22 §

THE EVIDENCE—PART FIVE:
THE TEN COMMANDMENTS

THE FOCUS OF THIS CHAPTER will be on the Ten Commandments, as to whether or not God has abolished them. We'll begin by reading the verses *used* by those in the Church who teach that God's law has been eliminated. These texts are:

[Ephesians 2:11-16] Paul states that the law of commandments "contained in ordinances" was abolished.

[Colossians 2:14-17] Paul mentions "handwritings of requirements" which were nailed to the cross.

[2 Corinthians 3:7-11] Paul states that the ministry of death engraved on stones was passing away.

[Romans 10:3-4] Paul says that Christ is the end of the law for righteousness.

[Romans 7:5-6] Paul writes that we are delivered from the law.

[Romans 3:28] Paul maintains that we are justified by faith, apart from the deeds of the law.

[Ephesians 2:8-9] Paul stresses that we are saved by grace through faith, and not by our works.

[Galatians 2:16-21] Paul says we are justified by faith, and not by the works of the Law.

[Galatians 5:14] Paul declares that the law is fulfilled by loving your neighbor.

[Galatians 3:10-13] Paul declares that as many as are *under the works of the law*, are under a curse.

[Galatians 3:23-25] Paul stresses that the law was our tutor to bring us to Christ, but that we are now no longer "under" a tutor.

[Romans 6:14] Paul writes that we are not *under the law*, but under grace.

In the first text, Ephesians 2:11-16, the issue context is to eliminate the separation between Jew and Gentile, and make them *one*. Paul says that Christ abolished the *law of commandments contained in ordinances*, so that Jew and gentile could be *one*. Is Paul talking about the Ten Commandments? That is highly unlikely. Even the famous Protestant reformers, Martin Luther and John Wesley, agreed that this passage is not talking about the Ten Commandments. There were numerous civil, ceremonial and health statutes, ordinances and laws that distinguished Jew from gentile. All of these extra requirements, which separated Jew from gentile, ended at the cross. God still required adherence to the Ten Commandments, as will be proven from numerous Bible texts.

In the second passage, in Colossians 2:13-17, we are simply told that some "handwritings" of requirements which were *against us*, were wiped out and nailed to the cross. Some important points need to be made regarding this text. To begin with, it does not say that it was the Ten Commandments! It simply says that it was some type of *handwriting of requirements*. The entire Bible could be described as containing *handwritings of requirements*. Should we also assume that the entire Bible has been wiped out and nailed to the cross? Of course not! Neither should we assume that the Ten Commandments have been.

Additionally, whenever the Ten Commandments are mentioned throughout the Bible, they are referred to as the *law, statutes, precepts,* etc. They are never referred to as *handwritings of requirements*. To apply this term to them is unreasonable and unprecedented.

Also remember, as with the first text in Ephesians, the respected early Protestant reformers agreed that these texts are not referring to the Ten Commandments.

However, it is clear from all of the aforementioned Bible texts, that obedience to God's commandments cannot and does not justify or save us. It is also evident that the Bible is emphasizing the point that we are not *under the law*. It makes it very clear that we have been delivered from being *under the law*.

It is significant to note that the apostle Paul wrote all of these Bible verses. Why? Because we can, therefore, ascertain what he meant when he said that we are not *under the law*, by simply examining other biblical texts that were also written by Paul.

I believe it is clear from the following Bible verses that Paul did not mean that the law had been abolished or eliminated.

> [Romans 7:12-14] Paul says that God's law is holy, just, good and spiritual.

> [Romans 2:13] Paul says that it is the "doers" of the law who will be justified.

> [Romans 3:31] Paul asks the question of whether or not we make void the law because of our faith, and then answers it himself saying, *"certainly not."*

Therefore, when Paul states that we are not *under the law*, we know that he is not saying that the law has been voided or eliminated, because he has already told us that this is not the case, in Romans 3:31. After all, why would God want to eliminate something that Paul himself said was holy, just, good and spiritual in Romans 7:12-14?

What did Paul mean when he said that we're not "under the law"? According to the gospel message presented in the New Testament, Jesus, God's Son, took our place and lived a perfect life in our behalf. He also died to pay the price for our sins.

According to the Bible, when we place our faith in Him, His perfect life is credited to our account. In other words, God views us as righteous because of what Jesus has done. Therefore, we no longer have to trust in our own perfect obedience to God's law in order to attain righteousness and to qualify for salvation. We are not "under the law" as a means of receiving these precious gifts.

Even more important than what the apostle Paul has said, is what Jesus Himself said concerning God's law and commandments. What did Jesus say?

[Matthew 5:17-18] Jesus said that He did not come to destroy the law. In fact, He said that heaven and earth would pass away before any part of God's law does.

[Matthew 19:16-17] Jesus declared that if we want to enter into life, we must keep God's commandments.

[Mark 7:6-9] Jesus stated that it is "vain" (worthless) worship to set aside God's commandments and to replace them with doctrines of men.

[John 14:15] Jesus tells us to keep His commandments if we love Him.

[John 15:10] Jesus claimed that He had kept His Father's commandments. And, we are told to walk as He walked in 1 John 2:6.

[Luke 6:46] Jesus asked why we would even call Him Lord, if we won't do what He says.

It is obvious that Jesus did not believe that God's commandments had been eliminated. Is there additional biblical evidence? Yes! The following list of Bible texts clearly reveal that God's commandments have not been abolished, and that His law is important and good. The Bible reveals and declares the following:

[Psalms 119:142,151] God's law and commandments are truth.

[Psalms 119:86] God's commandments are faithful.

[Psalms 119:172] God's commandments are righteous.

[Psalms 119:165] Those who love God's law will have peace.

[Psalms 1:1-3] Those who delight in God's law will be blessed.

[Psalms 19:7] God's law is perfect and converts the soul.

[Psalms 119:21] Those who stray from God's law are cursed.

[Psalms 119:53] It is the "wicked" who forsake God's law.

[Psalms 119:44] God's law is to be kept continually forever and ever.

[Ecclesiastes 12:13-14] Man's whole duty is to fear God and to keep His commandments.

[Isaiah 8:20] Those who do not speak in accordance with God's law have no light in them.

[James 2:10-12] We will be judged by the Ten Commandment law.

[1 John 5:3] We know we love God, by keeping His commandments.

[Revelation 14:12] God's true people at the end of the world will be recognized by their faith in Jesus, and also by keeping God's commandments.

[1 John 2:3] Keeping God's commandments is proof that we know Him.

[1 John 2:4] Anyone who says he knows God, but does not keep His commandments, is a liar.

[Psalms 119:126] It is time for the Lord to act, when they have regarded His law as void!

Did you pay close attention to the last reference from Psalms 119:126? The Bible states that it is time for the Lord to act when His law is regarded as void! Today, many theologians have regarded His law as void. They will be held accountable. God's word is clear. What does it say? It says that His law is everlasting, holy, just and good. It also states that His law helps to convert the soul and to bring peace; furthermore, that it is the duty of man to keep God's commandments. The Bible additionally declares that people who are truly saved will obey God's law; moreover, that God's people at the end of time will be distinguished by keeping His commandments, as well as by having faith in Jesus. And, finally, God's word states that keeping God's commandments actually proves that we know Him and love Him.

This is what the Bible says about God's law. It has not been done away with. In fact, according to Psalm 119:53, it is the wicked who try to get rid of God's law! Also, isn't it appropriate and reasonable for those who love Jesus, to want to please Him and obey His commandments out of love? Why would they want to disobey Him?

It is also significant that the Bible defines sin as "transgression of the law" in 1 John 3:4. Why is this significant? Because, according to this New Testament text, if there would be no law to transgress anymore, then there would also logically be no sin anymore. This is an extremely dangerous and slippery theological slope. The apostle John obviously did not believe that the law had been abolished, because he stated that when you transgress it, you have sinned. And, it is important to remember that 1st John was written more than thirty years after most of Paul's letters. Therefore, because we know that the Bible doesn't contradict itself, we also know that Paul never intended for us to believe that the law had been abolished either, because he would not be contradicting John's inspired statement concerning sin as being transgression of the law.

I will close this chapter with a few more scriptures that clearly reveal the perpetuity of God's law. In view of the clarity of these passages, as well as the numerous texts previously listed, it is truly an enigma that preachers are still welcome to proclaim such an obviously contradictory message within *so-called* "mainstream Christianity."

The Psalmist declared that he had inclined his heart to perform God's statutes *forever*. He stated that *everyone* of God's righteous judgments endures *forever*, or, as translated in the NIV version of the Bible, that *all* of God's righteous laws are *eternal*. He added that God's testimonies had been founded *forever*, or, as rendered in the NIV translation, that God had established His statutes to last *forever* (Psalm 119:112; Psalm 119:160; Psalm 119:152). Finally, in Psalm 119:111, he stated that he had taken God's "testimonies" as a heritage *forever*. The Hebrew word used for testimonies is *"eduwth."* And, according to *"Strong's Expanded Exhaustive Concordance,"* this Hebrew word refers to the "Ten Commandments" as being a solemn, divine charge or duty. In other words, Psalm 119:111 is literally stating that the solemn, divine charge of the *Ten Commandments* is a heritage *forever*.

It is time for today's theologians, teachers and preachers to come into agreement with the vast majority of biblical evidence concerning

God's Ten Commandments law. The ministers, priests and preachers should be the ones upholding God's law, instead of dismantling it. Probably never have the words penned by the prophet Malachi been more appropriate than at this time regarding this issue. God's word declares that people should be able to seek the *law* from the mouths of the priests, but that the priests themselves had departed from the *law*, and were causing the people to also stumble at the *law*! (Malachi 2:7,8). That is exactly what modern preachers, who proclaim the abolition of God's Ten Commandments, are guilty of. They, too, have departed from God's law, and are causing many others to also depart from it. It is important to note that some Bible versions have substituted the words *instruction*, *guidance or teaching* for the word "law." The King James and New King James versions, however, more accurately translate the Hebrew word used by Malachi, *torah*, as "law." Preachers have departed from the "torah" or *law*. In fact, the *"Strong's Expanded Exhaustive Concordance"* states that the word, "torah," *especially* refers to the "Decalogue" (The Ten Commandments)! The priests in Malachi's day, as well as many contemporary preachers, bear the same guilt of departing from the Ten Commandments.

Remember, the Bible states that God's law and commandments are perfect, holy, righteous, just, good, spiritual, faithful, continue forever and convert the soul. Now, based on the biblical evidence, does the Bible support or reject this popular church doctrine that teaches that the Ten Commandments were abolished? This is undoubtedly an easy question for us to answer after viewing the evidence, because it is obvious that the Church has chosen to ignore and disregard a multitude of biblical texts that clearly contradict this doctrine.

If church leaders can justify ignoring and disobeying the "once-revered" Ten Commandments of their Holy Bible, will they not also certainly be willing to justify ignoring and dishonoring the principles of freedom and liberty in our nation's constitution? Their duplicitous conduct in the Church should be a wake-up call for our secular society.

23

THE EVIDENCE—PART SIX: THE SABBATH

IN THIS CHAPTER, we examine the biblical evidence dealing with the Sabbath issue. The fourth commandment in Exodus 20:8-11 states: "Remember the Sabbath day, to keep it holy. Six days you shall labor and do all your work, but the seventh day is the Sabbath of the Lord your God. In it you shall do no work: you, nor your son, nor your daughter, nor your male servant, nor your female servant, nor your cattle, nor your stranger who is within your gates. For in six days the Lord made the heavens and the earth, the sea and all that is in them, and rested the seventh day. Therefore, the Lord blessed the Sabbath day and hallowed it."

This commandment clearly states that God has blessed and hallowed the seventh day of the week, Saturday, as the Sabbath of the Lord our God. We are told to remember the seventh day and to keep it holy, and to refrain from our normal labor on that day, just as God rested on the seventh day after completing creation. Why, then, are the majority of Christian churches honoring Sunday, the first day of the week, instead of the seventh day, Saturday?

Here follow the fourteen most common arguments or reasons given for replacing the seventh-day Sabbath with Sunday.

1. *"Who knows if Saturday is really the seventh day after the passing of cen-*

turies of time?"

This reason is only used by people with a limited knowledge of science, history and chronology. Most knowledgeable people in these areas agree that the current seven-day weekly cycle has been maintained back through Bible times. Even most theologians who keep Sunday, admit that Saturday is the seventh day. Also, the Jewish people have kept track of the correct Sabbath day down through the centuries, and they still honor Saturday as the seventh day. And, to eliminate any lingering doubt, read the following quotes from several authoritative sources in the fields of science, chronology and history, which verify the continuity of the current seven-day weekly cycle.

In the 1920s and 1930s, the League of Nations had considered altering the Gregorian calendar. Various ideas were considered and debated. In the League's official *"Report on the Reform of the Calendar,"* published at Geneva, August 17, 1926, we find the following statements by respected astronomers:

> "The week has been followed for thousands of years and therefore has been hallowed by immemorial use."
>> (Anders Donner, "The Report," p.51. Donner served as a professor of Astronomy at the University of Helsingfors).

> "I have always hesitated to suggest breaking the continuity of the week, which without a doubt, is the most ancient scientific institution bequeathed to us by antiquity."
>> (Edouard Baillaud, "The Report," p. 52. Baillaud served as director of the Pris Obervatory).

> "As far as I know, in the various changes of the Calendar there has been no change in the seven day rota of the week, which has come down from very early times."
>> (F.W. Dyson, personal letter, dated March 4, 1932. Dr. Dyson served as astronomer royal, Royal Observatory, Greenwich, London).

> "The week of seven days has been in use ever since the days of the Mosaic dispensation, and we have no reason for supposing that any irregularities have existed in the succession of weeks and their days from that time to the present."
>> (Dr. W.W. Campbell. Dr. Campbell served as the director of Lick Observatory, Mt. Hamilton, California).

"There has been no change in our calendar in past centuries that has affected in any way the cycle of the week"
> (James Robertson, personal letter, dated March 12, 1932. Dr. Robertson served as director of the American Ephemeris, Navy Dept., U.S. Naval Observatory, Washington, D.C.).

"The week is a period of seven days... It has been employed from time immemorial in almost all Eastern countries"
> (*The Encyclopedia Britannica*, 11th edition, Vol. 4, p. 988, article, "Calendar").

"The continuity of the week has crossed the centuries and all known calendars, still intact,"
> (Said Professor D. Eginitis; Dr. Eginitis served as director of the Observatory of Athens, Greece).

2. *"What difference does it make which day you honor, as long as you remember to honor **a** day each week?"*

The Sabbath commandment in Exodus 20:8-11, does not say to remember **a** day. The commandment says to remember the <u>seventh day</u>. God chose the day He wanted. He did not ask man to choose his own day. Also, we're told in Genesis 2:3 and in Exodus 20:11, that God blessed, sanctified and hallowed the seventh day. In other words, He made it holy! Only God can make a day holy. Man may try to honor God on a different day, but he will never be able to make it holy. And, even if you truly think that God allows you to pick a day yourself on which to honor Him, why wouldn't you still choose to honor the same day that He chose, blessed and sanctified, out of love and respect for Him? Why would you insist on picking a different day than the one He chose for you?

3. *"The Sabbath command is not specifically repeated in the New Testament, and therefore is not binding."*

This argument would eliminate over half of the Bible! The Old Testament is three times longer than the New Testament. You would have to eliminate at least <u>two-thirds</u> of the Old Testament to make it mathematically possible to repeat it in the New Testament. According to this argument, you could completely eliminate the Old Testament, because it would only be "in force" if it's repeated in the New Testament.

Also, using this argument would eliminate many beautiful Bible verses and promises in the Psalms and other Old Testament books, because they are not specifically repeated in the New Testament. After all, you must be consistent in applying this line of reasoning. I think most people would rather reject this faulty argument, than eliminate over half of the Bible.

We must also remember what the New Testament says about the Old Testament. In 2 Timothy 3:16-17, we're told that all scripture is inspired by God and profitable for us. When Paul wrote this, the only scripture they had was the Old Testament.

Also, this argument is not even accurate. The Sabbath is referred to numerous times in the New Testament. In Luke 4:16, we're told that it was Jesus' custom to keep the Sabbath. In Mark 2:28, Jesus declares Himself as Lord of the Sabbath. In the book of Acts there are several references to the apostle Paul keeping the Sabbath (Acts 13:42-44; Acts 17:2; Acts 18:1-4). Jesus even said in Matthew 24:20-21 that the Sabbath would still be important during the "great tribulation" at the end of the world! It's also interesting that the Bible says the seventh-day Sabbath will even be kept in the "New Earth" which God provides for His people at the end of this current sinful world (Isaiah 66:22-23).

4. *"The strict regulations and punishments related to the Sabbath commandment obviously disqualify it as a New Testament requirement."*

Opponents of seventh-day Sabbath observance point out that people were required to strictly adhere to the Sabbath or they would be put to death during the Old Testament era. They assert that because we would not consider applying such a drastic punishment in the New Testament era, the Sabbath commandment itself does not apply in the New Testament era. However, to be consistent, those who use this reasoning must also eliminate at least four more of the Ten Commandments, which also had extremely strict regulations and called for the death penalty. The commandments which forbid adultery, idolatry, blaspheming or using the Lord's name in vain, and the commandment commanding us to honor our parents; all required offenders to be put to death as well (Exodus 21:15-17; Leviticus 20:9-10; Leviticus 24:16; Deuteronomy 13:6-10; Deuteronomy 17:2-5). The commandment not to murder, of course, also called for the death penalty, although many would claim that the death penalty is justifiable in the case of murder. However, if you use this argument to eliminate the Sabbath commandment, you must also at least eliminate the commandments concerning adultery, idolatry, honoring your parents, and blaspheming or using the Lord's name in vain as well, because the death penalty would certainly seem to be just as extreme for these offences as it is for the Sabbath commandment. Therefore, proponents of this argument are not only contradicting the overwhelming weight of biblical evidence, but also would end up with only "five commandments" in their New Testament. This is obviously another faulty argument that must be rejected.

5. *"There are historical records of groups of Christians keeping Sunday instead of Saturday, as early as the late first century."*

So what? Does it matter when the error started? If an error starts sooner, does that make it less wrong? There are records of disobedience throughout the Bible. The Bible records that Abraham lied, Noah got drunk, and David committed adultery and murder. Does that mean it's all right for Christians to lie, murder, get drunk and commit adultery? Of course not!

It doesn't matter what any other historical books or famous theologians say. For a Christian, it only matters what God says in the Bible. And, God says we are to remember and keep the seventh-day Sabbath (Exodus 20:8-11). There are many books and teachers who contradict the Bible today. Therefore, we would be wise to remember what Jesus' disciples said to the false religious leaders of their day. Acts 5:29 quotes them as saying: "We ought to obey God rather than men." We are warned in Isaiah 8:20, that if people do not speak in accordance with the law and testimony of God, that there is no light in them. In other words, those who contradict the Bible are in darkness.

6. *"There are references to gatherings of Christians on Sunday in the Bible."*

There are only eight references to the first day of the week in the entire New Testament. Five of these references have nothing whatsoever to do with a meeting or gathering of Christians. They state that some women were going to the tomb to anoint Jesus' body for proper burial on the first day, or that Jesus appeared to someone on the first day (Matthew 28:1; Mark 16:1-2; Mark 16:9; Luke 24:1; John 20:1).

The other three "first-day" references are as follows: In John 20:19 we find the disciples gathered together on the evening of that same first day of the week. Why were they gathered there? Was it for a worship service? No! They were gathered together behind closed doors for fear of the Jews (John 20:19). They were afraid that they also might be arrested and crucified as Jesus was.

In fact, a few verses later, in John 20:26, we're told that they gathered together again eight days later. That would have been on a Monday. Was the Sabbath, therefore, changed to Monday? Of course not!

Christians gather together on many different days for many different reasons that have nothing to do with the Sabbath. For example: Wednesday night Bible studies, Tuesday night men's fellowship meetings, Monday night testimony services, Thursday night communion services, Friday night church socials etc. Does that mean that the Sabbath has been changed to Monday, Tuesday, Wednesday, Thursday or Friday? Absolutely not! Most Christians would agree that such a suggestion would be ridiculous.

Yet, that same absurd reasoning is used for the previous "first-day" text (John 20:19), and for the following "first-day" text in Acts 20:7-11. Here we find Christians gathered together to share a meal with Paul on the first day of the week, because Paul was going to depart the next day. In other words, it was a "farewell dinner." Churches frequently have farewell parties for important members and pastors. It is also interesting to note that this was almost certainly a night meeting, not a Sunday morning worship service, for Paul speaks until midnight. There is, in fact, no mention of any kind of change in the Sabbath day in this text.

The final "first-day" reference is found in 1st Corinthians 16:1-2. Paul is trying to put together a large donation for the poor Christians in Judea. He has asked all the churches that he has been associated with to participate in this offering. So, he reminds the Corinthians to "lay something aside" for this special offering, "first thing" at the beginning of the week. The word "day" is not even in the original Greek manuscripts. It simply says the "first of the week." English translators have simply supplied the word *day*, probably because of their own preconceived ideas concerning first-day worship, and because there are several instances where other New Testament writers seem to intend to indicate the usage of the word *day*, although they don't specifically use the Greek word for *day*.

However, the apostle Paul's letters are consistent in his usage of the words *day* and *first*. In each and every case when Paul wants to say the word *day* as referring to a specific day, he always uses the Greek word *hemera*. He never omits the word as he does here. If Paul has chosen not to use the word for day, because he obviously does not intend to convey that meaning, why do English translators insist on inserting it anyway?

Also, in all other cases when Paul uses the word *first* immediately preceding the noun that it describes, or to denote importance, order, place or time, as it would here if the insertion of the word *day* by modern translators is correct; Paul always uses the Greek word *proton* or *protos* for our English word *first*. He never uses the Greek word *mia* for those types of usages, as he does here in 1st Corinthians 16:2. This is another strong indication that Paul does not intend to say the word *day*, and that is why he did not do so. Paul simply told the Corinthians to lay something aside at the first of, or in other words, at the beginning of the week. He does not designate a specific day.

Paul even gives his reason for "laying aside" their offering on the "first of the week." He says so that there will be no collections when he comes. In other words, do it now so it will be ready when I get there. Paul does not mention anything about a church service on Sunday, or about a change in the Sabbath.

To attempt to use any of these previous eight "first day" verses to authorize changing the Sabbath from Saturday to Sunday is obviously incorrect and unbiblical! There are close to two hundred Sabbath references in the Bible. Many of them are stated as a specific commandment from God to honor, keep, obey or rest on His seventh-day Sabbath. And, dozens of these references to Sabbath observance or worship are in the New Testament. There is no comparison between the voluminous biblical authority for the seventh-day Sabbath, and the few unrelated "first-day" texts in the Bible.

7. *"The seventh-day Sabbath is for the Jewish people only, and is not meant for Christians.*

It is important to note that the Sabbath was instituted at the end of creation week according to Genesis 2:1-3. That means that the Sabbath was in existence for many centuries before Abraham and the Jewish people existed.

It is also significant that, according to the New Testament, Jesus Christ is the Creator of the world, which we read about in the creation account given in the book of Genesis (John 1:1-3; Colossians 1:16-18). Therefore, it was Jesus Himself who established, blessed and sanctified the seventh-day Sabbath after completing creation (Genesis 2:1-3). As you will see, the seventh-day Sabbath has numerous connections to Jesus Christ.

Another important point is that even after the Jewish people existed, the seventh-day Sabbath was still meant for the "foreigners" or "gentiles" too (Isaiah 56:1,2,6,7). In fact, even in the New Testament, when the gentiles asked Paul to preach to them also, the Bible states that they asked him to do it on the next Sabbath (Acts 13:42-44)! If the Sabbath had truly been changed to Sunday, why didn't Paul tell these gentiles that he would preach to them on the first day of the week, rather than having them wait for the next Sabbath? Obviously, no such change in the Sabbath had taken place.

Finally, the Sabbath is one of the Ten Commandments (Exodus 20:8-11). If the Sabbath commandment is only for Jews, to be consistent, the other nine commandments would also be only for Jews. Using this logic, God would only be requiring the Jews not to lie, steal, murder, commit adultery, etc. All non-Jews would be exempt from these commandments, and could lie, steal and murder all they want! Of course this is ridiculous, as is the argument that the Sabbath is only for the Jews.

8. *"Keeping the Sabbath is legalism."*

Once again, to be consistent, if obeying the Sabbath commandment is legalism, then obeying the other nine commandments would also be legalism. Is it legalism not to murder? Is it legalism not to commit adultery? Is it legalism not to lie or steal? Is it legalism not to worship idols? Is it legalism to honor your parents? This argument is obviously a poor one. Does God call obedience "legalism"? Quite to the contrary, according to the Bible, our obedience is a proof that we "know God" and love Him (John 14:15; 1 John 2:3; 1 John 5:3). Therefore, obeying God's Sabbath commandment is not legalism, but rather is a proper "love response" to God.

9. *"The Ten Commandment law was nailed to the cross and is no longer binding. Therefore, the seventh-day Sabbath is also no longer binding."*

This argument was dismantled in the previous chapter. Where does this idea come from, concerning the Sabbath not being binding? It is primarily from four texts. The first one is Romans 14:4–6. The issue and context in Romans chapter 14, most would agree, is not judging others and not putting a stumbling block in front of them.

It is significant that the word "Sabbath" is not mentioned in this text. Doesn't it seem unreasonable to eliminate God's Sabbath commandment by using a text that does not even mention the Sabbath?

This verse speaks of *special days*, which are "esteemed" by some, but not by others. Anyone with a knowledge of the Old Testament knows that the Jews had many *esteemed days* associated with various feasts, festivals, new moons, jubilees, etc. The Christian Church at Rome was composed of both Jews and gentiles (Romans 2:17; Romans 11:13). Therefore, the Jewish Christians would still probably esteem some of these other "special days," whereas the gentile Christians would not. So, Paul counsels them not to judge each other, but rather to allow each person to decide for himself if he wanted to esteem certain other special days. This text does not even mention the Ten Commandments or the Sabbath specifically.

The second text is Ephesians 2:11-16. As stated in the previous chapter, the issue or context here is eliminating the separation between Jew and gentile, and making them *one*. Paul says that Christ abolished the "law of commandments contained in ordinances," so that Jew and gentile could be *one*.

Is Paul talking about the Ten Commandments? That is highly unlikely. Even the famous Protestant reformers, such as Martin Luther and John Wesley, agreed that this passage is not talking about the Ten Commandments. There were numerous civil, ceremonial and health statutes, ordinances and laws that distinguished Jew from gentile. All of these extra requirements that separated Jew from gentile ended at the cross. God still required adherence to the Ten Commandments, as was conclusively proven in the previous chapter.

The third text used to try to eliminate God's Sabbath commandment is in Acts chapter fifteen. In Acts 15:28-29 the Jerusalem council writes to gentiles that they are only required to abstain from foods offered to idols, from fornication, from things strangled and from blood. Because their letter to the gentile believers doesn't specifically state that they must keep the Sabbath, it is suggested by Sunday advocates that the Sabbath must have been abolished. However, this letter does not state that the gentiles needed to keep any of the other Ten Commandments either. It does not tell them not to lie, steal, murder, covet, commit adultery or use the Lord's name in vain etc. Therefore, to be consistent, Sunday proponents who use this argument to eliminate the Sabbath commandment, must also be asserting that the other commandments had been abolished for the gentiles as well, due to the fact that they were not specifically mentioned either. If this is true, you have the ridiculous assumption that gentiles were required not to commit fornication, eat foods offered to idols, eat blood or things strangled; nevertheless, that it was ok for gentiles to worship idols, blaspheme the Lord's name, murder, steal, lie, commit adultery, etc.! Of course, this is absurd. It is obvious that the apostles in Jerusalem were assuming that the Ten Commandments "moral law" was already required, and that they were only asking for compliance with these four extra requirements in addition to the "moral law." I don't think anyone actually seriously believes that the apostles considered it to be more important for the gentiles not to eat improperly prepared meat, than for them not to murder, lie, steal and worship idols. The *moral law*, which includes the Sabbath commandment, was obviously assumed to be automatically still in force.

The fourth text often used to try to eliminate God's Sabbath commandment is Colossians 2:13-17. It has already been conclusively established in the preceding chapter that this text is not referring to the Ten Commandments. Therefore, it is very probable that the reference to "sabbaths" in verse sixteen, is not referring to the fourth commandment concerning the seventh-day Sabbath. Serious Bible students know that there were other types of sabbaths mentioned in the scriptures related to various other Jewish feasts and other requirements, as part of the Jewish ceremonies. Certain days involved with the *Feast of Tabernacles*, the *Blowing of Trumpets* and the *Day of Atonement*, were also referred to as "types of sabbaths," as well as "special sabbaths" for the land (Leviticus 16:31; Leviticus 23:24-32; Leviticus 24:39; Leviticus 25:2-6). It is probable that these "ceremonial sabbaths" are what Colossians is referring to, especially due to the related references to *festivals, food, drink* and *new moons*. These four related references are from the ceremonial laws, and not from the Ten Commandment moral law. Not one of the moral law commands deals with festivals, food, drink or new moons. Therefore we know for sure that four out of the five items mentioned in Colossians 2:16-17, as being shadows or symbols of things to come, which reach their substance and fulfillment in Christ, are strictly ceremonial law items, and have no connection to the moral law. Considering this context, doesn't it seem highly probable that the fifth item (the sabbaths), also being referred to as a symbol or shadow in Colossians, would almost certainly be a reference to the special ceremonial law sabbaths previously mentioned, rather than the moral law Sabbath contained in the Ten Commandments? This is especially probable in light of the reference to these items as being shadows or symbols of things to come concerning Christ, because the ceremonial laws did indeed point forward to, and were fulfilled by Jesus Christ, whereas this is not the case with the moral law. Most would agree that various Jewish ceremonies, feasts and special days related to these events have all been fulfilled in Jesus Christ and terminated. This is almost certainly what's being referred to in this text. However, even if one insists that the seventh-day Sabbath commandment is being referred to, several significant points can still be made which still prove that the Sabbath is not being changed or eliminated. In this passage, Paul says not to judge concerning the Sabbath, and that it is a "shadow" or "symbol" of things to come. This text does not say that the Sabbath has been changed from Saturday to Sunday, but only that we should not judge others regarding it. Not judging others isn't just limited to the Sabbath. The Bible tells us not to judge others, period (Matt. 7:1-2; Romans 2:1-2; James 4:12).

Also, even if the Bible is telling us not to judge concerning the Sabbath, does that mean that it's all right to disobey God and break His

Sabbath commandment? In Romans 2:1-2, Paul says we are not to judge the sinners listed in Romans 1:22-31. This list includes idolaters, murderers, liars, adulterers and haters of God. Therefore, if not judging concerning the Sabbath means that it's all right to break it, then, to be consistent, when we're told not to judge all these other sins in Romans chapter one, it would also mean that it's all right to do all of those things. Obviously that is not the case.

It is true that the Sabbath is a "shadow" or "symbol" of Jesus, because part of its message is about *rest*. However, the entire Bible is filled with symbols of Jesus. Jesus said in John 5:39, that the scriptures testify of Him. Water baptism by immersion and "communion" are also symbols of Jesus. Should we not practice or observe them either because they are symbols? And, we must remember that the Sabbath is much more than just a symbol of rest in Jesus; it is also a memorial of His completed creation of this world, which He has commanded us to keep. Once again, this argument is totally invalid and unbiblical.

Another significant point can be made from the position of common sense, sound judgment and logic. Is it reasonable to disregard multitudes of Sabbath texts throughout scripture because of one somewhat "challenging text" in Colossians? What if we did that with the multitudes of verses that tell us to love one another, in the Bible? Should we disregard all of these "love texts" because of one "challenging text" in Luke 14:26, where Jesus tells us that we must "hate" our parents, children, spouses and siblings if we want to be His disciples? Would it be reasonable to disregard all of the *love passages*, because of this one "challenging text" in Luke 14:26? Of course not! Instead, we find a reasonable answer to the one challenging text. A similar application of this principle would also be the doctrine of justification by faith. We know that numerous scriptures tell us that we are justified by faith, and not by works. However, in James 2:21-25, we're told that Abraham and Rahab were justified by their works. Do we disregard all of the "justification by faith" texts because of this one challenging text in James, which refers to being justified by works? Absolutely not! Instead we once again find a reasonable explanation for the one challenging text, rather than ignoring the numerous passages endorsing justification by faith. The same principle applies to the Sabbath. We also do not disregard all of the Sabbath passages, but rather find a reasonable explanation for the one *allegedly* challenging text in Colossians.

It is also very interesting that the author of Colossians is the apostle Paul. Why? Because, according to the Bible, Paul himself kept the Sabbath (Acts 13:42-44; Acts 17:1-2; Acts 18:4). Was Paul practicing the "do as I say, but not as I do" game? That is very unlikely.

It is probably even reasonable to assume that those who use this argument don't really mean it. Ask them if it's all right with God if we lie, steal, murder, commit adultery, worship idols, etc.? They will maintain that we still should refrain from these practices which, of course, accords with God's Ten Commandments. Their desire is to eliminate one commandment, but not all ten.

Finally, this argument directly contradicts the overwhelming weight of biblical evidence, which strongly supports the perpetuity of God's law, as was clearly established in the previous chapter.

10. *"Saturday might be the Sabbath, but Sunday is the Lord's Day in the New Testament."*

This is an easy argument to answer. Where does it say that Sunday is the Lord's Day in the Bible? Absolutely nowhere! There is not one single verse in the entire Bible that says that the first day of the week (Sunday) is the Lord's Day. In fact, the only day of the week that Jesus ever declared Himself to be Lord of, in the Bible, is the seventh-day Sabbath (Mark 2:28). And, it makes sense that the Sabbath would be the real Lord's Day. After all, Jesus was the Creator who established, blessed and sanctified the Sabbath in Genesis 2:1-3. Also, we're told that Jesus kept the Sabbath Himself as His custom in Luke 4:16. Finally, Jesus even kept the Sabbath in His death, but that is answered in the next argument, which follows.

11. *"Sunday is kept instead of Saturday, to honor Jesus' resurrection."*

This argument might sound good on the surface, but unfortunately, it lacks any biblical authority whatsoever. God chose the day He wanted, and He blessed, sanctified and hallowed the seventh day of the week as a perpetual memorial of His completed creation.

There is not one single verse in the entire Bible that ever removes God's blessing from the seventh day. There is not one text in all of scripture that says that the Sabbath has been changed from Saturday to Sunday. And, there is not a single passage in the entire Bible that says to honor Sunday because of the resurrection. In other words, this argument is completely unbiblical.

The truth is, that Jesus honored the Sabbath, even in His death. The Bible says that the Lord does not change (Malachi 3:6). It also says that Jesus Christ is always the same (Hebrews 13:8). Therefore, it is probable that the reason Jesus arose on Sunday, was because He was honoring the Sabbath that He Himself had established, by resting in the tomb on the seventh day after completing redemption, just as He had rested on the seventh day after completing creation.

We also see, in Mark 7:6-13, what Jesus thinks of men ignoring one of God's commandments, in order to establish or honor a tradition of men. When the religious leaders of Jesus' day were ignoring God's commandment to *honor their parents*, in order to practice a man-made tradition, He accused them of vain worship, of teaching commandments of men, of rejecting God's commandment in order to keep their own tradition, and of making the word of God of no effect.

If Jesus felt that way about ignoring one of God's Ten Commandments, wouldn't He feel the same way today? Remember, according to the Bible, He does not change (Hebrews 13:8; Malachi 3:6). If it was "vain" or "worthless" worship to replace one of God's Ten Commandments with an unauthorized tradition back then, wouldn't it also be "vain" or "worthless" worship to replace God's Sabbath commandment with the unauthorized tradition of keeping Sunday today?

The answer is obvious. Today's religious leaders who advocate disregarding the Sabbath, are just as guilty as the religious leaders who disregarded the commandment to "honor your parents" in Jesus' day.

12. *"The Sabbath commandment is different from the other nine, because it is not really a <u>moral issue</u>. Therefore it is not actually a <u>moral law</u>, and accordingly is not truly a part of God's moral law.*

This argument actually places man in judgment of God's wisdom. God knew what He was doing when He chose to include the Sabbath commandment within His Ten Commandment moral law. After all, who determines what morality is, man or God? Who establishes what a

THE EVIDENCE — PART SIX:

moral law is, man or God? If God has included the Sabbath as part of His moral law, we can be sure that it belongs there. Why shouldn't God consider it to be a moral responsibility for mankind to obey His Sabbath command and to honor the day that He has instituted, blessed, sanctified and hallowed? What gives mortal man the right to sit in judgment of God, by deciding which of God's commands are important and moral, and which are not? It would be much better to obey God, rather than question His judgment.

13. *"The Sabbath was a sign or symbol of our rest in Jesus. Now that Jesus has come and fulfilled that rest for us, we do not need to keep the symbol."*

Unfortunately for proponents of this argument, there is no specific Bible text that actually states that the Sabbath was only a symbol of our rest in Jesus. In fact, the Sabbath commandment does not point forward to some future rest, but rather points us backward to remember and honor God as Creator. That's what the Bible says! Also, it is significant that in Hebrews chapter four, where adherents to this argument try to establish their case, there is actually an interesting *twist* in the Greek language, which suggests the perpetuity of the Sabbath. After repeated references to the "katapausis" rest that we receive in Jesus, it almost seems as if God is trying to make sure that we don't <u>throw the baby out with the bath water,</u> by reminding us that even after receiving that "katapausis" rest from Jesus, there still also *remains* a "sabbatismos" or "Sabbath rest" for God's people (Hebrews 4:9). In other words, the observance of a Sabbath rest continues.

14. *"Even if the seventh day is the Sabbath, and is the day to rest according to the Bible, the first day, Sunday, is the day we are to worship together on."*

As with all of the other arguments, this one also is completely unbiblical, and in fact, directly contradicts scripture. There is not one single verse in the entire New Testament that says to worship on the first day of the week. There is not one single text in the entire Bible that suggests that the seventh-day Sabbath is not a time to worship together on; implying it is only a time for rest. In fact, the Bible calls the Sabbath a time of *holy convocation,* which means a time of sacred or religious assembly (Leviticus 23:3). Scripture also states that God's people in the

"New Earth" will come to worship before God from one Sabbath to another (Isaiah 66:23). There are no such references to worship regarding the first day of the week, Sunday. Also, seventh-day Sabbath corporate worship is endorsed throughout the Bible by example. There are dozens of references to worship services on the seventh day, whereas there are no such references regarding the first day of the week. Additionally, the Bible states that both Jesus and the apostle Paul made it their custom to worship on the seventh-day Sabbath (Luke 4:16; Acts 17:1-2). The biblical evidence overwhelmingly supports seventh-day worship, rather than first-day worship. Once again, this argument is nothing more than an excuse to ignore God's seventh-day Sabbath commandment. And, it is fair to say, that most people who worship on Sunday, are not also honoring the seventh day as a blessed and holy day of rest to God. In most cases, the seventh day, Saturday, is used as a time to do yard work, clean the house, buy groceries, go golfing, patronize shopping malls or attend sporting events. The Sabbath is not being honored, and proponents of this argument know this.

There you have it. These are the fourteen most common arguments used for honoring Sunday instead of the seventh-day Sabbath. As you can see, all of them are faulty and unbiblical. And, as you can also see, there is obvious confusion among those who advocate the observance of the first day, Sunday. What confusion? Even those who defend Sunday and reject the seventh-day Sabbath can't agree as to why they do so. Some say that it's because the Ten Commandments were abolished. Others say that this is not the reason, but rather that it's because the Sabbath was transferred from Saturday to Sunday to honor the resurrection. However, others say that this is not the reason either, but rather that each person is allowed to choose a day each week on which to remember and honor God. Then there are still others who say that this is not the reason either, but who claim that keeping the Sabbath is not required at all, because it was only a symbol of our rest in Jesus, and has been fulfilled. First-day advocates cannot seem to agree among themselves as to why they ignore the seventh day, and replace it with the first day. Why? It is probably because there is no clear scriptural authority for their position. They cannot go to any specific Bible verses to authorize and defend their stance. They have no clear *"thus saith the*

Lord." All they have is human opinions, which often vary from one person to the next.

There is no biblical mandate for Sunday keeping. There is no Bible text authorizing a change in the Sabbath. There is no scripture removing God's blessing from the seventh day. There is no passage stating that God ever blessed, sanctified and hallowed the first day. There is no Bible verse declaring Sunday to be the Lord's Day. There is no reference in scripture authorizing the keeping of the first day of the week in order to honor the resurrection. There is no Bible text calling obedience and Sabbath-keeping *legalism*. In fact, the Bible states that obedience is proof that we love Jesus! And, the Bible even states that keeping the Sabbath is a "sign" between the Lord and us, that He is our God, and that He sanctifies us (Ezekiel 20:12,20).

In closing, I again ask you to consider some passages from the Psalms, as you ponder this Sabbath issue. The Sabbath is unquestionably one of God's Ten Commandments; number four to be exact. The Psalms state that _all_ of God's commandments are faithful, true and righteous (Psalm 119:86; Psalm119:151; Psalm 119:172). Therefore, the seventh-day Sabbath commandment is also being declared to be faithful, true and righteous. Why would God change or eliminate a faithful, true and righteous commandment?

The Psalms state that _everyone_ of God's righteous judgments endures _forever_, or, as the NIV translation renders this text, that _all_ of God's righteous laws are _eternal_ (Psalm 119:160). If all of God's laws are eternal, and the seventh-day Sabbath commandment is undeniably one of those laws; then the seventh-day Sabbath is also _eternal_ and obviously was not changed or eliminated.

Psalm 119:152 states that God's testimonies were founded _forever_, or, as rendered by the NIV translation, that God established His "statutes" to last _forever_. Once again, the seventh-day Sabbath is unarguably one of God's statutes. Therefore, the seventh-day Sabbath was also established to last _forever!_ It has not been abolished or changed.

In Psalm 119:44 the Psalmist declared that he would keep God's "law" continually, _forever and ever_. The Hebrew word used for "law" in this text is *torah*, which according to *Strong's Expanded Exhaustive Concordance*, especially refers to the Decalogue (the Ten Commandments).

According to Scripture, the Ten Commandments were to be kept continually, *forever and ever*. Therefore, the seventh-day Sabbath commandment, which is indisputably one of the Ten Commandments, was also obviously intended to be kept continually, *forever and ever*. It is probably fair to say that we have now reached the point of *overkill* regarding the biblical evidence for honoring the seventh-day Sabbath, and for rejecting the Church's exalting of the first day, Sunday.

From a biblical standpoint, the Sabbath issue is an *open and shut case*. How open and shut? Our church has run several ads in the *Minneapolis Star and Tribune* and *Minnesota Christian Chronicle* newspapers, where we offered $10,000 to anyone who could produce *just one Bible text* specifically stating that the Sabbath has been changed from Saturday to Sunday. No one has ever come forward to collect the money.

Most "fair-minded" and reasonable people would certainly agree that if a Bible was handed to someone from another culture, who had never heard of either Saturday or Sunday worship; then asked him to read the Bible from the opening book of Genesis through the final book of Revelation, in which he will find close to two hundred references to the seventh-day Sabbath that endorse, command or bless its observance, while not reading one single passage that endorses or commands first-day observance; then asked him which day of the week that he should honor, based upon the Bible alone; that his response would unquestionably be the seventh-day, Saturday! It would be an absolute "no-brainer" for any previously unbiased and "unbrainwashed" reader. When you eliminate the non-inspired input from other books and from finite, fallible human beings, the Sabbath issue becomes "crystal clear." Based solely upon the Bible, there is only one day of the week that God commands us to honor and keep, the seventh day, Saturday. Now it is up to each individual Christian to decide if they will be as faithful and obedient as the disciples were when they confronted the wayward religious leaders of their day, by boldly telling them that they were going to "obey God rather than men" (Acts 5:29). The evidence concerning the Sabbath issue is overwhelming. It is clear that the Church's *Sunday doctrine* is being taught in blatant disregard of the indisputable biblical evidence.

§ 24 §

THE EVIDENCE—PART SEVEN:
FAVORING ISRAEL

I
T IS TIME to analyze the evidence related to the subject of Israel.
Are those in the church who place such a great emphasis and focus
on the literal nation of Israel, biblically justified in doing so?

In this book, the study of *Israel* is based on the Bible alone, and not
upon the opinions and interpretations of other religious books and
authors. And, you will probably be surprised to find that so many scriptures are being completely ignored when it comes to this topic.

It is also important to remember to distinguish between the Jewish
people collectively as a nation, and individual Jewish persons. God deals
with nations in certain ways, while dealing with individuals differently.
God can punish a nation, while still blessing and loving various individuals within that nation. The Bible clearly states that God is *no respecter of persons,* so we can be sure that He loves and accepts all who
come to Him in repentance through faith in Jesus Christ, whether they
are Jew or gentile.

Even when God rejects or punishes a nation, individuals within that
nation can still receive salvation. God loves both Jew and gentile, and
desires them to repent and put their faith in Jesus Christ. Please remember this important distinction between the nation of Israel, and
individual Jews.

Israel is the center of attention for the religious and secular worlds. From a secular perspective, Israel's importance is one of political and diplomatic concerns and foreign affairs. Israel's presence in the midst of the Arab world creates a scenario that influences the entire world.

From a religious perspective, Israel's importance is related to spiritual concerns and biblical truth, thus the subject of Israel influences the entire Christian Church. And, just as Israel divides the world politically, it also divides the Church spiritually and biblically.

There is a large segment of the Christian Church that still views Israel as being God's "chosen nation" or *chosen people*. They believe that the nation of Israel's significance, importance and *chosen nation status*, is the same in the New Testament as it was in the Old Testament. Therefore, they tend to be "pro-Israel" in most political issues as well as religious concerns. They view the Jewish people as being much "closer" to Christianity than the Islamic Arab world. They believe that Christians and Jews worship the same God, whereas Arabs worship a different god. This results in a natural alliance between pro-Israel Christians and the nation of Israel, which favors the Jewish people over the Arab world in just about everything.

There are other Christians, however, who have a different view of Israel today. They believe that the New Testament presents a change regarding the subject of Israel, which accords with Old Testament scriptures that proclaim God's promises and covenants with Israel to be conditional, based upon their obedience and fidelity. These Christians believe that the nation of Israel no longer enjoys a "favored nation" status, and that the Jewish religion should not be exalted any more than the Islamic faith, because the Jewish religion also worships a different god than Christianity.

We shall thoroughly examine this subject of Israel from a biblical perspective, and shall also examine whether Christians should be favoring the "Jewish people" over their Arab neighbors.

So, what is the "truth" concerning Israel? Where can we go to find the truth? In John 17:17, Jesus said that "God's word" is truth. Therefore, we shall base our decision concerning Israel, upon God's word alone as revealed in the Bible.

We know that there are numerous blessings, covenants and promises that God gave to Israel in the Old Testament. And, we also know that there are scriptures which state that these promises and blessings are everlasting, or will continue forever. For the sake of brevity, we will simply acknowledge that these scriptures exist.

Having acknowledged the existence of these scriptures, how can some Christians still assert that Israel has changed in the New Testament, and no longer enjoys their "chosen nation" status, forfeiting their promises and blessings from God? Do these Christians ignore the Bible, or do they have a biblical explanation for their position?

As we begin our quest for the truth about Israel, please approach this with an "open Bible" and an *open mind*. Remember what Jesus said concerning God's Word, that it is *truth*. What is the "truth" concerning Israel—what does the Bible say?

To begin with, an important consideration regarding Israel's ceremonies, covenants, promises and blessings, is that the continuation of these promises, covenants and blessings was conditional based upon Israel's obedience and fidelity. In Jeremiah 18:5-10, God says that if a nation which He had promised to build and to do good for, turns to disobedience, then He will not do the *good things* that He promised them.

In fact, God told Israel "up front" that if they persisted in disobedience, they would forfeit the blessing He offered them, and would receive curses instead (Deut. 28:15-68). These curses included disease, drought, crop failure, hunger, thirst, nakedness, persecution, plundering and enemy invasion; even to the point of their resorting to cannibalism of their own children because of their hunger. And, within these curses, God clearly and specifically states that Israel will not receive their promised blessings, but will receive the exact opposite, which is the curses. Instead of becoming as the *stars in multitude*, as God had promised in Genesis 15:4-5, they would be reduced to being "few in number" (Deut. 28:62). Instead of Israel being the *head* and others being the *tail*, as God had promised in Deut. 28:13, Israel would become the *tail*, while their enemies would be the *head* (Deut. 28:44). Instead of the Lord's multiplying and doing good for Israel, giving them their land forever, and having other nations and kings serve them as He had promised (Genesis 13:14,15; Genesis 17:6-8); the Lord would rejoice in destroying Israel and bringing them to nothing, and would pluck them from their land; moreover, Israel would serve its enemies and be destroyed by them, and no one would save Israel (Deut. 28:29,48,63). In fact, God says that all of these curses would continue to be upon Israel and overtake Israel and its descendants "forever" (Deut. 28:45-46).

As you can see, God's "everlasting" promises, covenants and blessings upon Israel, were conditional based upon Israel's obedience. And, the Bible also clearly states that Israel's disobedience would negate these promises and blessings, and would replace them with the curses we've mentioned. What does biblical history tell us about Israel? Was Israel a faithful and obedient nation, who could expect to receive God's promised covenants and blessings? Or, was Israel an unfaithful and disobedient nation, who forfeited its covenants and blessings, and who could expect God's curses?

Any Bible student knows that the history of Israel is filled with rebellion, disobedience and infidelity. And, any student of history also knows that Israel has indeed had a cursed history of persecution, oppression and enemy invasion resulting in hunger, thirst, starvation and even cannibalism when surrounded by Babylonian and Roman armies. This persecution has continued throughout modern history via Nazi Germany, Islamic terrorism, and so on. This is a precise fulfillment of the curses pronounced upon Israel for their rebellion. Israel rejected their God throughout the Old Testament. Israel rejected, persecuted and martyred the faithful prophets God sent to her. Finally, Israel even rejected its Messiah, Jesus Christ, declared that His blood was upon its own hands and its children's, and that they recognized no king but Caesar (Matthew 27:25; John 19:15). The New Testament records the continued obstinacy and rebellion of the Jewish nation, as they continued to persecute and martyr the disciples of Jesus. Paul even states in 1 Thessalonians 2:14-16, that the Jews were *always filling up the measure of their sins*, and that God's wrath had come upon them to the uttermost because they did not please God, and were contrary to all men. Jesus even declared to the Jewish religious leaders that they could no longer claim God as their father, but that their father was now the devil (John 8:37-44). The apostle John even refers to Jews who blaspheme and persecute Christians, as being a "synagogue of Satan" (Rev. 2:9; Rev. 3:9). Of course, we know the New Testament historical record of the persecution of Christians and Jesus Himself by the Jewish nation, as well as their blasphemy of Jesus and His followers. (Mark 15:29-32; John 5:16; Acts 7:51-52; Acts 13:44-51; Acts 18:5-6; 1 Thess. 2:14-16).

It is also interesting that John states that "they say they are Jews, but are not." Why? Because a "true Jew" in the "spiritual sense" in the New Testament, has nothing to do with physical genealogy or bloodline descent. A "true Jew" is someone who has had their heart circumcised, rather than their flesh (Romans 2:28-29; Colossians 2:11). Likewise, when Stephen spoke to the Jewish leaders, and traced their history of rebellion and disobedience, he declared that their hearts were *uncircumcised.* In other words, they were not "true Jews" in the New Testament "spiritual sense," which is in perfect agreement with John's statement about those who claimed to be Jews but really weren't, and whom he declared to be a *synagogue of Satan.*

Please remember that we are talking about the Jewish nation, and not individual Jewish people. Biblically, the nation of Israel had been rejected and was under God's curse, but individual Jews could still be saved by placing their faith in Jesus Christ. Jesus loves and receives individual Jew and gentile believers alike, but the Bible is clear that Israel, as a nation, had rejected God, thus, had forfeited the blessings, covenants, and "good things" that God had promised them, and instead, was heir to His curses (Jeremiah 18:5-10; Deuteronomy 28).

According to the Bible, the Jewish people no longer enjoy a "chosen people" status. This is clearly demonstrated in the New Testament. 1st Corinthians 16:22 states that "anyone" who does not love Jesus Christ is accursed, not blessed. Does the Jewish nation love and esteem Jesus Christ? The Jewish religion actually holds Jesus in lower esteem than does the Islamic faith. Islam at least acknowledges Jesus as a prophet of God, whereas the Jewish religion only acknowledges Him as a good man. The Jewish nation does not love and esteem Jesus as Lord and Christ, and is therefore pronounced as accursed in the New Testament, and not blessed.

In 1 John 2:22-23 we are told that whoever denies that Jesus is the Christ, which also means Messiah, is a liar and an *antichrist.* The Jewish nation denies that Jesus is the Christ/Messiah. Therefore, rather than still being God's *favored chosen people,* according to this passage, they are declared to be the complete opposite – antichrist! And, this text also reveals that they do not worship the God of Christianity, because it states that by rejecting Jesus, they have denied the Father as well. Therefore, the Jewish religion, which has rejected Jesus Christ, is just as distant from the God of Christianity as is the Islamic faith. Why? Because both have rejected Jesus Christ as being the divine Son of God and the Messiah, and the Bible clearly states that the only way to God is through Jesus Christ (John 14:6). Therefore, the Jewish and Islamic religions are both at an equally great distance from the God of Christianity. That distance equals acknowledging Jesus Christ as Messiah, Lord, Savior and the divine Son of God.

Some might say that Israel's more favorable acceptance of Christianity places them on a higher moral plane than that of Islamic nations. However, Israel desperately needs the assistance and friendship of the United States in order to survive. And, it is appropriate for America to help them protect their national sovereignty. Nevertheless, because of their reliance upon the United States as their only powerful ally, perhaps Israel is motivated to be respectful of American customs and practices, which includes Christianity. I believe that "pro-Israel" Christian evangelicals overlook this fact when they contrast Islamic nations' persecution of Christians, with the warm reception Christians receive from the Jewish nation of Israel. Perhaps these evangelicals should ponder how Christians would be received in the nation of Israel, if Israel were the superior power, and had no need of the friendship and support of the United States. What makes us think, in that scenario, that Christians would be treated much different in a non-Christian Israel, than in a non-Christian Islamic nation?

Let us remember that, to a strict orthodox Jew, a profession of faith in Jesus Christ as being God, constitutes heresy and blasphemy just as much as it does in the Islamic world. Furthermore, we also know that it is not uncommon for converts to Christianity to be "disowned" by strict orthodox Jewish families, just as they are in Islam.

The only real difference in the treatment of Christianity between Judaism and Islam is the additional "church-and-state-sponsored" persecution of Christians that occurs in many Islamic nations. That brings us back to my question of how Christians would be treated if Israel were the *superior power*, and had no need of America's friendship, assistance and support. In that scenario, would a non-Christian Israel treat Christianity much different than does a non-Christian Islamic nation? Does history help answer this question?

In the days of Jesus and the apostles, the first-century Christian Church was located in non-Christian Israel, which had a limited semi-autonomy. Of course, at this point in history, Israel was not relying upon the friendship and support of a Christian nation. How were Christians treated by the "non-Christian" nation of Israel back then? Were they treated better than they are by Islamic nations today? Not according to the historic record given in the New Testament. Homes of Christians were raided. Believers were imprisoned, beaten or put to death. The property of Christians was confiscated. This is how Christians are treated by any and every non-Christian people who have the ability to do so without fear of serious imminent repercussions.

It is time for evangelical Christianity to follow the scriptures, and stop playing favorites. As Peter said in Acts 10:34,35: "In truth I perceive that God shows no partiality, but in every nation whoever fears Him and works righteousness is accepted by Him." God loves both Jew and Muslim the same, and wants both to place their faith in Jesus Christ. Until they do so, they are equally lost, according to the Bible.

I am not attempting to establish any kind of moral equivalency regarding the present Palestinian conflict. The current suicide bombings are evil and reprehensible, and can never be justified. The brutality and inhumanity demonstrated by radical Islamic terrorists in the recent beheadings in Iraq should be an offense to all civilized human beings. My emphasis is strictly from a biblical perspective regarding the spiritual condition of "all" who have not accepted Christ. In this regard, from a biblical standpoint, a non-Christian Jew is no better off than a non-Christian Muslim. And, a non-Christian Islamic nation that has rejected Jesus Christ, stands under no greater condemnation than the non-Christian nation of Israel, which has also rejected Jesus. In fact, the physical city of Jerusalem is actually said to represent Hagar and legalistic bondage in Galatians 4:21-31. It is interesting that Hagar is actually the "mother" of the Arab world, which has descended from Ishmael, Hagar's son. So, according to the New Testament, literal physical

Jerusalem and literal physical Jews who have not accepted Christ, are viewed the same as Hagar and her descendants. In other words, they are viewed the same as the Arab world. Not only is the physical city of Jerusalem referred to as Hagar in the New Testament, but it is also said to spiritually represent the ancient and wicked city of Sodom in Revelation 11:8. These are not complimentary terms that God has chosen to use to describe the literal city of Jerusalem in the New Testament. Sodom and Hagar are clearly used to represent the physical city of Jerusalem as a place of bondage and iniquity.

On the other hand, the Bible speaks of a *Jerusalem from above*, spiritual or heavenly Jerusalem, which represents the child of promise, Isaac, through whom the ultimate "Child of Promise" would come, Jesus Christ. Do you get the picture? The physical city of Jerusalem in the New Testament now represents the rejected child, bondage and iniquity, whereas this heavenly or spiritual Jerusalem now represents Isaac, the promises and *freedom in Christ.*

This accords with Hebrews 12:18-24, which states that Christians' focus and citizenship is in the *heavenly Jerusalem*, not the earthly Jerusalem. Also, Hebrews 13:10-14 tells us that as Jesus suffered *outside* the "gate" or "camp" of Jerusalem, we as Christians are also to go to Him *outside the camp of Jerusalem.* Verse fourteen plainly states that Christians have <u>no city here</u>, but that we seek the one to come. The earthly city of Jerusalem is of no more spiritual significance in the New Testament than any other city. Its previous significance was forfeited.

Israel's persistent disobedience and rebellion, culminating with their rejection and murder of their Messiah, Jesus Christ, has resulted in their rejection by God, and forfeiting the blessings, covenants and "good things" that God had promised them, and instead making them heir to God's curses (Jeremiah 18:5-10; Deuteronomy 28).

That is why the covenant blessings promised Israel in the Old Testament regarding a temporal millennial reign, the reinstitution of temple services and festivals, and other nations coming to serve and bow before them, are not mentioned in the New Testament. These covenant promises and blessings could have been theirs if they had accepted their Messiah, yet they culminated their history of disobedience and rebellion with the murder of their Messiah, the Son of God. In the process, they forfeited the covenant promises and blessings, and became heir to the curses. The literal, physical, geographical nation of Israel, with all of its feasts, ceremonies and covenants, is no longer focused upon in the New Testament. In fact, it has been replaced by a *new nation*, a *spiritual Israel*, with a "new covenant." This is not *replacement theology*, as some like to call it, but is correct biblical doctrine based upon numerous New Testament scriptures, which clearly state that this is the case. We shall examine many more of these texts.

However, it is quite interesting and contradictory that the same preachers who accuse people, such as myself, of practicing *replacement theology*, also simultaneously justify rejecting the seventh-day Sabbath of the Ten Commandments. Why is this interesting and contradictory? Because one of their main reasons given for rejecting the seventh-day Sabbath commandment is that it's primarily mentioned in the Old Testament, and not stressed nearly as much in the New Testament. These same preachers then turn and rely upon the Old Testament for the vast majority of their biblical basis for their teaching about the literal nation of Israel. Is this not a blatant double standard? If the Old Testament is good enough to support their doctrine about Israel, it should also be good enough for them to obey the seventh-day Sabbath of the Ten Commandments in the Old Testament.

Conversely, if they refuse to accept and acknowledge the seventh-day Sabbath commandment, based upon its heavy reliance upon Old Testament references, then they should also abandon their emphasis on the literal nation of Israel, due to its heavy reliance upon Old Testament references. It seems that these "pro-Israel" teachers have adopted the convenient policy of using the Old Testament when it serves their purpose, while rejecting it when they are not willing to do what it says.

It is indeed ironic that the same preachers who accuse me of practicing "replacement theology," have themselves replaced the seventh-day Sabbath of the Ten Commandments with first-day (Sunday) observance; accepting and endorsing this change with no biblical authority whatsoever. In reality, they are the ones guilty of "replacement theology," by replacing the seventh-day with the first day.

In the Old Testament, the literal nation of Israel was God's chosen nation. The Jewish people were favored over the gentile nations in various ways. There were promises and blessings offered to them, which were not offered to any others. However, this is not true in the New Testament era. We shall examine numerous scriptures that help us understand those texts that referred to Israel's covenants and blessings as being everlasting or continuing forever. We shall present many scriptures which specifically state that Jews are no longer favored over gentiles, but are regarded as one and the same; that being a "true Jew" is a *heart issue*, not a bloodline descent issue. In fact, we shall see that the literal nation of Israel was rejected by God, and has been replaced by the Christian Church.

In Ephesians 2:11-18, the Bible states that Jew and gentile have become *one new man*, and that the "wall of separation" which used to distinguish between them is gone. Romans 10:12 also declares that there is no more distinction between Jew and gentile. In fact, the Bible says that being a Jew or a *child of Abraham*, in the true sense, has nothing to do with Jewish descent, but rather is defined by a faith relationship with God through Jesus Christ. Galatians 3:7 states that only those *who have faith are sons of Abraham*. Galatians 3:26-29 declares that it is those who are *in Christ*, and who belong to Christ, who are *Abraham's Seed*, and also that there is no Jew or gentile anymore. Galatians 6:15,16 states that those who have become "new creatures" in Christ, are the *Israel of God*. This "new" *Israel of God* comprised of new creatures in Christ, stands in stark contrast to literal, physical Israel which Paul refers to as *Israel after the flesh* in verse eighteen of 1st Corinthians chapter ten. From these two texts alone it is obvious that there is a "spiritual Israel" and a literal, physical Israel, and that they are not the same. Philippians 3:3 proclaims that those who worship God in the spirit and rejoice in Christ Jesus, are the real circumcision (Jew). Romans 2:28-29 actually specifically declares that being a Jew has nothing to do with outward fleshly things (being a physical Jew), but is defined by inward issues of the heart (being a spiritual Jew). This text makes it clear that, in the New Testament gospel era, you become a Jew by having your heart circumcised, and it has nothing to do with the flesh! Romans 9:6-8 tells us that being part of Israel is now attained by faith in God's promise, and not by Jewish descent. Paul says that it's not the "children of the flesh" (physical Israel), but rather "children of the promise" (spiritual

Israel). In fact, he specifically states that not all the "seed of Abraham" are true children of Israel. This text makes it clear that being part of Israel, in the New Testament gospel era, has nothing to do with bloodline descent. As Paul says in verse six, *they are not all Israel who are of Israel.* In other words, Israel is not limited to literal physical Israel.

Why has this New Testament change in "Israel" occurred? As previously mentioned, it was because of Israel's persistent and continual rebellion and disobedience, culminating with their rejection of Jesus Christ. The nation of Israel continued to reject God, until God ultimately respected and honored their persistent choices to reject Him, and accordingly also rejected the nation of Israel. This is not just a statement of my opinion. It is exactly what Jesus Christ said in Matthew 21:33–43. Jesus told the parable of the vineyard to illustrate the history of Israel's stubborn and persistent rebellion. God had sent His servants repeatedly throughout centuries of time to try to bring Israel to repentance, and to bring forth the appropriate fruit of repentance, but Israel had responded by persecuting and murdering the prophets that God sent them. Finally, God sent His Son Jesus Christ, but they also rejected and murdered Him. The parable concludes with the declaration that the vineyard would be taken from them and given to others, and that they would be destroyed. Here, in Matthew 21:43, Jesus plainly states that the kingdom of God would be taken from Israel, and given to a different nation. Who is that nation? 1 Peter 2:9 calls the Christian Church a *holy nation,* a *royal priesthood* and *God's own special people.* The Christian Church has replaced Israel, and is a type of a *spiritual Israel.* This is not *replacement theology.* This is what the Bible says!

Jesus also told Israel that their house (the temple) was now "desolate" (Matthew 23:38). Desolate means unoccupied. Israel had rejected God, and was about to publicly reject their Messiah, Jesus Christ; they would publicly proclaim His blood as being upon them and their children, and that they recognized no king but Caesar. Now, according to Jesus Himself, God was going to honor their request, and would no longer be dwelling in their temple. Their house was desolate, and unoccupied by God. It's also interesting that Jesus had previously referred to the temple as His "Father's House," but now He calls it "your" house. Israel had persistently rejected and abandoned God, and now God was rejecting the nation of Israel. Of course, Jews on an individual basis could still receive personal salvation by accepting Jesus Christ, but their "chosen nation" status had been forfeited. They had exchanged the blessings for the curses in Deuteronomy 28. As Jesus also said in Luke 19:42, the things that could have been theirs, had they accepted Jesus, were now hidden from their eyes.

In an effort to give their *Israel focused doctrine* some appearance of New testament support, proponents of this teaching refer to Romans 11:1, where Paul asks if God has cast away His people of Israel, and then answers his own question by saying "certainly not." They mention Romans 11:26, where Paul states that all Israel will be saved. And, they remind us that Paul's declaration in verse twenty-six, immediately follows his statement in Romans 11:25 that "hardness in part has happened to Israel, until the fullness of the gentiles has come in." They also mention Paul's statement in Romans 11:29, that "the gifts and calling of God are irrevocable or without repentance." As always, consideration of the context of this passage in Romans chapter eleven is essential for correct understanding. Is Romans chapter eleven focusing on a nation's exaltation as a special people, or upon the availability of *acceptance and salvation* to <u>*individuals*</u> within that nation? The proper context is clearly established within the text of this chapter. In the first five verses of the chapter we are reminded of the presence of 7000 faithful <u>*individuals*</u> within that nation at an earlier time in history. The emphasis here is on faithful individuals, and not on a faithful nation. In verse fourteen Paul states that he hopes to save <u>*some*</u> (individuals) from within that nation, but not the entire nation itself. In verses seventeen through twenty-four, Paul describes God's people as an "olive tree," and states that people, both Jew and gentile, are grafted in or broken off based on their belief or unbelief. Once again the emphasis is on individuals and their choices to believe or disbelieve, and not on the exaltation of any particular nation.

Regarding the specific verses in Romans chapter eleven that are used by those who attempt to offer some New Testament support for their pro-Israel doctrine, it is important to consider the following biblical facts. Romans 11:1 simply states that God has not cast away all of the Jewish people, so that they are hopelessly lost without having any hope of salvation. Salvation is still available to each and every Jew.

Paul's statement that all Israel will be saved in Romans 11:26, is in perfect harmony with all of the New Testament evidence I have presented concerning Israel. Remember that Israel has been *redefined* in the New Testament, as has been clearly demonstrated. As previously documented, Jesus told the Jewish leaders that the Kingdom of God was being taken from them and would be given to a new nation (Matthew 21:43). Paul said that Israel is *bigger* than literal Israel, and that bloodline descendants of Abraham are not necessarily a part of Israel, because it is a faith issue rather than a physical descent issue (Romans 9:6-7). Paul also said that being a "true Jew" has nothing to do with being a *literal, physical, outward Jew,* but rather is an "inward heart issue" (Romans 2:28-29). Romans chapter 11 plainly states that the *"new Israel olive tree"* is comprised of both Jew and gentile alike! There is only one tree now! That tree is the Christian Church. As Jesus said in Matthew 21:43, there would be a new nation replacing Israel. Peter then designates the Christian Church as being the "holy nation," "royal priesthood" and *"new" special people of God* (1 Peter 2:9). The New Testament clearly defines the Christian Church as now being God's special people. The New Testament presents a new type of "spiritual Israel" comprised of *inward, heart Jews;* an olive tree comprised of Jews and gentiles alike. As Paul states in Romans 11:26, "all" of this newly redefined olive tree of *spiritual Israel,* consisting of both Jews and gentiles, will indeed be saved! This is, in fact, the only acceptable way to explain this passage in Romans chapter 11, which maintains the proper context of the passage, and which also accords with the overwhelming amount of New Testament evidence already presented regarding the subject of Israel. It is also noteworthy that Paul had earlier stated in verse fourteen that he only hoped to save "some" of those who were of his flesh (physical bloodline Jews). This is another strong indication that the *"all* Israel being saved" in verse twenty-six, can't be referring to literal, physical Israel, because Paul would not be contradicting his previous statement that he only hoped to save "some" of them.

Regarding the argument that Paul's declaration, that all Israel would be saved, immediately follows his statement in Romans 11:25 that "hardness in part happened to Israel until the fullness of the gentiles has come in," the following important biblical facts need to be remembered. Romans 11:25 is essentially a summarized restatement of the points that Paul previously made in verses eleven through fifteen. In Romans 11:11-15, Paul gives a somewhat more detailed description of how God sovereignly used the nation of Israel's rejection of the gospel, in order to bring the gospel to the gentiles. It is important to remember that, as Paul is writing verses eleven through fifteen, he is preparing to present the New Testament Church as an "olive tree" comprised of both Jews and gentiles in the verses that immediately follow. Furthermore, he is about to present God's *olive tree* (the Church) as being accessed only by faith on an individual basis for both Jew and gentile. People are grafted into this tree as branches through belief in the gospel, and they are broken off as branches through disbelief in the gospel.

In the process of studying Romans 11:11-15, it becomes apparent that Paul is demonstrating a characteristic of God that he has pointed out earlier in the book of Romans. In Romans 8:28 Paul previously stated that God works all things together for the good. We see a demonstration of this principle in the eleventh chapter of Romans. As Paul is preparing to discuss God's "olive tree" (the New Testament Church), which is clearly comprised of both Jews and gentiles, he begins by showing how God is sovereignly *working all things together for the good,* for Jew and gentile alike. In Romans 11:11-15, Paul plainly implies that God's sovereign purpose in the Jews' initial choice to reject the gospel, was to sovereignly use their "bad decision" to bring about the *good result* of the conversion of the gentiles; furthermore, that God was also using the gentiles' conversion to cause the Jews to be jealous of the gentiles' good fortune, which God would also sovereignly use to cause *some* of the Jews to make the "good decision" of accepting the gospel. This principle of God's ability to work all things together for the good, in order to bring about the salvation of both Jews and gentiles, introduces Paul's presentation of God's "olive tree" (the New Testament Church), in the verses that immediately follow in Romans 11:16-24.

After Paul has carefully and specifically discussed how Jews and gentiles are *grafted in* or *broken off* God's "olive tree" in the same manner, without partiality or favoritism to either group; Paul concludes his *olive tree* presentation by restating the points he made in his introduction of the "olive tree passage" in Romans 11:11-15. Unquestionably for emphasis, Romans 11:25 basically conveys the same message as Romans 11:11-15: God is working all things together for the good for Jews and gentiles, in order to bring them to salvation.

A thorough, analytical study of Romans chapter 11 reveals that Romans 11:25 is the culmination and conclusion of the preceding *olive tree* verses, rather than the introduction of the following verses, beginning with verse twenty-six. Romans 11:25 clearly concludes Paul's "olive tree teaching" by restating the points made by Paul in the introduction of his *olive tree* message in Romans 11:11-15.

It is noteworthy that Paul's message is not only clear, but also encouraging! God is on our side! He is working to bring salvation to everyone, Jew and gentile alike. And, He offers this salvation to everyone in the same manner, through faith. Regardless of ethnicity, if you believe, you are *grafted in* to His *olive tree* (the New Testament Church). Likewise, regardless of ethnicity, if you disbelieve, you are rejected and *broken off* from His *olive tree*. However, in Romans 11:25 Paul chooses to conclude by briefly restating the "positive side" of the message that he began with in Romans 11:11-15. He chooses to focus on the "God is on our side" part of the message, in which God is working to get us into His *olive tree*, not to remove us from it. For both Jew and gentile, God is sovereignly using everything, even our bad decisions, to bring about the *good result* of our salvation. He is working all things together for the ultimate good of including us in His *olive tree* (His New Testament Church, "Spiritual Israel").

Subsequently, after this powerful presentation of God's *olive tree*, comes Romans 11:26, where Paul states, "And so all Israel will be saved." This is a very appropriate statement after delivering the message contained in Romans 11:11-25. It seems that Paul is basically saying that: "In view of the fact that God is on our side; in view of the fact that He is working all things together for the good of everyone, Jew and gentile; in view of the fact that He allows both Jews and gentiles to become part of His *olive tree*, moreover, in view of the fact that He is sovereignly using *all things*, even our bad decisions, to get us grafted into that tree; therefore, Paul confidently states in Romans 11:26 that all of this *olive tree* (the New Testament Church, "Spiritual Israel"), now comprised of both Jews and gentiles, _will be saved_ ! It is reminiscent of Paul's earlier statement in Romans 8:31 that, "if God be for us, who can be against us?"

Regarding Romans 11:29, which is translated in many Bible versions as follows: "The gifts and calling of God are _irrevocable_"; it must be remembered that the original language in which the New Testament was written was Greek. The original, inspired Bible writers did not use English words. They used Greek words. Then, hundreds of years later, those Greek words were translated into our English vernacular by modern translators. Although the original Bible writers were certainly inspired, as were the Greek words that God impressed them to use; notwithstanding, it would be a "stretch" to claim a similar and equivalent inspiration for modern translators who are responsible for the exact wording chosen for usage in the many versions of the Bible available today. Modern translations often choose different English words when translating the same Greek word. God does not have a "split personality" that causes Him to inspire different translators to use different English words while translating the same Greek word. In truth, translating from one language to another is often an imprecise science. It is common for one Greek word to be able to be translated into several different English words. It then becomes up to the translators to decide which word to choose. These modern translators don't always agree on which word is the best choice, and that is why various versions of the Bible often render the same passage of Scripture differently. The human agent involved in the translation process is certainly a factor, and unfortunately these human agents are sometimes inconsistent and inaccurate. It is almost certain that we have such a case of inconsistency and inaccuracy in the translation of Romans 11:29.

As previously mentioned, many modern translations have rendered Romans 11:29 to state that God's gifts and calling are "irrevocable." The original King James Version, which is usually quite accurate and consistent, has rendered this passage to state that God's gifts are "without repentance." The Greek word used by the Apostle Paul in Romans 11:29, that is being translated as _irrevocable_ or "without repentance," is _ametameletos._ This Greek term is only used one other time in the entire New Testament, in 2nd Corinthians 7:10. How do modern translators render the Greek word *ametameletos* in 2nd Corinthians 7:10? They translate it as "not to be regretted," "never regret," "leaves no regret" or "never brings regret." These are the same translators who render that same Greek term as *irrevocable* in Romans 11:29! It is obvious, from their unanimous agreement in their translation of 2nd Corinthians 7:10, that *ametameletos* can be accurately rendered as "without regret." If these translators were consistent in their translation of this Greek word, by translating it as "without regret" in Romans 11:29, the meaning conveyed in this passage would be dramatically changed, and would be in accordance with the rest of Scripture. Romans 11:29 would state that God's gifts and calling are "without regret," *not irrevocable.*

God does not make mistakes, and He is working all things together for the good. God knows the end from the beginning. He knows beforehand who will accept or reject His salvation and His callings. Yet, He offers them to everyone, because He loves everyone. He gives everyone a chance, and He has *no regrets* for having called them. Does any good earthly parent have any regrets for having offered and given good things to their children, although some of them may have rejected them? Even so, God has no regrets for having extended His good gifts and calling. As the original King James Version rendered this particular passage, God does not "repent" of having made these gracious offers. After thorough study of Romans chapter eleven, it is apparent that this chapter offers no *true* New Testament support for the pro-Israel doctrine being espoused by so many today.

Another significant consideration involves the New Testament book of Hebrews. Hebrews is written specifically to Hebrew Christians. If the literal nation of Israel is to regain its Old Testament prominence, and to have its temple, sacrifices, temple services and other Old Testament rituals reinstated, then isn't it strange that there is no mention whatsoever in this letter to Hebrew Christians concerning these momentous events? In fact, anyone who has studied the book of Hebrews is certainly aware that no such restoration to prominence, or reestablishment of their services and rituals is promised to Jewish believers. Actually the complete opposite is the case. Hebrews warns Jewish Christians to *stop focusing* on the earthly temple and its services, and to fix their eyes on the heavenly. There is no exaltation of literal, physical

Israel or Jerusalem whatsoever. In fact, <u>Hebrews</u> 13:12-14 reminds Hebrew Christians that Jesus suffered *outside* the gate of Jerusalem, and that Jewish believers should also go *outside the camp* of Jerusalem to meet Him. Verse fourteen then reminds the Hebrews that they have <u>*no*</u> <u>*continuing city here.*</u> Instead, it says to seek the *one to come*, which has already been identified as the "heavenly Jerusalem" in Hebrews 12:22. In other words, stop focusing on literal, physical Israel and Jerusalem, and focus on heavenly, spiritual realities instead. It would be wise for today's preachers and teachers to remember and heed this biblical counsel in the book of <u>Hebrews</u>.

What about those Old Testament scriptures that state Israel's covenants, promises, blessings and ceremonies were to be everlasting, and continuing forever? First, we need to remember that all of these things were conditional, based upon Israel's obedience and fidelity, as was previously proven from scripture (Jer.18:5-10; Deut. 28).

Additionally, there are numerous references to other things, practices, events and requirements in scripture, which are also stated to be everlasting, eternal or continuing forever; notwithstanding, they have been terminated or eliminated.

Consider the following examples:

Jeremiah 17:4 states that God's anger against Judah will burn *forever*. Is He still angry now? Will He still be angry when all the redeemed are at home in heaven?

Deuteronomy 15:17 declares that if an Israelite has a servant who wants to stay with him, he can pierce his ear, and then he will be his servant *forever*. Yet, it is obvious that the servant would die at some point, and therefore his service to his master would come to an end.

Leviticus 6:13 states that the fire on the altar in the Old Testament tabernacle of Israel would "ever" burn, but it is not still burning. And, Leviticus 24:1-4 declares that the lamp in the tabernacle would burn continually, with Aaron in charge of it *forever*, but that lamp has been extinguished for thousands of years, and Aaron and his descendants have not been in charge of that lamp for thousands of years.

According to Leviticus 7:34 and Leviticus 10:14-15, the priests would continue to receive and eat the breast and thigh of the "wave" and "heave" offerings from the animal sacrifices *forever*, but that has not happened for thousands of years either. Numbers 18:8-11 also says that the priests would eat the animal offerings *forever,* which of course, terminated long ago as already mentioned.

Leviticus 16:29-34 declares that the animal sacrifices on the "Day of Atonement" would continue *forever* and were *everlasting.* Yet, we know that they also were discontinued thousands of years ago. And, we know they were terminated because they were only symbols of the real sacrifice, the Lamb of God, Jesus Christ. Hebrews 10:1-10 clearly states that these animal sacrifices could not take away our sins, but were only a reminder to us of our sins; therefore, a reminder of our need of a Savior from sin. Hebrews declares that God did not desire animal sacrifices and offerings, and had no pleasure in them. It then records Jesus' wonderful statement: *"Behold, I have come."* Hebrews 10:9-10 specifically states that God took away the "first" (the system of animal sacrifices), and established the "second" (the offering of the body of Jesus Christ).

In the case of most of these scriptures that declare certain things to continue forever or to be everlasting, you may have noticed that they refer to things that are symbolic of Jesus' coming, His ministry and atonement. The animal sacrifices, which the priests ate, were symbolic of the *Lamb of God,* Jesus Christ. The lamp in the tabernacle was symbolic of the *Light of the World,* Jesus Christ. The animal sacrifice on the "Day of Atonement" was symbolic of the *true atoning sacrifice* of Jesus Christ on the cross.

Consider three more examples. In Exodus 40:12-15, the Bible states that Aaron's priesthood was to be "everlasting" throughout his generations; yet, we're told in Hebrews 7:11-19 that this was changed, and that the former commandment concerning Aaron's priesthood descendants was annulled or cancelled. Why? Because Jesus Himself was the *true High Priest,* and the perfect fulfillment of the high priestly office, of which Aaron's priesthood had only been a symbol.

In Genesis 17:13 the Bible speaks of circumcision as being an "everlasting" covenant, which not only applied to Abraham's descendants, but also to all others who wished to join them and become part of God's people. This everlasting covenant was a strict requirement for everyone, and anyone who was not circumcised was "cut off" from God's people (Genesis 17:14). Circumcision was absolutely required as an everlasting covenant. However, in Acts chapter fifteen the apostles' council officially proclaims that the gentiles are not required to be circumcised when joining the New Testament Christian Church. And, in Galatians 5:1-4, Paul says that if you become circumcised in order to become part of God's Church, you have become estranged or separated from Christ, you have fallen from grace, and Christ profits you nothing. Why? Because circumcision of the flesh was only a symbol of the *spiritual circumcision* of the heart, which Jesus performs when we accept Him into our hearts. Jesus is the perfect fulfillment of the true spiritual meaning of circumcision. Just as Jesus is the true High Priest, He also performs the "true circumcision" of the heart (Romans 2:26-29).

Another example is found in Jude verse 7. The Bible calls the fire that destroyed Sodom and Gomorrah an *eternal fire*. However, the fire is not still burning today. The fire went out after destroying the cities.

So, what does this tell us about the usage of the terms *forever*, *eternal* or *everlasting* in the Bible? Obviously, from all of these examples, and others that could be given, when the Bible uses the terms *forever*, *everlasting* or *eternal*, it does not necessarily mean continuing forever and ever, and never coming to an end. Otherwise the "eternal" fire that destroyed Sodom would still be burning; Aaron's "everlasting" priesthood would not have been annulled; the "everlasting" covenant of circumcision, strictly required in the Old Testament for acceptance among God's people, would not have been eliminated as a requirement for believers in the New Testament in Acts 15, and would not have been discouraged and spoken against by the apostle Paul in Galatians; and the animal sacrifices and the burning of the lamp in the tabernacle, which were all to continue "forever," would not have come to an end thousands of years ago.

It is clear that, in the Bible, the words *everlasting* or *eternal* can simply mean that it will continue until it has accomplished or fulfilled its purpose. The *eternal* fire that destroyed Sodom, continued until it had fulfilled its purpose of destroying the wicked city. Aaron's "everlasting" priesthood continued until it had fulfilled its purpose, when the real High Priest, Jesus Christ came. The *everlasting* covenant of circumcision continued as a spiritual requirement until it had fulfilled its purpose, when the new covenant was instituted by Jesus Christ, where the real circumcision of the heart occurs when Jesus comes into our hearts. The animal sacrifices, which were to last *forever*, continued until they had fulfilled their purpose, when the true atoning sacrifice of the "Divine Lamb of God" was offered on the cross. From all of these examples of things that were stated to be *everlasting* or *eternal*, yet have been terminated and ceased long ago, it is obvious that the Bible's usage of these terms does not necessarily convey the meaning of perpetual continuance forever and ever without end. In the numerous examples I've presented we see that "ongoing continuance" can be *conditional*, based upon obedience and fidelity, or upon *"fulfillment of original purpose."* Therefore, there is no scriptural contradiction for the nation of Israel's *everlasting* promises to have been terminated and forfeited based upon its infidelity and disobedience, as well as its *being replaced* by a "new nation" (*Spiritual Israel/The Christian Church*), which God is now using to fulfill the *original purpose* of Israel.

In addition to the termination of Israel's "chosen nation" status in the New Testament, we find that the religious feasts and ceremonies associated with Israel were fulfilled and terminated as well. This is an important issue due to recent trends by some church leaders, to implement the ceremonies of Judaism within Christianity. We will examine numerous New Testament scriptures that clearly reveal the fulfillment and termination of these Old Testament religious events. Ephesians 2:11-16 says that Jesus abolished a law of commandments with ordinances, which separated Jew and gentile. Colossians 2:13-17 states that Jesus wiped out some *handwritings of ordinances* or requirements, and nailed them to the cross; because He did this, no one should be judged concerning food, drink, holy days (feasts), new moons or sabbaths, because they are only a "shadow" of things to come.

What law of ordinances and requirements is the apostle Paul declaring to have been abolished and nailed to the cross? What law full of *shadows* or *symbols* of things to come contained requirements concerning food, drink, holy days (feasts), new moons and sabbaths?

We know that Paul is not referring to the Ten Commandments Moral Law, because it makes no mention of food, drink, new moon or feast requirements. Any good Bible student knows that the only possible and logical biblical answer is the various Old Testament ceremonial laws and ordinances regarding the feasts and holy days, which did indeed have requirements and instructions concerning food, drink, new moons, "special sabbaths," etc. Additionally, all of these things were *shadows* or *symbols* of the *things to come* concerning the coming Messiah, His ministry and His atonement. Therefore, the ceremonial laws and ordinances containing these feasts, holy days, new moons, food and drink requirements, and the "special sabbaths" of the Old Testament, are what Paul states that Jesus has abolished and nailed to the cross. Why would He do that? Because they were only symbols of Him, His ministry and atonement that He had fulfilled, so there was no more need of the symbols. In 2nd Corinthians 1:19-20, we're told that *all* of the promises of God receive their "Yes" and "Amen" in Jesus Christ. In other words, Jesus is the fulfillment of them all.

Although it is already obvious from these scriptures that the ceremonial requirements have been terminated, we will examine additional scriptures to even more conclusively prove that these Old Testament ceremonies, ordinances and rituals were indeed fulfilled and terminated by Jesus. The totality of evidence is overwhelming.

The book of Hebrews contrasts the differences between the "first" or "old" covenant of the Old Testament, with the "second" or "new" covenant that Jesus established in the New Testament. Hebrews specifically states that the old covenant was only symbolic of the new covenant that was to come, and that the old covenant is now obsolete and was taken away by Jesus! Hebrews also clearly defines that old covenant as representing the Old Testament earthly tabernacle and its services and sacrifices. It refers to them as being only a *shadow* of *good things to come.* That is the exact wording used by Paul in Colossians to describe what had been "wiped out" and *nailed to the cross,* and which included *feasts* or *holy days,* and *new moons.* The New Testament leaves no doubt that the various ceremonies, ordinances and feasts of the Old Testament have been fulfilled and terminated in Jesus Christ. The specific texts from Hebrews that I have referred to are as follows.

Hebrews 9:1-5 tells us that the first covenant had an earthly sanctuary with ordinances of service. Hebrews 8:1-5 says that this earthly tabernacle with its priests, sacrifices and services, was only a *shadow* of the heavenly reality, and that Jesus is the true High Priest, who ministers in the true tabernacle in heaven.

Hebrews 8:6-8 states that the first covenant proved faulty, so a new and better covenant was established related to Jesus' more excellent ministry. Hebrews 10:1-8 proclaims that the old covenant with all of its sacrifices, was only a *shadow* of *good things to come,* and could not make people perfect. It is also significant that this old covenant and its sacrifices were referred to as a "type of law" in Hebrews 10:1 and 10:8. Remember that the New Testament book of Ephesians said that a "law" containing ordinances had been abolished by Jesus Christ.

Hebrews 9:9-10 declares that the earthly sanctuary and its ordinances of service were only symbolic or figurative; only being imposed until the *time of reformation,* because these earthly services could not change the conscience. Hebrews 9:11-15 states that Christ came to mediate a "new covenant," which would accomplish what the first covenant could not, which is the *cleansing of the conscience.* Hebrews 10:9 then tells us that when Jesus established the second covenant, He took away the first! Hebrews 8:13 additionally states that this new covenant made the first covenant obsolete, and caused it to be vanishing away.

The New Testament makes it "crystal clear" that the *first covenant* in the Old Testament, with all of its ceremonies, ordinances, feasts and services, was fulfilled and terminated by Jesus Christ, and is no longer binding upon Christians. That is probably why the Bible uses different terminology when mentioning the feasts in the New Testament, than it does in the Old Testament. On numerous occasions in the Old Testament, the feasts are referred to as the *Lord's feasts* or as *feasts of the Lord.* For example, the Passover was called the "Lord's Passover" (Exodus 12:11; Exodus 12:27; Leviticus 23:5). The Feast of Tabernacles was called a "feast of the Lord" (Leviticus 23:34; Leviticus 23:39). They were the "Lord's feasts" because He had established them, and also because they were reminding people of the coming Messiah, His ministry and atonement. However, once Jesus had come and completed His mission, in fulfillment of these Old Testament ceremonies, feasts and rituals, they were unnecessary and irrelevant. That is probably why the New Testament <u>never</u> refers to them as the *Lord's feasts.* Once Jesus had fulfilled His mission, these Old Testament feasts and ceremonies were nothing more than unnecessary rituals. In fact, in the gospel of John, which was one of the last New Testament books written, probably at least twenty years after the destruction of Jerusalem in fulfillment of Jesus' prophecy; John repeatedly refers to these feasts as *Jewish feasts*, rather than the *Lord's feasts*. Instead of the *Lord's Passover*, he calls it the "Passover of the Jews" (John 2:13; John 6:4; John 11:55). Instead of calling the Feast of Tabernacles a *feast of the Lord*, he calls it the *"Jews' feast of tabernacles"* (John 7:2). Additionally, in John 5:1, he refers to another *feast of the Jews*. This is also why you do not find any references to gentile converts to Christianity in the New Testament, being required to keep the "feasts" of the old covenant. In fact, when the apostles held their official meeting to discuss the requirements for gentile believers in Acts 15, the only additional Old Testament rules they placed upon them, were to abstain from blood, things strangled, fornication and from foods offered to idols. There were no required *feasts* or *new moons*, because these things had been fulfilled and terminated by Jesus, as has been thoroughly documented. However, it should be mentioned that the Ten Commandments moral law was obviously assumed to still be binding. Why? Because the apostles certainly would not be telling the gentiles that they could not eat food offered to idols, but that it was ok to worship idols. They would not be saying that the gentiles could not commit fornication, but that it was ok to commit adultery. They would not be saying that the gentiles could not eat things with blood in it, but that it was ok to murder and shed blood. Therefore, it is logical to conclude that the Ten Commandments moral law was unquestionably assumed to still be binding.

In addition to all of the clear specific biblical evidence we've examined concerning the fulfillment and termination of the Old Testament ceremonies and feasts, the New Testament also issues stern warnings against those who try to require obedience to these *old covenant* ordinances. Paul warns us not to be brought into "bondage," by observing *days*, *months*, *seasons* and *years* in Galatians 4:9-10. It is also significant, that those who teach people to observe circumcision and these extra "old covenant special days," are denounced in the Bible. They are called *false brethren* and *spies* in Galatians 2:4. They are accused of "bewitching" people (Galatians 3:1), and of "perverting" the gospel of Christ by preaching a *different gospel* (Galatians 1:6-7). They are called "accursed" (Galatians 1:8-9), and are said to be *under a curse* (Galatians 3:10). They are accused of bringing people into "bondage" (Galatians 2:4; Galatians 5:1), and of causing people to become estranged or separated from Christ, and thus to *fall from grace* (Galatians 5:4). Finally, the Bible declares that these false legalistic teachers will *bear their judgment* (Galatians 5:10).

This is serious business! God obviously does not tolerate people adding onto the gospel. He plainly states that all who do so will bear their judgment. Why? The New Testament clearly teaches that Jesus has fulfilled all of the Old Testament ceremonies, ordinances and festivals. He was the "perfect fulfillment" of every single old covenant ceremony, service, holy day and feast. That is why Paul even stated that Christ Himself *is our Passover* (1 Corinthians 5:7), which was one of the most esteemed Jewish feasts. The Passover and every other feast and holy day were only symbols of the coming Messiah, His ministry and atonement. Jesus Christ is the reality and fulfillment. Therefore, we do not need the symbols anymore. We are to trust that Jesus fulfilled everything completely and perfectly. For someone to require our continued performance of these Old Testament symbols, in addition to Jesus' fulfillment of them, is to imply that He didn't perfectly fulfill them. It is going back to a "Jesus Plus" system, which contradicts the Bible, perverts the gospel, and indirectly insults Jesus by implying that He did not perfectly and completely fulfill and finish His mission. It is no coincidence that as Jesus was proclaiming *"it is finished,"* while on the cross, simultaneously the veil which separated the Holy and Most Holy places in the temple was being torn apart. (The Most Holy Place was only visible and accessible to the High Priest, and only once each year on the *Day of Atonement,* which was probably the most sacred of all the holy days and festivals). The tearing of the veil, exposing the Most Holy Place to the open view of all as Jesus was proclaiming *"it is finished,"* testified to the conclusion of the "old covenant" ceremonies, rituals and festivals; it revealed that even the *Most Holy Place* of the temple, which was entered only during the most sacred "Day of Atonement" festival, had reached its ultimate fulfillment at the cross, and had truly *finished* its course, even as Jesus proclaimed *"it is finished."* What Jesus had finished and completed, man should not attempt to continue. Jesus' proclamation of *"it is finished,"* also encompassed more than what I've presented in this paragraph. I am only dealing with its application to our current discussion.

Some contemporary legalistic teachers proclaim that the New Testament reveals that the Apostle Paul, who wrote many of these scriptures we've examined, still regularly attended the Old Covenant feasts himself. However, a thorough biblical study of Paul's writings and journeys reveals that these teachers are either biblically ignorant or dishonest. Paul did **not** regularly attend these feasts.

There were three main feasts each year that truly religious Jews would unwaveringly attend. All Jewish men who sincerely believed and practiced the religion of Judaism would be sure to be present at these feasts. Paul's life as a Christian spanned approximately thirty years, from the "mid-thirties" to the "mid-sixties" AD. That means that Paul would have had the opportunity to attend about *ninety* of these major feasts during his life as a Christian, but the Bible reveals that Paul only attended, *at most,* four or five of those ninety feasts!

Galatians 1:18 explains that Paul did not even visit Jerusalem for over three years after his conversion, and that he only stayed for fifteen days. Galatians 2:1 states that he did not return to Jerusalem again for fourteen years. Acts chapters thirteen and fourteen cover Paul's first missionary journey through the cities of the gentiles. It is commonly agreed by most theological historians that this journey must have encompassed at least two years. Acts 15:40 through Acts 18:18 reveals that, during his second missionary journey, Paul spent at least three years traveling through numerous gentile cities. Acts 18:23 through Acts 21:15 reveals that Paul's third missionary journey among the gentiles also spanned a period of at least three years. Acts 24:27 states that Paul spent two years in "house arrest" under a Roman governor named Felix in Caesarea. And, Acts 28:30 tells us that he spent an additional two years under house arrest in Rome. Furthermore, there were additional time periods of house arrest under the Roman governor Festus in Acts chapters twenty-five and twenty-six; of being shipwrecked and stranded on the island of Malta in Acts chapters twenty-seven and twenty-eight; of being imprisoned a second time in Rome before his eventual execution according to 2nd Timothy and early church historians; and of the time period spent evangelizing among the gentiles between Paul's fist and second imprisonments in Rome. When Paul's life is carefully charted out in the Bible, it is clear that, with the exception of "at most" four or five brief visits to Jerusalem, he spent his entire Christian life away from Jerusalem. Since the Apostle Paul only attended, *at most*, four or five Jewish feasts in his thirty years of being a Christian, it is obvious that these feasts were _not_ religiously significant to Paul.

It is also noteworthy that Paul explains the motivation that probably prompted his participation in the few feasts that he did attend. In 1st Corinthians 9:19-22 he basically states that he would meet people wherever they were at, in order to win them to Christ. He says that he became *all things to all men*, so that he might save them. He specifically states that to those who were "Jews" or *under the law*, he also conducted himself as *under the law*. In fact, he even clearly states that he did so in order to win the Jews and those who were *under the law*. Paul occasionally practiced and adhered to some of the old covenant ceremonies and ordinances as an "inroad" to evangelize the Jews. He, in fact, only rarely participated in them himself, and never encouraged others to do so. The assertion by contemporary, pharisaical teachers that Paul regularly attended these Jewish feasts is blatantly in error.

You have read the biblical evidence concerning the religious rituals of Judaism. God has clearly stated that the Old Testament ceremonies and festivals have been fulfilled and terminated in Jesus Christ. He has issued strong warnings and rebukes against those who try to require their observance in the New Testament gospel era. The Bible has plainly revealed that all of God's covenants, promises and blessings upon Israel were conditional, based upon their obedience. In fact, God's word clearly stated that if Israel persisted in disobedience, they would receive God's curses, instead of His blessings. The Bible also revealed that Israel's history of rebellion and disobedience culminating with their rejection of their Messiah, Jesus Christ, had resulted in their rejection by God, and in being replaced by a *new nation*, the Christian church. It is unwise for Christians to attempt to revive the old ceremonies, festivals and practices of the Jewish nation. God declared that the old covenant has been taken away or removed, and is now obsolete

(Hebrews 8:13; Hebrews 10:9). Therefore, Christians should come into agreement with God's Word. When Jesus said, *"it is finished,"* it was finished! As the apostle Paul said: "Stand fast therefore in the liberty by which Christ has made us free, and do not be entangled again with a yoke of bondage" (Galatians 5:1).

Another related "Judaistic issue" concerns the additional require-ment that many "old covenant" teachers are attempting to impose upon Christians, by stressing the great importance of stating our Savior's name as "Yahshua," instead of Jesus. These teachers point out that Mary and Joseph would have spoken Hebrew, and that the angel Gabriel, therefore, would also have spoken Jesus' name to them in He-brew. This may be true, but the fact of the matter is, that in the original language of scripture, Jesus is not called by the Hebrew word *Yahshua* one single time in the entire Bible.

The Old Testament, which was written in Hebrew, never speaks the actual name of the coming Messiah. Therefore, Jesus is not called *Yahshua* in all of the Old Testament. *Yahshua* is used numerous times for Joshua in the Old Testament, but never for Jesus.

The New Testament, which was written in Greek, speaks Jesus' name hundreds of times, and every single time it is written in Greek as "Iesous" (ee-ay-sooce). The original Hebrew word of *Yahshua* is not used one single time for Jesus in all of the New Testament either. Therefore, as previously stated, Jesus Christ is never referred to as *Yahshua* in the entire Bible.

It is noteworthy, that the Bible states that all of scripture is inspired by God, and that holy men of God spoke as they were moved by the Holy Spirit (2 Timothy 3:16; 2 Peter 1:21). Therefore, we also know that God used the original wording that He wanted when the scrip-tures were written. If it were so important for Christians to be speak-ing our Savior's name as *Yahshua*, certainly God would have made sure to include the original Hebrew word *Yahshua* for Jesus' name someplace in the Bible, but it never appears in the original language as our Savior's name in all of scripture.

It is also interesting that in Mark's gospel, Mark uses at least six original Hebrew or Aramaic words (henceforth simply cited as Hebrew for the sake of brevity), mixed in with his gospel written in Greek. He uses the Hebrew word "ephphatha" in Mark 7:34, also the Hebrew words "talitha" and "cumi" in Mark 5:41, as well as the Hebrew words "Eloi," "lama" and "sabachthani" in Mark 15:34. However, Mark never uses the original Hebrew word *Yahshua* to refer to Jesus. Mark refers to Jesus by the Greek word "Iesous" 96 times, but not once does he call Him *Yahshua*. Why not? Mark uses at least six other original Hebrew words in his gospel account.

In the gospel of John, we also find the same scenario. John uses a Hebrew derivative for "Messiah" in John 1:41 and John 4:25. He also uses a Hebrew derivative for "rabbi" or "rabboni" six times (John 1:38; John 1:49; John 3:2; John 3:26; John 6:25; John 20:16). John chooses to use Hebrew derivatives several times in the midst of his letter written in Greek. However, John never uses the Hebrew word *Yahshua* to refer to Jesus. John refers to Jesus over 250 times, and uses the Greek word "Iesous" every time. If saying *Yahshua* is as important as these modern-day *old covenant teachers* claim, certainly Mark or John would have used *Yahshua* at least once, for they used other Hebrew words and derivatives. Why didn't they? The answer is obvious. This modern-day "Yahshua doctrine" is nothing more than a new form of legalism, with absolutely no foundation in scripture. God meets us all wherever we are. He communicates with the Chinese in the Chinese language. He communicates with the French in the French language. He communicates with the Greeks in the Greek language. And, He communicates with the English-speaking world, in the English language. Our Savior is known to us as Jesus.

Remember the words of the Apostle Paul, and "do not be entangled in a yoke of bondage." There is a modern-day "pharisaism" gaining popularity in some circles, requiring adherence to the "old covenant" and using the name *Yahshua*. Don't be deceived into this system of bondage. Recall that Jesus was harder on the legalistic Pharisees than He was on prostitutes and publicans. Jesus declared that the "harlots" would enter heaven before these legalistic teachers (Matthew 21:31).

New Testament Christians should not be attempting to "reconstruct" the Old Testament nation of Israel and its related practices. And, we should also be careful to not repeat the mistakes of the past, regarding the church's focus concerning Israel.

History has a tendency to repeat itself. As Solomon stated in the Bible, "There is nothing new under the sun." We tend to repeat the same mistakes over and over again. This is also true concerning Israel. The Church in Jesus' day was not prepared to receive Him because their focus was on the literal nation of Israel, and their expectation of its forthcoming exaltation to political and military supremacy, because of the anticipated arrival of a conquering military Messiah. Due to this improper focus on the literal physical nation of Israel, and expected political and military events, the church leaders of Jesus' day were not prepared for His *first coming*. Jesus came to offer spiritual blessings and deliverance, but their focus was on physical worldly blessings and deliverance. Of course, we know the end of the story. The church leaders' incorrect teaching caused many to reject Jesus Christ.

Many church leaders today are making the same mistake. Once again, they are focused on the literal physical nation of Israel, and on expected political and military events, just as the church leaders did in Jesus' day. Will this improper focus by many of today's church leaders also cause them to be unprepared for Jesus' *second coming*, just as the Jewish church leaders were for His *first coming*?

It almost seems as though the Church tends to forget what the central and primary focus of the Bible is. It is not Israel. It is Jesus Christ! The Bible is *Christ-centered*, not *Israel-centered*. Jesus said the scriptures testify of Him, not of Israel (John 5:39). We're told in 2 Corinthians 1:19-20, that all the promises of God are fulfilled in Jesus, not in Israel. It's time for today's "pro-Israel" teachers to take their eyes off of Israel, and to fix them upon Jesus. Our hope is in Jesus, not in Israel.

In conclusion, I want to repeat that I am not attempting to establish any moral equivalency regarding current events in the Middle East. I am neither *pro-Israel* nor *pro-Palestinian*. I am *pro-Jesus*, and *pro-Bible*. Again, I plainly state that the suicide bombings being inflicted upon innocent Jewish civilians are evil deeds that can never be justified, as are any abuses by the Jewish state inflicted upon the Palestinians. My emphasis is strictly from a spiritual and biblical perspective. God loves Jew and gentile alike, and He desires both to place their faith in Jesus Christ. It is time for the Christian Church to adopt the same perspective, and to stop favoring one side over the other based upon the Church's bias.

25

THE EVIDENCE—PART EIGHT:
FINAL CONSIDERATIONS

I N SUMMARY, it is appropriate to close this book with several final considerations. If the Church refuses to literally follow the teachings of its "founding document," the Bible, on such basic issues as obedience and the Ten Commandments, is it proper for the Church to reprimand the *political left* for not literally interpreting and following the founding documents of our nation?

If the Church decries the materialistic, wasteful and self-serving attributes of *big government*, is it right for the Church to accept the concept of today's mega-church, with all of its materialism, waste and selfish inward focus?

If the Church denounces the moral decay in our nation, and attributes it to liberal, political and social philosophies of the *political left*, shouldn't the Church also denounce its own equally sinful condition, and then "connect the dots" to its own liberal "anything goes" theology of *"once saved always saved"?*

If the Church deplores the removal of the Ten Commandments from our schools and other public arenas, isn't it hypocritical for the Church to teach that the commandments have been removed from the Church, by being nailed to the cross?

If the Church is concerned about the *political left* "dumbing down" our society with "feel good," "emotion driven" agendas in our public schools, which either ignore or reinterpret the historical records of our nation, shouldn't the Church be equally concerned with today's trend of "feel good," "emotion driven," "church light" services spreading across our nation, which also ignore or reinterpret the Bible? And, if the Church perceives that our public schools have exchanged the *solid truths* of education, for political and social *"warm fuzzies,"* why doesn't the Church also perceive that many of the *solid truths* of the Bible, have also been exchanged for *"spiritual warm fuzzies"*?

If the Church complains about liberal, arrogant, activist judges who exalt themselves in defiance of the constitution, why do Christian leaders exalt themselves in defiance of their *founding document*, the Bible?

If the Church detests the manipulation and distortion of words and phrases, in order to make changes in the constitution, why does the Church also manipulate and distort words and phrases in order to make changes in the Bible, as revealed in chapter twelve of this book?

If the Church asserts that the biblical "creation theory" should also be taught in our public schools, shouldn't the Church be honoring the only commandment which commemorates God's creation, the Sabbath commandment?

Should the churches in America be *sitting on* hundreds of billions of dollars in assets, while millions of children starve around the world, and millions in American streets are homeless? Should our churches be building elaborate and luxurious facilities for themselves, or should they be building homeless shelters and feeding starving children?

Are some of the ideas and arguments of the Church correct? Yes. Has our nation become materialistic? It certainly has, but so has the Church. Has our nation fallen into moral decay? Indeed it has, but so has the Church. Has our nation removed God's laws? It may have, but so has the Church. Has our nation reinterpreted and revised our founding documents? You could argue that it has, but so has the Church done to the Bible, which is its *founding document*. Has our nation distorted and censored those who oppose modern agendas that deviate from the constitution's original intent? It may have, but so has the Church maligned and censored those who expose the Church's deviation from Scripture.

Therefore, if the Church refuses to acknowledge and repent of its own compromises, contradictions and double standards, shouldn't it cease from rebuking the *political left* for its contradictions and double standards? When the Church has dealt with its own problems, it will be better prepared to deal with our nation's problems. After all, Jesus said that Christians should remove the *log* from their own eye, before they attempt to remove the *speck* from the eyes of others (Matthew 7:3-5). The apostle Peter also said that judgment begins with the "House of God" (1st Peter 4:17). It is time for the Church to examine and judge itself concerning these issues, before judging those outside the Church.

As a Christian pastor, I am part of today's Christian Church. According to the Bible, all Christians are part of the same Church, the Body of Christ. Therefore, I am addressing my brothers, sisters and friends in Christ. I may have wounded some in the Church with this book. However, the Bible states that "faithful are the wounds of a friend" (Proverbs 27:6). The Bible also declares that wise men accept rebuke, and even love you for rebuking them (Proverbs 9:8). I pray that this will be the response of the Church.

The Church has three options in response to this book. It can attempt to prove me wrong, and I welcome that. However, the Church's response must be based solely on the Bible. It doesn't matter what other books or preachers say. For a Christian, it only matters what the Bible says. The Church's second possible response would be to accept the message of this book, to acknowledge its errors, and then to repent and reform. The third possibility is for the Church to ignore both of the previous options, and to resort to attacking and disparaging the messenger, rather than dealing with the message. My hope and prayer is that the Church will take the noble path and prove itself to be wise, by accepting the biblical rebukes and criticisms delivered in this book, and then responding with repentance and reformation.

I apologize to our nation on behalf of the Christian Church in America. We have set a terrible example and we are not qualified to be criticizing anyone else, until we have done our own "house cleaning." I am not apologizing for the Bible or for Jesus. There is nothing wrong with Jesus or the Bible. Unfortunately, today's Church in America has not represented Jesus or the Bible very well.

I challenge the Church in America to repent and get back to following the literal teachings of the Bible, and thereby begin setting a much better example for our nation, by truly representing and reflecting the character of Jesus. Once the Church has experienced true repentance, reformation and transformation, it will then be truly qualified to address the problems in our nation.

It is probably appropriate for me to conclude this book by personally addressing the Christian, conservative leaders who have become very active in the political arena. The God whom you claim to serve and honor sees what you have done in His Church. He sees how you have slandered His character with your eternal torment and Calvinism doctrines; moreover, He sees your stubborn pride and arrogance that keeps you from admitting and confessing your error, in spite of the enormous amount of biblical evidence that contradicts your position. He sees how you have rejected His commandments, while trying to force the secular world to honor them. He sees how you have squandered the massive wealth that He has entrusted to you, by spending it on luxurious buildings and huge salaries, while millions of children die of starvation and millions of Americans are homeless and lacking health care.

God sees how you have exalted yourselves with religious titles, although the Lord Jesus Himself has told you not to do such things. He sees how you have self-righteously attacked and condemned the *political left* and the mainstream media, while you have been guilty of many of the same strategies and practices within the Church. You are guilty of slander, disobedience, self-exaltation, dishonesty, hypocrisy and embezzlement via financial misappropriations within the Church; notwithstanding, you arrogantly continue to attempt to expand your sphere of influence within the political arena. If you have justified betraying your Church and your God, why should we trust you to be faithful as leaders within our government?

I also am a conservative Christian, but your behavior sickens me! God has sent me to expose you because you have betrayed Him, and you have set a terrible example for Christianity through your unholy conduct and despicable doctrines.

I encourage all true Christians throughout America to withdraw your support from these unfaithful leaders, both within the Church and in the political arena. You must honor God and His Bible more than any human leaders. I have conclusively proven in the "Evidence Chapters" that most church leaders have betrayed God and His word. I have truly exposed *Right-Wing Christianity* as being <u>*the unholy alliance*</u> in need of repentance and reform, rather than further expansion and exaltation. I hope and pray that this book will help to initiate the kind of true repentance and reformation that is so desperately needed within our Christian Church hierarchy.

Henry Bechthold is the pastor of a non-denominational Christian church in Minneapolis, Minnesota. He has been studying, teaching and preaching the Bible for more than twenty-five years. He is also the founder of Inner City Outreach, a ministry that provides new clothing for the poor and homeless.

His passion for the Christian Church is to have it return to true ministry, following the example of Jesus by feeding and clothing those who are in need, and also to set a more consistent example, by practicing what it preaches. His personal experience within the Church and his biblical studies have prompted him to write this book, because of his deep conviction that today's Christian Church in America is guilty of numerous compromises, double standards, dishonest practices, sadistic teachings, financial abuse and blatant hypocrisy.

You can reach the author by mail at, H.E. H.A.D. Faith Ministries, P.O. Box 535, Rogers, MN., 55374-0535.